BLACKBERRY®

BLACKBERRY

THE INSIDE STORY OF
RESEARCH IN MOTION

ROD McQUEEN

KEY PORTER  BOOKS

To Sandy
the love of my life

Library and Archives Canada Cataloguing in Publication

McQueen, Rod, 1944-
          BlackBerry : the inside story of Research In Motion / Rod McQueen.

ISBN 978-1-55263-940-5

          1. BlackBerry. 2. Research In Motion Ltd. I. Title.
QA76.8.B53M36 2010   004.165   C2007-901838-6

ONTARIO ARTS COUNCIL
CONSEIL DES ARTS DE L'ONTARIO

The publisher gratefully acknowledges the support of the Canada Council for the Arts and the Ontario Arts Council for its publishing program. We acknowledge the support of the Government of Ontario through the Ontario Media Development Corporation's Ontario Book Initiative.

We acknowledge the financial support of the Government of Canada through the Book Publishing Industry Development Program (BPIDP) for our publishing activities.

Key Porter Books Limited
Six Adelaide Street East, Tenth Floor
Toronto, Ontario
Canada M5C 1H6
www.keyporter.com

Text design and electronic formatting: Martin Gould

Printed and bound in Canada

10 11 12 13 6 5 4 3 2 1

TABLE OF CONTENTS

FOREWORD   7
by Jim Balsillie and Mike Lazaridis

INTRODUCTION   9

CHAPTER ONE   THE EARLY YEARS   19

CHAPTER TWO   STUDENT START-UP   39

CHAPTER THREE   A WIRELESS WORLD   59

CHAPTER FOUR   DIVIDING THE DUTIES   79

CHAPTER FIVE   TUCSON AND SHOW LOW   95

CHAPTER SIX   SUCCESS LIES IN PARADOX   111

CHAPTER SEVEN   GOING PUBLIC   127

CHAPTER EIGHT   MILLIONAIRES' ROW   147

CHAPTER NINE   BIRTH OF BLACKBERRY   167

CHAPTER TEN   TAKING MANHATTAN   187

CHAPTER ELEVEN   DREAMS FULFILLED   205

CHAPTER TWELVE   FAMILY VALUES   225

CHAPTER THIRTEEN   POSTER CHILD FOR PATENT REFORM   237

CHAPTER FOURTEEN   GLOBAL REACH   257

CHAPTER FIFTEEN   A PEARL OF GREAT PRICE   275

CHAPTER SIXTEEN   THE FUTURE UNFOLDS   291

INDEX   309

FOREWORD

ENTREPRENEURSHIP IS THE CORNERSTONE of a successful marketplace and the story of Research In Motion's first twenty-five years is indeed an entrepreneurial tale of initiative, skill, innovation, hard work, risk and reward.

Of course, RIM's growth did not happen overnight. It is the result of many people's efforts over many years. We operated for years as a small, innovative and successful company that was grounded in solid business and technological principles. Over time, the company's initiatives became increasingly larger and we attracted more and more talented people, but RIM's entrepreneurial spirit has always remained intact.

RIM was one of the first companies in the world to focus on developing wireless data technologies in the late 1980's and quickly decided to concentrate and invest all of its resources on establishing industry-leading competencies in this field. At the time, most of the wireless industry was naturally focused on the booming cellular phone market. The wireless data sector was an untapped, niche market opportunity and posed incredibly difficult engineering challenges, but RIM stayed focused and grew the opportunity one forward-looking step at a time.

RIM's focus on the wireless data sector led to the development of wireless data and email gateways, wireless modems and two-way pagers, which then led to the BlackBerry wireless email solution and eventually to the incredible smartphone market opportunity that exists today.

BlackBerry was introduced in North America in 1999 and continues to be the top selling smartphone brand in North America. With already over 75 million BlackBerry smartphones sold worldwide, RIM and its partners now offer BlackBerry products and services in over 170 countries.

As can be expected on such a corporate journey, there are lots of twists and turns with both smooth and bumpy patches along the way, but it continues to be an absolute pleasure to work in this industry and we are grateful every day for the privilege of working alongside so many extraordinary people at RIM. A broad range of people were interviewed in an effort to capture many of the events and turning points that occurred during that time.

RIM has grown from a student start-up in 1984 to become an international corporation with over 12,000 employees and one of the world's most valuable technology brands. We thank you for your interest in RIM and we hope you enjoy this book.

Jim Balsillie and Mike Lazaridis, co-CEOs

INTRODUCTION

MIKE LAZARIDIS, THE FOUNDER AND CO-CEO of Research In Motion (RIM), moves to the microphone with the easy self-assurance of a successful inventor whose creation, BlackBerry, is as well known in the family room as the boardroom. As he looks out at the shareholders attending RIM's Annual General Meeting in July 2009, he knows that he has a room full of happy investors. The market capitalization of the firm—the number of shares times the per share value—is $43 billion, making RIM three times bigger than Motorola, a major competitor founded in 1928, more than half a century before RIM's brave beginnings in 1984 as a two-man shop on borrowed money. The share price has recovered to $75, more than double the levels reached during the global financial crisis that battered all companies six months earlier. (All figures in US dollars unless otherwise indicated.)

At the peak of his powers, Lazaridis is one of those rare people in business who rightly deserves to be called a genius. "It's a privilege to work with experts every day," he said, referring to the more than 12,000 RIM employees, including

5,000 in research and development, up from a total of only 100 employees in 1997. "We knew we were building a company for the long term," he said. "We're just absolutely obsessed with customer quality, the reliability of the product, and the value we're providing the carrier, the enterprise, the IT manager, and the user. You turn it on and it just works," he said. The device works so well that the company sold 75 million BlackBerry smartphones by the end of 2009, nearly half of those in the previous year alone. BlackBerry commands a 51 per cent market share of the U.S. smartphone market, and a 21 per cent global market share, as Research In Motion increasingly becomes the first choice for the world.

RIM's other co-CEO, Jim Balsillie, matches Lazaridis's intellect and passion. He shared the stage with Lazaridis at the annual meeting, and provided the shareholders with an overview of another successful year at RIM. Balsillie thanked employees for their accomplishments during the year in terms of revenue and earnings growth, continued global expansion of the company's operations and customer base, and a record number of new and successful products. Despite RIM's substantial growth to date, Balsillie appears more optimistic than ever about the opportunities ahead. In baseball terms, he says, "We are in the second or third inning of a nine-inning game."

RIM has already become Canada's most valuable tech company with annual revenues approaching $15 billion and a five-year revenue growth rate of 910 per cent, a meteoric rate usually reserved for start-ups. In fact, *Fortune* magazine ranked RIM at the top of its 2009 list of the 100 Fastest Growing Companies in the world. RIM's position at the top of the 2009 "Tech 100" list published by *Canadian Business* magazine also illustrated RIM's tech-titan status in Canada, with a market cap that was actually more than double the combined value of the other ninety-nine publicly traded Canadian technology companies on the list. And according to a Millward Brown brand study published in 2009, the BlackBerry brand value grew 390 per cent in the past year and is now worth $28 billion, ranked as the sixteenth most valuable brand in the world and tenth in North America. In just ten years, the Black-Berry brand grew from cult object to icon status and ranks higher than other household names such as Intel, Amazon, American Express, Disney, and Pepsi.

Unlike some firms that might be content to rest on their laurels, innovation continues apace at RIM. In the last year RIM has launched a flurry of new smartphones—including Bold, Curve, Pearl, Storm, and Tour models—with more expected in the months ahead. "These are iconic designs," Lazaridis told shareholders. "They capture the imagination of the market. More and more people are starting to be attracted to these devices; they realize there's depth to these devices. It's not just the push email (which allows messages to be automatically delivered to users), but it's the multimedia, the multitasking. They're great phones with usable features packed into something that's so small and so light."

As recently as 1998, RIM sold only one pager through two carriers in two countries, Canada and the United States. As of the summer of 2009, RIM distributed a dozen different models via 530 carriers and distribution partners in 170 countries. Moreover, RIM's global BlackBerry infrastructure incorporates one of the largest private networks in the world. As a result of this global reach, over one-third of BlackBerry subscribers live beyond RIM's original North American base. After BlackBerry was launched in 1999, it took five years to sign up the first one million subscribers. These days, over a million incremental users join every month. After relying on larger enterprise customers in the early years, today more than half of BlackBerry subscribers are consumers or people in smaller businesses.

Research In Motion is based in Waterloo, Ontario, a university city of 100,000 an hour west of Toronto, first settled in the nineteenth century by Mennonites who came for the fertile land and can still be seen driving their horse-drawn buggies on rural roads. Over the years, manufacturing firms in the region, like those in most other increasingly urban areas in North America, have gone through boom-bust cycles. Button makers and leather tanneries gave way to tires and televisions, only to see low-wage countries take those jobs, too.

High tech is the new saviour. The twin cities of Kitchener-Waterloo are part of what's called the Technology Triangle, which includes the nearby cities of Cambridge and Guelph, with a total regional population of about 500,000. Among the other high-tech companies such as Open Text, Sandvine, ATS, COM DEV, Dalsa, and Descartes, RIM is by far the biggest, representing more than 90 per cent by value of the fourteen publicly traded local high-tech firms.

But RIM stands out from the others in an even more important way. In the entire history of the country only a handful of Canadian manufacturing firms have achieved anything approaching sustained success as a global brand. They include Massey-Ferguson in the nineteenth century and Bata, Bombardier, Magna, and—for a time—Nortel Networks in the twentieth century. BlackBerry is the first Canadian brand of the new millennium to have the same kind of commanding international presence as those giants of yesteryear.

Even the sites of the annual meeting have resonance, both

historically and for RIM's co-CEOs, Mike Lazaridis and Jim Balsillie. The annual meeting rotates between the Perimeter Institute, founded by Lazaridis, and the Centre for International Governance Innovation (CIGI), a think tank launched by Balsillie in what was formerly the barrel warehouse for aging whisky by distiller Joseph E. Seagram and Sons Ltd. That operation, bought in 1928 by Sam Bronfman, successfully exported Seagram's VO for decades until it was abandoned in 1997 by Edgar Bronfman Jr., the scion of the third generation who turned his back on liquor in order to acquire media and entertainment baubles en route to losing three-quarters of the family fortune.

In 2001, those whisky barrels gave way to higher thinking when Balsillie secured the building and donated C$20 million to create CIGI. By mid-2009, Balsillie's investment totalled over C$160 million, including C$50 million to build the Balsillie School of International Affairs on three and a half acres of vacant land beside CIGI and C$57 million to create the Balsillie Centre of Excellence.

Across Erb Street, a five-minute walk away, sits the Perimeter Institute for Theoretical Physics, a sleek glass-and-steel edifice where more than eighty physicists ponder the future thanks to a C$100 million endowment in 2000 from Mike Lazaridis that launched the unusual mid-career philanthropy practiced by RIM's co-CEOs. In 2008, Lazaridis increased his endowment by another $50 million, making his total investment in the Perimeter Institute C$150 million. The Institute for Quantum Computing, on the nearby campus of the University of Waterloo, represents another C$100 million donation by Lazaridis.

RIM has made four major contributions to the region, according to University of Waterloo president David Johnston.

"First, RIM has employed a very large number of our students in their co-op program. Second, there has been a very large transfer of technology back and forth. Third, the wealth they have brought to this community has helped the community and the university. Fourth, Jim and Mike and others of their colleagues have set the bar for philanthropic investment in the community and leadership in many institutions."

Beyond such local impact, RIM has also become an essential component of global investment portfolios. As of June 30, 2009, approximately 70 per cent of RIM shares are owned by 800 institutional investment firms that in turn represent tens of millions of individual investors. The two largest firms are Denver-based Janus and Boston-based Fidelity with approximately 5 per cent of the company each, followed by TD Asset Management and Barclays Global Investors. In total, those four firms owned approximately 17 per cent of RIM as of June 30, 2009.

Unlike many entrepreneurs who unload shares along the way to bring in more partners, pay for growth, or reward themselves, Lazaridis and Balsillie remain major shareholders. In October 2009, Lazaridis owned 33.2 million shares and Balsillie 33.7 million shares, meaning that the co-CEOs' shares were each worth about C$2.5 billion and they owned almost 12 per cent of the company between them.

Although the two entrepreneurs are the same age, with Balsillie born five weeks before Lazaridis in 1961, they couldn't be more different. Lazaridis is from Turkey, immigrated to Canada with his parents in 1966, and grew up tinkering with electronics in the basement of the family home in Windsor, Ontario. Born in Seaforth, Ontario, and raised on the other side of the province in Peterborough, Balsillie was so eager to earn pocket money that he sold Regal greeting cards door to door when he was only seven years old. Lazaridis left university to start RIM. Jim Balsillie has an undergraduate degree in commerce, a chartered accountant designation, and a Harvard MBA.

At six feet and a solid 210 pounds, the silver-haired Lazaridis dominates a room with his manner and mien. Balsillie stands just under six feet tall, and looks slimmer than his 190 pounds, as if he's built to go where others can't. Lazaridis is smooth and cerebral; Balsillie is energetic and charismatic. Both men enjoy full and balanced lives. They accomplish a lot during an average day while still ensuring plenty of downtime, and they both highly value their family life. Lazaridis likes to read and think in his spare time, and has no trouble keeping quiet in a room with nothing but his own inventive thoughts. Balsillie regularly participates in various sports, including cycling and hockey, and enjoys both social gatherings and private relaxation.

They bring distinct strengths to RIM, and their seventeen-year reign as co-CEOs of RIM works precisely because they are so different. Balsillie drives corporate strategy, business development, and finance and has enjoyed considerable success at striking a broad range of deals for RIM. "I guess I have a knack for understanding the crux of opportunities and situations and I have spent a lot of time ensuring that the company is focused on the things that matter most. I have also placed a lot of importance on identifying and building successful partnerships for RIM. That has been and continues to be a critical part of our business plan," said Balsillie.

Lazaridis is the innovative visionary who remains amazed by his own entrepreneurial success. "In a life of this fast pace, after you throw twelve double-sixes in a row, you start to wonder what's going on. There's just been too many cases where things just seem to work out. The first time it happens, it's good luck, the second time it's coincidence, the third time you're starting to wonder. After the sixth or seventh time you just accept it," he said.

The dissimilarity between their personalities is further expressed by specific items displayed in their respective offices. Lazaridis has a wooden model of the Avro Arrow, the supersonic jet cancelled in 1957 by federal government fiat, a reminder of Canada's engineering prowess and lost opportunities. Balsillie has a glass case containing an electric guitar autographed by the band members of Barenaked Ladies, a signal he likes having fun and hanging out where there's action. "They complement each other really well. Jim enjoys the business side, the wheeling, the dealing. He was just a blur whizzing around Bay Street in the early days. He was everywhere. He had that characteristic that you're not going to keep someone like that back," said David Neale, former vice-president of Rogers Communications and now with Telus, who has seen other entrepreneurial firms fly apart because there were too many egos to feed. "Quite often, by this stage, they're trying to determine if it can continue being about 'us' or is it about 'me.' For Mike and Jim there's enough for the 'me' bit to make the 'we' bit work."

Even after spending a quarter of a century building his business, Lazaridis remains deeply passionate about what he's doing. "Mike is still a little-boy gadget freak. Whenever I see him at a trade show, he takes me aside, pulls out the latest toy, and he oohs and he aahs all over it," said California-based wireless consultant Andy Seybold. "Mike is not driven by money. He is driven by 'What can I do next to take this platform and turn it into something super cool yet again?' And he keeps doing it."

Balsillie equates their roles at RIM in a roiling, competitive world with the wild ride of surfers. "It's like a beach which has got three or four series of waves. You have the rolling waves here, but then you sort of have a semi, loosely coupled set of rolling waves over here, and you have a set here, and they're all one body of interrelationships, and wave by wave by wave, you have to understand that they're separate but not. Between Mike and I they're highly, highly interrelated. You're surfing these waves but you are not in control, you are definitely not in control. You just aim and hold on and tweak where you can."

Well, surf's up. According to the Wireless Intelligence Group, in 2009 there were four billion mobile phone subscribers worldwide, a number expected to rise to six billion by 2013. "What I like about RIM is that they target a market that's huge. There's a lot of opportunity there. It's a global market in every context," said Deepak Chopra, technology analyst with Genuity Capital Markets. "It's very difficult for companies to find spaces where there are multi-billion opportunities. RIM has a shot to become a $30 billion revenue company. We need more companies like that. They are very driven people. They are passionate about what they do."

Concept and commitment sets RIM apart from other high-tech companies. "They're smart and they learned. They had faith that people wanted a keyboard-based device that could fit inside their pocket and transmit and receive messages," said Alan Reiter, one of the earliest and foremost experts in the field. In 1988, Reiter launched the first newsletter on wireless communication, *Mobile Data Report*, and now runs his own consulting firm in Chevy Chase, Maryland. "It was a killer concept. Mike Lazaridis had the technical brilliance, the technical expertise to pull it off."

"Little by little, the machine will become a part of humanity," wrote French author Antoine de Saint-Exupéry, best known for *The Little Prince*. He was writing about how people become accustomed to new technology, in his case the train, but his comments could also refer to BlackBerry, the wireless handheld that grew from a cult brand to create a cultural revolution. Along the way the device changed the daily habits of so many millions of people that it has been given a nickname—CrackBerry—a playful reference to the addictive drug, crack cocaine. CrackBerry is now in such common use that a Google search turns up more than a million references. In 2006, Webster's dictionary declared CrackBerry "New Word of the Year."

At Research In Motion, the future has only just begun. "We see a tremendous number of opportunities and strategies. After oxygen, we're right up there," Balsillie jokingly told the assembled shareholders at the annual meeting. Added Lazaridis: "The BlackBerry evolution will continue and it is accelerating. Our customers are going from deploying hundreds to thousands of BlackBerrys, from thousands to tens of thousands. Stay tuned."

CHAPTER ONE

THE EARLY YEARS

ON SEPTEMBER 6, 1955, mobs in Istanbul attacked, looted, and destroyed hundreds of houses and businesses owned by Greeks, Jews, and Armenians. Churches were incinerated and more than a dozen died in the pogrom aimed at non-Muslim residents. As long-suffering Greeks, Nick and Dorothy Lazaridis had lived for years under punitive policies that included severe limitations on some professions. The Istanbul community of 300,000 Greeks in the 1920s had shrunk to 100,000 by 1955, the result of scapegoating by Turks who envied the business success of Greeks like Nick Lazaridis, who operated a shop that sold women's wear and perfume. Among the Greeks who tried to rebuild their lives and businesses after the riots, some were boycotted, others were deported, and many left of their own accord.

It was into this repressive regime that Mihal (Mike's given name) Lazaridis was born in 1961. Paul, his father's brother, fled with his family to Germany, where he made arrangements in 1964 for Nick, Dorothy, and Mihal to join him. "My parents left for a couple of reasons. First was the hardship and second was the automatic military training. My father had a hard time being a Greek Christian in a Turkish Muslim army. He just felt it was something he'd avoid with respect to his children. There was some violence in the neighbourhood against the nationality and culture, but I don't remember any specifics. For me, it was an adventure getting away, it was something special."

In addition to new-found freedoms, Germany provided an opportunity for Nick to become a tool-and-die maker. Too young for school, Mihal had to find things to do while his mother worked at home assembling cardboard hats and partyware in the apartment they'd rented on the second floor of a house in southern Germany. The landlord, who lived a floor below, didn't like noisy children; Mihal learned to play quietly and be inventive. Among his earliest recollections was being told that music came from the grooves in vinyl records, so he built his own phonograph from Lego, a paper cup, a pin, and a platter driven by rubber bands. "It made sounds," he said. "It wasn't high fidelity, but it made sounds. Everyone in the house thought it was neat until they realized I was ruining all the records."

Playtime with an electric train set was curtailed after complaints from the landlord. "I was only allowed to play with it if I didn't run it. What's the fun of that? I had to push it by hand on the track. My dad showed me how I could light up the lights in the engine with a few batteries. If I put wires from the batteries to the track the lights would come on. I thought that was the coolest thing ever."

At four, Lazaridis was already learning life lessons about electronics and adapting to circumstances. "That's probably the most important thing in electronics, understanding that circuit.

With a circuit and Ohm's Law [the relationship between voltage and current] you can derive everything. Later, when we were learning about electronics at school, none of this stuff looked strange to me. I knew it by instinct."

Lazaridis's uncle Paul went ahead again, this time to Windsor, Ontario, across the St. Clair River from Detroit, Michigan. Late in 1966, Mihal and his parents set out to join Paul, sailing the Atlantic Ocean with all their worldly possessions in three suitcases, two large and one small. Five-year-old Mihal would stand for hours at the stern of the Montreal-bound ship, holding the wind in his hands as he flew a plastic airplane kite with spinning wings out over the water en route to a new life.

Nick found a job in Windsor at Canada Bridge, but the firm went bankrupt. Next, he worked briefly at a tool-and-die shop and then joined the production line at a Chrysler assembly plant where salaries were high and the benefits generous. Dorothy waitressed at a curling club until she opened a seamstress shop to earn her own spending money, as well as enough to afford an annual holiday for the family, which by then included a daughter, Cleopatra.

At first they shared an apartment with Paul and his family, but Nick scrimped and saved, obtained a mortgage, and was able to buy a house on Pillette Street, one of the city's main thoroughfares. Ada C. Richards Public School was so close that Dorothy could watch Mike, as he was by then called, walk through the neighbour's yard, across the playground, and right into the school.

The basement of the family home became Mike's private preserve, a place where he and his grade-six friends could pursue their hobbies. While he explored electronics, Doug

21

Fregin built model airplanes. Ken Wood's mother was a chemistry teacher who provided ingredients for the trio's youthful experiments, such as iodine bombs that were so unstable they would explode unannounced and produce a mushroom cloud of smoke. The trio bought walkie-talkies and improved the antennae to increase the range so they could talk long into the night from their neighbouring homes. In his quest for knowledge, Lazaridis spent so much time at the Windsor Public Library that he was given a prize by the institution for reading all the science books on the shelves before turning twelve.

One Halloween, Lazaridis and Wood built a haunted house in a hallway at the local church. "By today's standards it was rather pathetic, but it did raise money for the church. We had ghosts and loud noisemakers; you'd step on plates, and lights would come on. It was completely automated, not the traditional version with people dressed up doing the scaring." Doug and Mike won first prize at the school science fair with a parabolic reflector that tracked the sun. Their creation was featured on a local TV newscast after a reporter covering the event in the school auditorium realized that the device would turn and follow his camera lights.

Lazaridis learned his work ethic by helping his father clean and repair rental apartments in several buildings Nick acquired as income properties. "Life was quite good at home even though we didn't have any money. When you learn to scavenge and build your own stuff it doesn't matter. All the kids had sleds and there was a big hill in the schoolyard. My dad couldn't afford a new sled but that was no problem. He went into the garage and got two pieces of wood. There was some corrugated metal left over from building the garage. We cut the wood so it had a curve to it. We had some cross braces, a top of corrugated metal, and a few nails to hold it in the wooden frame. We put a rope in it, painted it white and blue, and I had a sled. It took all of one afternoon."

At W. F. Herman Secondary School in Windsor, Lazaridis and Fregin combined academic subjects with technical shops, a difficult curriculum that few students attempted. Lazaridis also studied art and soon realized that what got talked about the most was believed to be the best. One work, a series of intertwined coloured circles done in Styrofoam, hung in the gym and was widely admired. "The more ridiculous you were, the more seriously you were taken. The real art that I did was hard work. It would take weeks, months to do. The wacky stuff you could do in a couple of days got all the attention. It was so easy to do once you understood the process."

In addition to generous government funding at the time, a local industrialist had donated money for school equipment, so Herman had two well-equipped shops in each of five areas: automotive, machine, architecture, woodworking, and electronics. Lazaridis became skilled at a wide variety of pursuits: turning brake drums on a lathe, using shapers to cut metal, and operating an annealing oven. "Mike first came to my attention when he was in grade nine. He was very bright and had a thirst for knowledge. He was exceptional. He had a very strong work ethic, an excellent sense of intuition, was a fast learner, and problem solver," said shops teacher John Micsinszki. "While the rest of my class was finishing an experiment on the first module of automotive lighting, Mike would be using the next three or four modules together to test out some theory. Mike was not a braggart or in any way boastful. He was actually a very patient teacher if another student asked him for help."

The healthy budget meant there were two dozen unopened boxes in the lab containing the most up-to-date equipment, including some early digital items. Micsinszki gave Lazaridis full access to everything as long as he read the manual from cover to cover before opening any box. "I believe that we learn by experimenting, making mistakes, and then trying another approach. However, preparation for the experiment is the key—hence my insistence that the manual be studied before starting an experiment. Mike was definitely the most interested student that I ever taught," said Micsinszki.

After a fire created billows of foul-smelling selenium smoke and disabled the system that supplied power to the individual workbenches in the lab, Micsinszki told Lazaridis that his assignment for the term was to fix the electrical system. "I opened the back door, found a comfortable place to put all my equipment and then—before taking it apart—made notes of every cable and every wire. I marked them all so I knew how to put it together again," said Lazaridis. "I was in there with a mask and gloves working on early integrated circuits. He helped me, but he never did my job. He'd find the information, he'd show me where to look, he would order the parts, but he would never tell me what was going on. In the end I got it working, but it took me a long time."

That successful restoration established Lazaridis's school-wide reputation as a repairman extraordinaire. Teachers would invite Lazaridis to fix their home TVs and stereos, paying him for his successful efforts with a Coke and cookies. "To me it was what my dad taught me: 'You just have to have faith you can do it and then you have to do it step by step using all your skills. When you don't understand something, start from first principles. Walk your way through it.'"

Among those who sought his help was the school librarian who coached Herman's *Reach for the Top* team. *Reach for the Top*, a quiz show that first aired nationally in the 1960s on CBC-TV, featured two teams of four students from different high schools. The show's host would ask a question from a broad range of categories and the first student to press a button that sounded a buzzer would attempt an answer. Points given for correct answers grew until the end of the thirty-minute show when a winner was declared. The top team would return the following week to meet a new quartet of bright young challengers from another high school.

Herman's team had a makeshift device they used to simulate the show conditions so they could practice for regional playoffs and a chance to appear on national television. The buzzer system was constantly breaking down and Lazaridis finally became frustrated not just because of the frequency of the requests but also because he concluded that the setup didn't replicate actual game conditions. On his own initiative he devised a new system that had only one cable instead of eight so there was less wiring to become tangled and cause trouble, replaced the master control panel using a reset device that automatically sped up the process so the next question could be asked immediately, and then added individual lights that came on when a participant pressed the button so there was no debate about who was first off the mark. When word spread about his invention, other high schools as far away as Toronto ordered similar systems that he and his father built together at home and sold at a profit.

Lazaridis also built his own oscilloscope, an apparatus that looks like a small television with a screen that displays an electrical signal in graph form. The oscilloscope is a diagnostic tool that can be used, for example, to determine a signal's voltage or tell if some component in a piece of equipment isn't working. As with many such advanced projects tackled by Lazaridis that weren't part of the regular curriculum, Fregin worked right alongside his friend, knowing where Lazaridis was headed next, always poised to smooth the path. "When he's working on his oscilloscope, I'd have the screwdriver. I already knew that he's going to need the screwdriver so we're both thinking the same train of thought: OK, this is where the problem is; this is what you're going to do to solve it," said Fregin. "It was a great learning experience."

Just as his father had showed him how to build a sled from items already available in the family garage, Lazaridis used parts for the oscilloscope that had been cannibalized from a wide range of sources, including some from Ernie Hales, a neighbour of Fregin's, who was an avid ham radio operator and supplied the pair with tube amplifiers, among other items. The only component Lazaridis had to purchase was the cathode ray tube that displayed the signal. Even though he stretched his money to buy the best tube he could afford, it was too long and the signal was weak. "You could barely see the beam; I was really disappointed. My teacher already knew that I could never drive that big tube, so he had bought a proper tube at a trade show. The day I finished and it didn't work as well as I'd hoped, he gave me this little box and inside was the exact tube I was looking for." Help from others, Lazaridis concluded, was always welcome. Sometimes you just couldn't do it all on your own.

Among Lazaridis's broad range of interests beyond what everyone else was doing, however, one began to dominate: computers. After Ken Wood moved with his family to

Goderich, a city on Lake Huron north of Windsor, Lazaridis took a bus to visit his boyhood chum. During that trip, as Lazaridis finished the last in a series of books he'd been reading on microprocessors, he was struck by a thought. "It wasn't an epiphany, but it was like everything came together and I understood what was going on. I knew how a computer worked," said Lazaridis.

Having figured out the inner operations of what would become the key ingredient for so much innovation in the future, Lazaridis knew he wanted to get his hands on one. While some lads might have simply read catalogues and yearned, or others might have had the money to buy one, he decided he would build his own computer. He and Fregin spent the next weekend designing a computer on a blackboard and then turned their chalk drawings into reality using various pieces of equipment scrounged from Micsinszki's lab. "We built a computer that was a four-bit bus and had something like twelve instructions. You put it in a loop and it could branch, make a decision, add, and subtract. It was very basic, but the lights would blink and it was pretty cool. We could program it to do things." They even created a high-low game. Lazaridis's mother would say, "Put on the game," and then go down to the basement where the computer was housed and enjoy the game. Her eager response taught him another lesson. It was fine to create something for yourself, but it was even better if someone else could use it, too, and have fun at the same time.

When Lazaridis started high school, he had originally intended to get his four-year diploma and then attend a technical college. During his early years at Herman, he felt segregated, like some lesser being, spending most of his time in the shops programs, far removed from academic pursuits, which were made to seem more worthy. "There was this barrier, two classes of society. There were shop teachers and shop programs and then there were the honors programs, maths and sciences. It really was upstairs, downstairs," he said. That divisive arrangement began to fade after his math teachers saw how much trigonometry, calculus, and algebra Lazaridis learned on his own in shops. They encouraged him to take a fifth year of studies so he could go on to university. "What really impressed them," Lazaridis said, "was that we understood how the math could be used to predict physical effects. The math teacher talked to the shop teacher and all of a sudden they got respect for what was being taught down there because we were looking at things like temperature co-efficients, leverage theory, pneumatics, and ratios. One day he asked if we could put together a lecture for the math students because he wanted to show them how what they were learning was relevant to physical things."

While most young people work their way through high school as best they can, Lazaridis's experience was unusual. In addition to achieving far more than most of his fellow students, he also learned that his inventiveness knew no bounds. His self-confidence, which had a solid base because of his parents' belief in him, was further strengthened by other adults who let him know how much they admired his native talents and problem-solving ability. He further learned the importance of mentors as well as the open-mindedness necessary to follow their guidance. Among the many pieces of savvy advice that Lazaridis received, one particular comment from John Micsinszki stood out and stayed in his mind. "Don't get too hooked on computers," said Micsinszki. "Someday the person who puts wireless and computers together is really going to make something." The door to his future swung open.

As Mike Lazaridis began assessing various universities to see which one he would attend, one candidate stood out: the University of Waterloo. As one of Canada's top institutions for engineering, mathematics, and computer science—his main areas of interest—Waterloo was three hours east of Windsor, more than halfway to Toronto. He toured the campus, visited the Math and Computer Red Room, and was excited to learn that Waterloo had just installed the powerful IBM 3031, with plans afoot to bring in the next iteration, a 4341. The clincher, however, was the school's co-op program that combined study terms with paid work experience. Because his parents couldn't afford to pay for all costs associated with his university education, he knew that whatever he could earn through the co-op program would greatly help. Lazaridis also applied for and won two scholarships, which, when added to his earnings from the *Reach for the Top* invention, meant he could cover his tuition fees and books. His parents agreed to pay for him to stay in student residence.

The co-op program was unique among post-secondary schools in Canada. Students at Waterloo alternated between four-month academic terms on campus and pre-arranged work terms of a similar duration in industry. When Waterloo was founded in 1957, some educational purists greeted the co-op program as heretical, but it worked. Students not only earned a degree, but also gained specific knowledge of occupations they might pursue and, very often, received job offers from firms where they'd worked. The program has migrated from engineering to other faculties and now involves 10,000 of the school's 24,000 students.

From day one, there was another key cultural difference at Waterloo. Professors were permitted to retain ownership of personal inventions or patent an idea for commercialization rather than cede all rights to the university, as was the case at most places of higher learning. As if to underscore the private sector focus of Waterloo, the university's first president was not an academic, but a businessman: Gerry Hagey, a former advertising and public relations manager with B. F. Goodrich Canada. "Waterloo was very visionary. It created a set of entrepreneurial academics and, hence, entrepreneurial students," said Gerry Sullivan, a Waterloo grad who obtained his doctorate in England, worked at Imperial Oil, and then joined the Waterloo faculty. "As a prof, especially in third and fourth years, you had to show students the most up-to-date stuff because they'd already seen a lot of it in the co-op program," said Sullivan. "They'd pull you over the carpet, right in front of the class, saying, 'What are you teaching us this old stuff for?'" Sullivan taught from 1980 to 1990, at which point he gave up his tenured position to start his own process control company, Dantec Systems Corp., and has since launched half a dozen other firms.

By the time Lazaridis arrived in September 1980, Waterloo, which began in temporary quarters in a farmer's muddy field, had grown to a 300-acre campus of modernist buildings in concrete, brick, and glass, rather than the usual staid collection in the Collegiate Gothic style. While engineering remained a major focus, other faculties had been added that included kinesiology, architecture, environmental studies, and the first math faculty in North America. Former farmland along University Avenue had been replaced by commercial development and residential subdivisions. The Faculty of Engineering had an international reputation; the Waterloo Pump, designed to be built with cheap and locally available materials, was supplying drinking water to millions in Africa.

Lazaridis immediately felt he was among kindred spirits. "In high school it's all about football, track and field, and social events, so I was kind of cloistered in the shops program. I had a few really good friends and we pretty well stuck to ourselves. All the popular people lived on a different stratum. When I came here [to Waterloo], it was the opposite; everybody was like those people that I spent time with in high school," said Lazaridis. "This was an engineering school. This guy built a computer, that guy built a radio control system, everybody built something or at least had an interest in building something. Here the most popular students were the ones who knew how to run the labs. I knew how to run the labs, so it was a different world."

This new world was also more competitive; Lazaridis would be able to probe the far reaches of his intelligence. In first year, no marks were assigned. Instead, a certain proportion of students were promoted into second year; the rest were jettisoned. "Work like you're going to fail," faculty warned them. "You put your head down and you worked like crazy," said Lazaridis. "But once you made it into second year, life changed again. You're in a whole new cream of the crop. You're with the top students, you've gone to co-op, made some money, and got some work experience. Plus, you're able to select your courses so you can start doing things you like. When you start taking more electives, the whole school opens up."

Lazaridis enrolled in a new program, electrical engineering with computer science, so he studied compilers, word processing, input files, output files, and systems directories. Students had access to local area networks (LANs)—short-distance data communications that linked campus computers via telephone lines—as well as the opportunity to work with early models of air-cooled minicomputers, conduct diagnostic tests, repair hardware, and write program code for UNIX, a computer operating system.

One of the most exciting revelations was learning about a networked world known only to a relatively small coterie of scientists in government and academe. Begun by the U.S. Department of Defense in 1969, the Advanced Research Projects Agency Network (ARPANET) gave cold warriors a secure means of communicating during an enemy attack. ARPANET became a network of networks that grew to include scientists, academics, and engineers who collaborated on projects, gained access to databases, emailed messages, or posted questions on bulletin boards that brought answers from total strangers—and all of this through linked, local telephone systems.

"We thought this was just normal, every university had this," said Lazaridis. "But very few universities had this, let alone businesses. It became apparent, as we started to go on work terms, just how advanced the training we were getting was. We were learning the future."

Lazaridis spent one work term with a Waterloo prof, Dr. Mohamed Elmasry, a world-renowned specialist in integrated circuits, but most of his time was at Control Data Corp. (CDC), an hour or so from Waterloo in Mississauga, the site of a major research and manufacturing facility. Lazaridis wrote microcode diagnostics and was able to devise on his own an automated process that worked away quietly overnight to identify failed circuit boards, thereby reducing the time previously taken by an individual who was forced to check all boards to figure out which one was causing the problem. CDC recognized his talent and installed Lazaridis in the office of his boss, right beside the chief software architect and across the hall from the chief hardware architect.

Lazaridis was assigned to the Canadian facility's most important venture: an air-cooled minicomputer that could simultaneously run CDC's network operating system (NOS) as well as UNIX, another popular system. Because such developmental projects can take five years before a product is brought to market, Lazaridis learned how to think ahead by imagining things that did not yet exist. "They told you to first invent the components that you would have available to you, and then design the product based on your component predictions. If you didn't do it that way, you ended up with products that were basically obsolete the day you delivered them." So important was the Mississauga minicomputer to the prospects of the company that CDC headquarters in Minneapolis, Minnesota, made available three Cyber 205s, the fastest computer of its day, each worth in excess of $100 million. The team on which Lazaridis worked was able to design and build a computer that not only outperformed the Cyber 205 but at $125,000 was far more affordable.

Their feat was short-lived; the project was derailed by internal politics. Head office was so worried that profit margins would be too slim on this less expensive model that they ordered the engineers in Mississauga to modify the invention by slowing the performance they had been able to achieve. In response to such meddling, the head of microcode quit. "I remember his door slamming, him leaving the building, and I heard his Porsche squealing out of the driveway," said Lazaridis. "I saw, the next day, a hardware architect disappear, I saw people in the memory section start to leave, the people who were working on the silicon technology, people who were working on our CAD [computer-aided design] tools."

Many of them moved to Silicon Valley to join Trilogy Systems, launched in 1980 by Gene Amdahl after he left his namesake company. "The stuff that was happening at Control Data, that was a singular experience," said Lazaridis. "We'll never see it again, not in my lifetime. What we were working on was brand-new integrated technology, new packaging, a new physics. The fact that we had this research and manufacturing environment in Canada, that was pretty special. We're not talking about a satellite office here, we built and designed our own stuff. Those are one in a million, one-of-a-kind intellects that had tremendous experience. We lost a lot of those people to Silicon Valley."

The episode gave Lazaridis a good reason to start his own firm where he could have more control of events. "There are a small number of visionaries within an organization and they're important, they're key developers, you don't want to lose them. You don't want to make mistakes that appear to penalize them for being really clever. If you make that kind of heavy-handed move, you start losing people because they see the place is not open to new ideas. These guys are working fifteen-, sixteen-, seventeen-hour days, they think they've come up with a breakthrough and it has been taken out of their hands. It was the kind of thing you see in a bad movie."

He resolved that any firm he headed would honour engineers with innovative ideas.

During his study terms, Lazaridis lived in Waterloo Co-op Residence with Greg Anglin, a math student from Alberta, and four others in the same "pod." Each student had a separate bedroom; they all shared a sitting room, washrooms, and showers. Anglin, in turn, introduced Lazaridis to Chris Shaw, a math student who owned the same microcomputer as Lazaridis, an S100 box with its eight-inch floppy discs and Z80 assembler. By second year, Lazaridis was showing leadership tendencies as he held discussions with Anglin and Shaw about starting their own business together in an era when most graduates preferred finding salaried jobs at established firms. "We had an idea to have an idea," said Shaw. "One of the problems is, we want to start a business, but start a business doing what?" Lazaridis was most interested in hardware, the nuts and bolts of equipment, while Shaw liked software programming, particularly games. He had even created a naval war game called Ironclads from which he earned modest royalties.

Lazaridis wasn't much of a drinker—a beer or two was plenty in an evening—and the campus pub, The Bomb Shelter, was noisy, so most of the trio's conversations took place in someone's dorm room or a school lounge. In addition to the planning of an entrepreneurial start-up, other topics included Carlos Castaneda, who wrote about his magical experiences as a shaman in *The Teachings of Don Juan*, as well as *Zen and the Art of Motorcycle Maintenance*, Robert Pirsig's iconic book about his travels and philosophy. "There was a whole bunch of literature at the time that was trying to connect quantum theory with the mystical stuff that came out of the seventies," said Anglin.

Lazaridis was drawn to the kind of thinking that promised high energy and human happiness. On a weekend, while most students attended football games or wondered where the next party was, Lazaridis organized a trip for himself, Anglin, and eight other students to Ottawa in a borrowed van. The keynote speaker at the conference they attended was physicist David Bohm, who linked science with spirituality and had studied with Jiddu Krishnamurti, a swami who taught the importance of self-knowledge. "It was an eye-opening experience that gave you a lot of energy. We came back and talked about this stuff a lot, what was happening in physics, how these problems had not been solved. I guess they eventually called it New Age," said Lazaridis. "We would stay up all night and it wouldn't affect us. You'd just go to class the next day so energized. You didn't need alcohol, you didn't need anything, you could get high on just these ideas, what they meant and what the implications were, where things were going and then start to apply them."

For business advice, Lazaridis turned to Larry Smith, adjunct associate professor of economics at the University of Waterloo. In his twenty-five years on faculty, Smith has taught entrepreneurship to more than 16,000 students. He has counseled five hundred teams of students, one hundred of whom started their own businesses, none anywhere near as successful as Lazaridis. "He was an exceptional student. What stood out was his approach to what he wished to do, rather than his ideas," said Smith, who met with Lazaridis half a dozen times. "When I was speaking with him the ideas still were speculative, quite broad based. He was very turned off by his co-op employers because he felt they were making compromises. One of the reasons he wants his own business is because he doesn't think excellence can be achieved with respect to the employers he had. At twenty-two, twenty-three, that kind of maturity stands out. What he wanted was fairly clear: freedom to design to a high standard of excellence in an environment where he could have control of responsibilities. He's an engineer, so he's interested in innovation. He wants to make something new."

Lazaridis, Anglin, and Shaw were usually on different schedules, but in the summer of 1983 all three happened to be on study terms in Waterloo, so they rented a townhouse together at 80 Churchill Street, in an area near campus that was popular with students. None of them owned a car; they used bikes for the ten-minute trip to classes. Their typical student digs had computer equipment strewn around the living room and junk in the basement. One time they dragged a couch into the backyard, where they lolled about while roasting a leg of lamb on a hibachi. A regular weekend visitor was Doug Fregin, who had enrolled in engineering at the University of Windsor and continued to live at home.

In the fall of 1983, as Lazaridis began his fourth and final year at Waterloo, the North American economy was still struggling to recover from a recession that had begun almost three years earlier. During what had been the worst downturn since the Great Depression, many firms had slashed employment and were slow to start hiring again. The University of Waterloo's co-op department had just been through the worst winter term in its history, with nearly 25 per cent of all students unable to find work. For Lazaridis, ever the optimist, the difficult business environment simply offered proof that the time was right to be his own boss.

CHAPTER TWO

STUDENT START-UP

DOUG FREGIN'S SUMMERTIME TRIPS between Windsor and Waterloo continued once school started that fall as the two long-time friends began another one of their joint projects. Rather than build something that already existed, like a computer or oscilloscope, this time they worked on a brand-new idea that had been bubbling inside Mike Lazaridis's brain. His inspiration flowed from two of the ham operators he'd known in high school, Ernie Hales and John Micsinszki, who would broadcast television signals carrying their call letters so other radio buffs would learn about them and make contact. Wondered Lazaridis: Why not adapt similar thinking to a TV screen that could show words typed on a keyboard, words that would serve as a point-of-sale device beside a cash register to attract a shopper's attention to special deals?

With Fregin's help, Lazaridis worked weekends on the project all fall, often using University of Waterloo facilities. To a cathode ray tube that could replicate those ham radio video signals they added read-only memory (ROM) for the computer program, random access memory (RAM) to store data in the form of words typed in by the user, a Z80 central processing unit (CPU) similar to the one used in Radio Shack computers, and a shift register to move data from the box onto the TV screen. The device also included a power supply, two RCA jacks to connect the box to a standard television monitor, and a keyboard so the user could enter the message to be displayed.

Fregin and Lazaridis had known each other so long and had worked together so often that each instinctively knew his place. There might be heated discussions about what to do next, but once they'd decided how to proceed, Fregin would operate the wire-wrap gun used to coil wire around a terminal to make the circuit board layout while Lazaridis determined the overall architecture. What they created was a device that allowed users to write specific messages for onscreen display using a series of pages that automatically flowed one after the other. The display was limited to words up to eleven characters long and five lines deep on the TV monitor, but the shift register controlled the timing between page displays and how long each page remained on the screen so that a shopper would see a passing parade that added up to a complete sales pitch. The message might begin with the store's name, and then cycle automatically through pages announcing special deals, hours of operation, and other helpful product information. Lazaridis designed two demonstration pages: the first contained the word "Super," the second "Sales," with the words rotating on the TV monitor in order to catch the eye of a passerby. Chris Shaw wrote most of the software code.

By January 1984, the prototype was ready; it just needed a name. "He wanted to deliver the subjective impression that this thing wasn't a heavy piece of technology, that it was easy for the user to program," said Shaw. He thought about naming his invention after a cat, like a cougar or a jaguar, but concluded, "All the good cats are taken." Lazaridis then moved to the other end of the spectrum in the animal kingdom and called his invention Budgie, as if the appliance were an irresistible Tweety in a world of wily Sylvesters.

Compared with such entrepreneurial progress, classes were beginning to seem irrelevant, even boring. "He was always coming up with neat little ideas on the back of an envelope, little things that might make some money," said Greg Anglin. "He was always at the forefront of what people were thinking." Typical of the concepts Lazaridis devised, both of which now exist, were a controller on a hot-water tank to save energy and a software program so pharmacists could keep track of a customer's medications in order to avoid drug interactions. Said Professor Smith: "I knew from the tone of our conversations he was getting impatient. He wanted to get at enterprise and design. He wanted his own shop and he wanted it sooner rather than later."

Lazaridis phoned Fregin in Windsor and said, "I'm thinking of starting a company. I need some help." That's all Doug Fregin needed to hear. He abandoned his studies at the University of Windsor and was soon sleeping on a mattress on the floor of Lazaridis's room in the married-student residence, which, despite its name, also housed single students. Every dreamer needs a detail man. Lazaridis knew he couldn't make a go of any business without his boyhood chum by his side. Most of the engineering had been done before Christmas, but they finished up the engineering work in Lazaridis's room. The two also drew up budgets, drafted operating manuals, and made some sales calls to sound out interest.

Exams for Lazaridis were mere weeks away, but graduation

seemed pointless, an unnecessary step on the road to being in business. After all, under University of Waterloo rules Lazaridis could take a two-year leave from his studies. If things didn't go well, he could return anytime during that period and pick up where he'd left off, no questions asked.

Such a step, however, required personal permission from the university president, Doug Wright, who also happened to be the former dean of engineering. Lazaridis met with Wright, who listened to his business plan and was supportive. "I have to do this, I have to try and dissuade you, so bear with me," Wright said, and then made a half-hearted case for him to finish his year. With the bureaucratic niceties out of the way, Wright leaned forward, looked directly at Lazaridis, and said: "But speaking personally, just between you and me, go for it."

If branding Budgie with precisely the right name was important, naming the company was crucial. When Lazaridis tried to register his first choice, Paradigm Research, he was told that name was already taken. He tried other words coupled with "Research," but none of the proposed combinations was available. The application process was slow and each submission cost $160. At this rate, he worried that he'd run out of money before the firm got off the ground.

Lazaridis and Fregin moved out of residence and rented the basement apartment in a house filled with students on Erb Street, a mile east of campus. One evening, a disconsolate Lazaridis slumped in a chair in front of an old black-and-white TV that he'd donated for general use. As he flipped through the channels in search of something to take his mind off the naming dilemma, he happened upon a story about football players who were trying to improve their running game by taking ballet lessons. As the footage showed a player dancing nimbly past members of the opposing team, the words at the bottom of the screen read: "Poetry in motion."

"That's when it hit me," said Lazaridis. "As soon as I saw that, I knew what to do. I applied with Research In Motion and it came back clean." And so it was that Research In Motion, agile and always moving forward, was officially incorporated on March 7, 1984, by Lazaridis, then twenty-three, and his childhood friend and co-founder, Doug Fregin, twenty-four.

While Lazaridis's parents were not pleased with his decision to postpone graduation, they did agree to lend him $15,000 to launch the business. He also obtained a matching Student Venture Loan from the Ontario government. He and Fregin rented a 500-square-foot two-room office on the second floor of a strip mall at 55 Erb Street East, across from where they lived. Monthly rent was $330. Their business phone number, 519-888-RIML (7465), remains the same today. The space consisted of a small room that Lazaridis used as his office, a workroom filled with battered desks from the Churchill Street townhouse, and some tables they built using old doors on metal trestles.

Chris Shaw spent a four-month work term finalizing the code for Budgie on his Apple II+ at a desk in the workroom with windows through which were visible a row of trees and the gallery of local artist Peter Etril Snyder. The small office used by Lazaridis had no view, but he could gaze longingly at a framed print hanging on the wall he'd been given by his friend Ophelia Tong at the company's launch party, which featured his mother's homemade food. Tong, who moved from

Hong Kong to Canada to attend high school, was a third-year math student at Waterloo who fully understood the immigrant experience and the deeply felt need to succeed. The inspirational object shown in the 24 x 18-inch print was a Porsche Turbo. "As time goes on, and you have your down moments," she told him, "just look at this picture and remember, one day you're going to be able to afford one." The two later began dating, were married in 1992, and have two children.

RIM signed a $10,000 contract with a local manufacturer, Corman Custom Electronics Corp., to make one hundred Budgies. The order was delayed that summer after Corman's factory roof collapsed during a thunderstorm, a portent of trouble to come. Remembering that his high school art was more appreciated if given some sizzle, Lazaridis pitched the local television station, CKCO, to do a story on Budgie. Among those who saw the broadcast were buyers at Home Hardware, a national chain based in nearby St. Jacob's. They asked Lazaridis to give them a demo and then added Budgie to their dealer catalogue.

Budgie worked, just as Lazaridis had designed it, and Home Hardware dealers did buy a few, but of the one hundred Budgies manufactured, only about one-third sold. The rest, packed in their original cartons, sat piled in RIM's office, a daily reminder of their marketing miscue. "We didn't know our customer. We were imagining that there was demand for this but there wasn't," said Shaw, who was halfway though his four-year degree. Rather than join RIM full-time, he decided to return to school after his work term ended in August 1984. "We had some of the necessary ingredients for a successful business, but we didn't have all of them. We were thinking like electrical engineers and computer scientists."

While Budgie was not a commercial success, the knowledge that Lazaridis gained and the profile RIM achieved did lead directly to a major contract. Computer Advertising Signs (CAS) of Toronto heard about Budgie and called Lazaridis to see if he'd join with them in building new signs for the General Motors truck plant in Scarborough, Ontario. The two companies met with GM to hear details about updating a system that displayed safety messages and production line information in a noisy setting where oral instructions might get missed or muddled. Lazaridis wrote a five-page proposal for a system that ran on a network and could accommodate any number of signs. Rather than depend upon highly paid union members to climb up a ladder and physically make changes to each sign, as was currently the case, his innovative method permitted updates and messages on a remote basis from a central console.

RIM and CAS won a $600,000 contract from GM to create a series of six-foot-long by one-foot-high LED (light-emitting diode) panels that could broadcast announcements using a word crawl. Lazaridis bought a surplus computer that did not work from the University of Waterloo for $650. He fixed the unit himself simply by tightening some transistors in the power supply circuit, and then used the computer to design the GM system as well as carry out other work for two more years. "That computer never failed. I knew how stable it was because I'd used it at the university. I was able to take apart the operating system and add my own pieces. I built a network for it; this was in 1984–85 when nobody knew what networks were. That network became the forerunner for the signs and the technology that came later."

A culture clash caused friction in the partnership between RIM and CAS. Where Lazaridis was penny-pinching, CAS was spendthrift. "They went through a lot of cash that should have been going to the project. I kept telling them, 'Go home, relax, take some time off. Let us get our job done. You're not helping.' They wanted offices, furniture, and a receptionist. I kept telling them, 'Look, I have no idea how long this is going to take.' It took us a year longer than we thought to finish and deliver. They couldn't sustain their expenses and got into debt," said Lazaridis.

For his part, Lazaridis knew RIM had to run lean to stay alive. "Doug and I were very frugal in those early days. We shared the lowest-cost basement apartment. We walked or biked to work. We lived on spaghetti. Occasionally, we'd have meat. Every morning when we'd go to work we'd smell the bagels in The Bagel Bin downstairs, which was driving us crazy. Eventually we were able to afford the bagels."

The young entrepreneurs kept detailed accounts of their expenses in a coil notebook showing where every nickel went. There was no money for an office fridge, so during the summer they stored soft drinks in the air-conditioning duct. In March 1985, Lazaridis turned to John Corman of Corman Manufacturing, who acquired the rights to the CDS-100 system from RIM and CAS, which by then was bankrupt. As part of the buyout RIM also received a 12.5 per cent royalty from every sign system sold by Corman, who found buyers in Ontario and Michigan. With the injection of funds from the sale to Corman, Lazaridis opened the corporate purse strings a little and leased a Honda Civic hatchback, blue with a blue interior. The $152 monthly payment included two optional items: fifth gear and floor mats.

Lazaridis also posted a notice on the university's bulletin board, Usenet, looking for RIM's first full-time employee. Among the applicants was Michael Barnstijn, who had just graduated from Waterloo with his master's in math and computer science. While his resumé was solid, it was the cover letter he'd done in calligraphy that caught the attention of Lazaridis and Fregin. The three men had lunch and Barnstijn was hired that afternoon to start in May at $400 a month. To that point, neither Lazaridis nor Fregin had paid themselves a salary. Local charities benefited before they did. In July 1984, RIM gave $300 to the food shelter at a local church. In June 1985, fifteen months after start-up, they finally paid themselves a total of $1,750 for the two months of May and June. After that, each began drawing $800 a month; Barnstijn's salary was increased to match that of the co-founders.

Lazaridis had written the initial network operating system for the CDS-100, but Barnstijn was able to find and fix several software bugs that had been causing the system to crash. "Michael was a genius. He wrote what today we would call elegant code. It worked first try, code that was scalable. He was doing stuff, quite frankly, that few people at the time understood," said Lazaridis. "We were using a compiler and it wasn't optimizing the code well enough, so he wrote his own optimizer. That optimizer got the attention of the company that made and sold the compilers, so we did a deal with the compiler company to licence what he built. NASA (National Aeronautics and Space Administration) ended up buying the compiler optimizer. He was able to write some amazing code. In my career, I don't think I've hired more than a few dozen geniuses. You can tell the difference."

In 1986 Lazaridis decided to reward Michael Barnstijn,

vice-president, software systems, and Doug Fregin, co-founder, with ownership positions in RIM. He gave them each 20 per cent and kept 60 per cent for himself. "I always wanted people in the company to have a vested interest. There's nothing like having vested ownership positions to really feel that they're accomplishing something," said Lazaridis. "They were paying themselves a fairly small amount compared to what they would be making if they were employed at some larger company with larger resources," said Barnstijn. "I was content to take the same kind of salary and they felt that if I was taking a much smaller salary than I could get elsewhere, it was fairer for me to be considered a partner because I was taking the same kind of financial risk that they were. Little did I know how much that might be worth to me in the future."

In addition to the sign system royalties, short-term projects provided revenue for RIM. Typical work included creating a local area network for an IBM plant, as well as building a special toothbrush for a local dentist who believed that patients brushed too hard and damaged their tooth enamel and gums, thereby creating breeding grounds for the bacteria that cause cavities. The dentist hired RIM to invent a toothbrush that would measure the pressure so that patients could learn the correct force to use when brushing. "Building that thing was a nightmare. It had to be hygienic, you had to be able to change it and clean it, it had to be indestructible because kids tended to drop it, and it had to be accurate because you're learning a pattern," said Lazaridis. The brush had an integrated circuit in the form of an EPLD, an electrically programmable logic device. Infrared signals sent results of the brushing to a base station, where a set of lights showed the pressure being used sideways as well as up and down. A green light indicated proper pressure was being applied, orange was borderline, and red too strong. Both technologies were used later in other RIM products.

By the spring of 1986, Lazaridis was overseeing installation of the first CDS-100 system at GM. He was able to use the same basic circuit as in the Budgie, but he came up with a way to double-scan the message so the letters looked less fuzzy and were therefore more readable than in other LED systems. "If you had two rows of dots going vertically, if you made them exactly the width apart of another dot, there would be a phantom LED down the centre. Once they started moving, your eye would see extra dots where there weren't any dots. It was an optical illusion. That's something we pioneered," said Lazaridis.

The satisfied client added the CDS-100 system to GM's approved product catalogue, and a second GM plant also bought one. Coincident with the success of the CDS-100, the two-year leave Lazaridis had taken from the University of Waterloo was over. After much thought, he decided not to graduate. "I tried going back, but we were hiring people, and I was going to GM a lot. It was just becoming too much," said Lazaridis. His parents were disappointed. "Taking a leave was a first step, but dropping out of school completely, they were not happy about it."

RIM's fortunes had improved to the point where the company was able to move to an office in Parkdale Plaza at 465 Phillip Street. While this was just another second-floor suite above another strip mall, it was both larger and closer to the University of Waterloo campus than the previous location. Eager to make a good impression on anyone who dropped in unannounced,

Lazaridis insisted that everyone wear a dress shirt with cotton or wool pants. No jeans were allowed. "State-of-the-art tools used by state-of-the-art minds," declared the firm's letterhead. The original corporate logo, designed by Michael Barnstijn's sister, Linda Gray, consisted of the three letters RIM with an overlaid pattern of lines that looked like rays of light emanating from a prism. Gray had no design training, but the price was right. She did not charge for her work. "That was kind of important in those days," said Barnstijn.

By April 1988, there was enough work and sufficient revenue to hire another employee, Terry West, a Waterloo grad in computer science with "triple E"—electrical engineering electives—at a salary of $30,000 a year. "Young engineers often have the idea that they are really, really smart and they need some employees to leverage them, but they believe they know most of the answers and that business is something that they can learn about from a book on the weekend," said Waterloo professor Larry Smith, who continued to advise Lazaridis during those formative years. "Mike never thought he was a one-note band. Mike said to me more than once, 'I've got to get a good team, get them the resources, then leave them alone.'"

While West and Barnstijn wrote software and Lazaridis dreamed up ideas, it was Doug Fregin who kept RIM running on a daily basis. "Doug was the glue that made the company work. Without Doug we would have continually screwed up. He did everything. He'd run to Kitchener to get parts, he'd run to Toronto to pick up something," said West. "Mike would get lost in a lab for days on end and Doug would be the one to remember to turn the lights on, turn the lights off. It was a really good complementary skill set."

The CDS-100 sign system provided some ongoing royalty

revenue, but by the summer of 1988 Lazaridis was looking for the next big thing. One possibility was a microprocessor development tool, called FIRE, for software engineers. Lazaridis thought if they could capture just 1 per cent of what was said to be a $1 billion market, RIM would have $10 million in annual sales. He had lined up a U.S. distributor, Intermetrics, of Cambridge, Massachusetts, and had obtained a grant from the National Research Council (NRC), but needed more development funds from an outside source.

People who invest their own money in early-stage companies with good prospects are known as "angels," a term coined on Broadway where new plays are always looking for help to pay for production costs before a show opens and begins bringing in revenue. Whatever the sector, there's never any ready-made list of individuals willing to take such risks; it's all just word of mouth. Lazaridis approached Michael Volker, a University of Waterloo engineering grad who had founded and later sold his own computer terminals company, and then worked with various start-ups as an investor, director, or officer.

While a commercial bank can spend weeks in similar circumstances looking at a loan application and still turn thumbs down, angels can make speedier decisions because they're backing the jockey, not the horse. Volker toured the RIM office, met Fregin and Barnstijn, but did no other due diligence. "Even to this day I rely a lot on my impression of the people involved more so than the product or the technology," said Volker. "For me, the most important thing is: Do the people involved have the makings of a good team, does it look like they can pull it off? You just had the feeling that this was a quality guy, someone who thinks about quality and wants to make something that's outstanding in its class."

Lazaridis, who regarded Volker as a local high-tech hero and was looking for a business partner as much as an angel, proposed that Volker invest $30,000 in RIM for a 15 per cent interest. Volker agreed but wanted to involve the Small Business Development Corporation (SBDC). If the program run by the government of Ontario approved his investment, Volker would receive a 30 per cent rebate, thereby reducing his actual outlay to $21,000. Volker says Lazaridis duly sent in the necessary application letter in September 1988 and, although Volker had handled other investments the same way, several weeks passed with no response from SBDC.

Lazaridis always liked to have more than one line in the water as he continued fishing for new projects that might lead to ongoing revenue. He met with John Corman and told him, "I can't just keep working on these signs; I have to start on something else. Is there anything on the horizon?" Corman handed over a fax he'd received from the National Film Board of Canada (NFB) calling for bids to build a prototype electronic counter for film synchronizers. Lazaridis could see that the deadline for applications was the next day and complained about the lack of notice. "Well," said Corman, "that's all I've got."

Lazaridis did some quick calculations on the information supplied and found a logical and technical flaw. He phoned the NFB official involved, Frederick Gasoi, who was so upset to hear directly from a possible participant that he swore at Lazaridis.

"Just hear me out for a second," said Lazaridis. "I'm not calling for any new information. I think there's a problem in your specification. How many people have submitted a proposal?"

"You can't ask me that," replied Gasoi.

"OK, that's fine, but have you gotten any proposals?"

"Yes."

Lazaridis described the methodology that he believed all bidders would have followed as well as their exaggerated claims about battery life. When Gasoi agreed the account was generally accurate, Lazaridis said, "They're all lying or haven't done their math. Here's some assumptions, do the calculation yourself." Gasoi did the math and realized the batteries would die after only a few hours even though the NFB specs demanded batteries that would last a month. His interest immediately piqued, Gasoi asked, "Where are you guys located?" Two days later he was in Waterloo explaining the project in more detail.

The key to a winning bid was the ability to read the bar code on the film's edge at a faster rate than any other product on the market. "Doug, Mike, and I sat down, and in one weekend wrote the code for that. Pretty much all of that software was done in seventy-two hours. We did that as a proof of concept. After that it was about turning it into a device that could be used," said Michael Barnstijn.

That next step was aided by Lazaridis's up-to-date knowledge of new technological developments. He was aware that Intel had just announced a microprocessor that was perfect for this product. "After we had finished writing the bar-code scanning software," said Barnstijn, "Mike chose this microprocessor. When I saw it, my mouth hung open. It made the difference between doing the same thing everyone else was doing or doing it ten times faster. We got back to the NFB and said, 'We can do this.'"

In addition to such technical know-how, personal presentation skills were paramount. "Mike has got confidence and he's got the depth of technical knowledge and understanding. Knowledge and understanding are not the same thing. He's got the

gift of being able to explain it in layman's terms so that who-
ever he's talking to will understand," said Barnstijn. The NFB
awarded RIM a $26,000 contract. The need for Volker's
money evaporated. Lazaridis ultimately walked away and the
deal to sell 15 per cent of RIM never got done.

Just as Lazaridis had hired Barnstijn for help with the GM
system, he now signed up Dale Brubacher-Cressman at
$27,000 a year as employee number five to work on the NFB
project. After Brubacher-Cressman graduated from Waterloo
in 1987, he spent a year at Ottawa-based software firm Cognos Inc., but wanted to return to the Waterloo region where
he'd been born. Brubacher-Cressman led the RIM-NFB team
that created DigiSync Film KeyKode, an electronic film
counter that replaced mechanical versions. Using the new bar
code technology an editor could find specific footage more
quickly or seamlessly create an action scene that had been shot
using multiple cameras. "The genius of that was Mike came up
with the comparative system," Fregin said. "To that point, all
the systems were using absolute values to look at the bar codes.
The problem was that you were dealing with prints and neg-
atives of different qualities and developments. What we did was
take a comparative look at an edge where it transitions from
light to dark. It could be a print film or it could be a negative,
it doesn't matter, it's looking for the difference. There had been
a couple of other attempts at doing this, but they all failed. We
succeeded and sold quite a few of those. They ended up all
over the world. They're still being used."

   DigiSync, sold through film labs and Evertz Microsystems,
captured 80 per cent of the market during the first half of the

1990s. "There was a period of time when it was the sustaining revenue for the company," said Brubacher-Cressman, who didn't expect any RIM shares at the time. "People weren't expecting or demanding anything in return. They were really enjoying the work. They were putting in a lot more hours than they might at a larger company. They could see the impact that their individual contribution was having on the success of the company," he said. "Mike is just an inspirational guy. His passion for the company, the work, and the technology is really what makes him such a motivator. People who were coming to the door were really keen to work in that kind of environment. You didn't get a clock-puncher from a large organization looking to be hired."

DigiSync won an Emmy in 1994 and an Oscar in 1998. In both cases, the technical awards were presented to Lazaridis, Brubacher-Cressman, and their NFB colleagues. The technical-Oscars ceremony was hosted by actress Anne Heche. The Emmy-event glitterati included *NYPD Blue* regulars Jimmy Smits, Sharon Lawrence, and Dennis Franz. RIM's Emmy presenter was Anne Ramsay, who played in *Mad About You*. Hollywood stars would hear more about this firm.

Shortly after the NFB contract was signed, Ernie Davidson, the National Research Council representative in Waterloo, urged Lazaridis to apply for a grant under the Industrial Research Assistance Program to investigate surface mount technology (SMT), a new way of making electronic circuits. Unlike the standard method of soldering wire leads into holes, SMT components were smaller and lighter and could be attached directly onto circuit boards.

"You've got to be kidding," said a dubious Lazaridis. "You can only get four surface mount components. Out of millions of parts, there's only four that are available in surface mount."

"Yes," replied Davidson, "but there will be more."

Lazaridis was able to obtain a grant and began working with Tasker Electronics, of Montreal, one of the first SMT manufacturers in Canada. "That was the breakthrough that got me the Sutherland-Schultz contract because we were probably the only company in town that even knew what surface mount technology was," said Lazaridis.

Among other engineering activities, local manufacturing firm Sutherland-Schultz Ltd. installed plant equipment containing a programmable logic controller that permitted testing how a new machine would function along with others in an existing production line before the new unit was actually put in place. The controllers that Sutherland-Schultz bought from Allen-Bradley were expensive, so Sutherland-Schultz asked Corman Manufacturing to design a lower-cost substitute. After Corman tried but failed, Sutherland-Schultz turned to RIM, which created a card containing thirteen integrated circuits that did the work of the three hundred in the Allen-Bradley product. "Everything could be reprogrammed from a floppy disk, all the hardware could be completely changed, and we could basically emulate any product that Sutherland-Schultz had in their stockpile. In fact, we were able to do things they couldn't do with this one very inexpensive card," said Lazaridis.

RIM paid Tasker $150 to make each SMT card, sold them for $250 to Sutherland-Schultz, which in turn sold the cards to clients at a profit and was still able to undercut Allen-Bradley. "For us to make a hundred bucks a board times a thousand boards, that was huge," said Terry West, who wrote the software. Sales to Sutherland-Schultz were so strong that RIM's annual revenue went over the $1 million mark in 1990 for the first time in the company's history.

For all his success with such "one-off" contracts, however, Lazaridis continued to look for a line of products that would yield permanent revenue and a prestigious reputation. He was almost pulled off course by the possibility of becoming involved in the International Space Station, a multinational effort involving the United States, Russia, Japan, the European Union, and Canada. Doug Fregin had an engineering friend from university who worked at Spar Aerospace Ltd., the Canadian company that developed Canadarm, the robotic manipulator used on shuttle missions. Spar hoped to build Canadarm2 for the space station and asked RIM to bid on the circuit board for the video camera used at the working end. "When I was younger it was always my dream either to get into space or make something that went into space," said Lazaridis. "For me, it was a dream come true. Here I am, going to build something for the space station."

Then he started asking basic questions, such as how many boards and when. It turned out Spar might need a grand total of six, two for research purposes and the rest at an unspecified pace. In fact, the entire project was just coming before Congress for debate. "It was risk compounded on top of risk on top of risk. I just looked at it and said, 'This is not for me.'" The International Space Station, first announced in 1989, was finally launched in 1998. "When I saw Canada's contribution with the Canadarm-equipped maintenance module, and at the end of that are two cameras, I knew that somebody built the boards for those two cameras, but we would have likely gone out of business before being able to see it through," said Lazaridis. After forgoing outer space, RIM was about to take the first tentative steps to a new frontier right here on earth.

CHAPTER THREE

A WIRELESS WORLD

WHEN LAZARIDIS LAUNCHED RIM in 1984, his business card included an email address. People would often ask, "What's email?" Such ignorance gave Lazaridis an edge. "I had something special, something new, something relatively few understood. The more I got people asking me, 'What's email?' the more I realized how important it was." That burning ember of interest was fanned in 1987 when Lazaridis attended a conference and heard a speaker from NTT DoCoMo, the Japanese phone company, describe a wireless system that monitored vending machines. As product became low, the machine would send a message to a truck driver asking for a delivery before the machine was empty.

By comparison, North America was far behind, but a Canadian carrier, Rogers Communications, was at least beginning to investigate wireless data systems. Toronto-based Rogers was founded in 1960 by entrepreneur Ted Rogers, who obtained a cable TV licence in 1965 and a national cellular licence in 1983. Rogers obtained the necessary cellular infrastructure from Ericsson, and by 1989 had also acquired Mobitex, a wireless network for two-way paging and mobile messaging, developed in 1986 by Eritel, a joint venture between Ericsson and Televerket, the Swedish Telecommunications Administration.

Mobitex was originally designed so dispatchers could direct fire trucks and police cruisers. Unlike the telephone, which used circuit switching, Mobitex used packet switching. Circuit switching requires a dedicated channel that's used continuously during communication while packet switching involves breaking the content down into standard-sized packets or segments, each of which is given the receiver's address. The packets don't have to travel together, be in the same sequence, or even go by the same path. Instead, they move independently on a variety of different channels. When the packets arrive at the destination, the receiver automatically reassembles them into the original message. The advantage of the packet-switched method is that more messages can travel on a narrower band. Unlike early cell phones that quickly used up all the available frequencies in a city, packet networks could stuff more data messages into a smaller transmission space and still have lots of room left over.

Rogers was the only carrier outside Sweden with a Mobitex network, but the unique licence yielded little revenue. The primary user of Mobitex in Canada was Rogers's own cable division. The receiver boxes cost $8,000 to $10,000 each and had to be bolted onto individual service trucks. "The reality was there wasn't humongous numbers of people who wanted to lug these things around," said David Neale of Rogers.

Mobitex was like a cellular network without any handsets for sale. Rogers needed a range of applications beyond these expensive boxes in order to create a market. In December 1989, Tom Pirner, vice-president of the Rogers Cantel data division, happened to be interviewing a possible recruit when serendipity's hand reached out to RIM. As Pirner described Rogers's need for Mobitex products, the interviewee said, "I know of a little company in Waterloo called Research In Motion. There are only six people, but these guys have technical knowledge in data modulation on radio." Pirner, who had gone to the University of Waterloo, was all ears. He called RIM and arranged a meeting with Lazaridis. "Mike immediately understood the problem. He didn't try to play Motorola. He didn't say, 'Give me a $100,000 open-ended contract and I'll call you when I've got something.' He said, 'I'll work with you, I'll experiment with this, I'll do the best I can. I'll charge you a fair price. We'll both learn and we'll see if there is an opportunity,'" recalled Pirner.

Lazaridis was familiar with packet switching because that's how messages moved on ARPANET, the email system he'd used at university. Although some corporations were beginning to set up their own internal email systems, for the most part, mass-market wireless transmission among individuals was still the stuff of science fiction. Like Sweden, home of Mobitex, Canada is a northern nation with a relatively small population that requires inexpensive ways to communicate over long distances. Previously, any programmer trying to create a new application for Mobitex had to reinvent the wheel every time by writing code for all the routines, right down to the initial handshake that acknowledged contact whenever a PC connected with a data radio modem made by Ericsson or Motorola. The other complicating factor was that a user could only run one Mobitex application at a time.

After the call from Rogers, RIM set out to create an application programming interface (API) used to link hardware and software. Some of the information Rogers provided came directly from Ericsson, so it was in Swedish, but Michael Barnstijn, who was of Dutch descent, was able to decipher enough of the manual to get started before an English version finally arrived. While Barnstijn worked on creating new applications, Rogers put on the best face possible for the Mobitex Operators Association meeting in Toronto in May 1990. Among the other member countries in the trade group—Sweden, Norway, the United States, and the U.K.—no one was any further ahead at developing uses for Mobitex. Despite pouring rain, three hundred people came to a Rogers-sponsored event held in the King Edward Hotel in downtown Toronto. In a valiant attempt to distract attendees from realizing that they really had nothing to demonstrate, Rogers filled the room with so many *ficus benjamina* trees draped in strings of tiny white lights that the event became forever known as "The Enchanted Garden." A few videos and a bottomless-glass bar service helped.

By fall 1990, Barnstijn had created two Mobitex applications. The first was MobiLib, an application that handled all details involving the radio modem and permitted multiple programs to run simultaneously. The second was MobiTalk, a wireless chat program with a split screen so both participants could see their messages in real time. As the first firm to develop products for Mobitex, RIM showed off its applications at the Mobile Data World Conference in Washington, D.C., in February 1991. "They stuck with it," said Pirner, "and as a result they became more knowledgeable about how to make Mobitex work than Ericsson. Ericsson never spent time on that side of the equation. They said, 'We'll put a signal on the air but somebody else had better work out everything else.'" Despite RIM's new products, Rogers was unable to attract many new customers. In March 1991, Rogers merged the firm's data and paging divisions, effectively giving up on Mobitex, in order to focus on other areas such as cellular with better prospects for profits. RIM retained ownership of both MobiLib and MobiTalk.

Mobitex was making little headway, not just because there were too few applications, but also because Mobitex was not yet as popular as X.25, a global packet-switched network developed in the 1970s by the telephone companies. X.25 allowed corporations and individuals to connect with one another, regardless of what system they used. To keep a foot in both camps, Lazaridis realized that RIM needed expertise not only in Mobitex but also in X.25, so in 1991 he hired Gary Mousseau because of his ten years' X.25 experience at Honeywell, Kaiser Resources, and Corman Manufacturing.

At thirty-four, Mousseau was the oldest RIM employee and the only one with children. Mousseau's starting salary was around $50,000 a year—13 per cent less than what he'd been making. He had to move houses because he could no longer afford what he had. Lazaridis kept such a wary eye on costs that Mousseau built his own desk and set up shop in what had been the fax and reception room.

Yet for all the financial scrimping and cramped working quarters, newcomers like Mousseau were swept away by the charm of Lazaridis and the challenges he issued. "Mike's charisma captured me. I felt like a kid in the candy store," said Mousseau, hired as employee number twelve. "There was a big hole in the technology, which from my experience was really obvious. I was pressing him, saying, 'Where are the gateways? How do you connect to stuff? You've got this network, but what are you talking to?' Before the Internet, X.25 connected to everything. It was *the* network worldwide. It made a lot of sense to get us on there."

Within six months, Mousseau produced MX25, the first general-purpose gateway that provided ready access to the Mobitex network. What MX25 did, in effect, was to increase transmission speeds tenfold. The "pipeline" between a dispatcher and a fleet of service vehicles was suddenly fatter, faster, and cheaper to operate. Mousseau also created RIMGate, a box with software that allowed a Mobitex user to hook up with hosts such as Compuserve or AT&T EasyLink.

Other RIM developers were busy, too. Herb Little, RIM employee number ten, wrote MobiLib-Plus, which compressed files and guaranteed delivery of a message. Michael Barnstijn devised MobiView to analyze traffic, and he created the RIM Box, a Mobitex protocol converter that could relay messages between corporate computers and wireless Mobitex paging networks. RIM now had a complete line of Mobitex products to connect users, evaluate and test applications, handle pilot projects, and offer "streaming compression" that reduced data packets to one twenty-fifth their original size, thereby slashing transmission costs.

RIM had built so many items bearing the Mobi prefix that there were jokes. A man named Richard at Rogers Cantel became known as MobiDick. The antenna on a mobile device was dubbed MobiSpike. But beyond the humour, RIM had begun to move into a wireless future at a quickened pace that no one else seemed able to match. "There's always a group of people who somehow find things that the rest of us don't know about. They make something happen, but it's a lash-up. They're the really early pioneers. It's their endurance that makes these things work," said David Neale of Rogers. "The next group mimic it, but they're still really early adopters. But the gap between the people who do the lash-ups and the early adopters is really serious. RIM, as individuals, are right up on the hairy edge. They're the guys who see two things that seem to be totally unrelated, bolt them together, and get it to do a third thing. Mike Lazaridis sees things that nobody else does. He is an integrator; there is some intuitive feel."

But no one person can do it all, not even a compelling leader like Mike Lazaridis. He had hardware engineers and software developers and innovative thinkers who could solve any technical problem, but he badly needed someone to help him with the business side of operations, the kind of savvy adviser he'd been seeking in the 1988 deal with Mike Volker that collapsed. Then—as has happened so often in the blessed life of Mike Lazaridis—the right man came along at exactly the right time.

James Laurence Balsillie was born in the small Ontario town of Seaforth in 1961, making him five weeks older than his future partner. In 1966, the same year Lazaridis arrived in Canada, Balsillie moved with his parents, Ray and Laurel, an older brother, David, and a younger sister, Carol, two hundred miles east to Peterborough, where his father serviced Xerox photocopiers.

As a boy, Balsillie was every bit as bright as Lazaridis but much more obstreperous. In grade seven he was expelled from math class, ostensibly because he didn't know the material, yet a week later came first in a province-wide math test. "This is the kind of stuff that drives teachers to distraction. Can you imagine being a teacher with a smart-alecky kid who disrupts your class? A lot of people have trouble with that. It's a bit of the Canadian way: mind your p's and q's, keep your head down, get in your place, the Family Compact, the monarchy, and the aristocracy," said Balsillie.

At various times while attending Peterborough Collegiate and Vocational School, Balsillie had five newspaper routes, ran a student painting business, and worked at a ski hill and the local General Electric plant. "We didn't have much money," said Balsillie. "I liked being able to get what I wanted and do what I wanted. I had to buy my own clothes from grade seven on. I played basketball games on Friday night, worked all day Saturday, partied Friday night and Saturday night, worked all day Sunday, did my homework on Sunday night, and couldn't understand why I was so tired on Monday. I did that for years. I never slept in. Now that I look at it, I was just crazy. I was centred and focused, but it was full on, working all the time, partying all the time."

Balsillie dated Mary Symons, daughter of Tom Symons, the founding president of Trent University in Peterborough. Symons, a historian who was educated at the University of Toronto, Oxford, and the Sorbonne, urged Balsillie to attend his alma mater, U of T's Trinity College. Balsillie's background as the son of a tradesman did not deter him from making an immediate impression on his Trinity classmates, most of whom were from more privileged families and had attended establishment prep schools. In September 1980, at the end of his first week at Trinity, Balsillie was elected president of his year. "Getting noticed has never been one of my challenges. I just have this way of finding the energy in the room. I don't go making it. I'm just the guy who figures a way," he said. "There's a whole bunch of fish, but someone figures a couple of little wiggles and waggles and people ask, 'How the heck did *you* get there?' I'm sure it's innate." Balsillie joined Zeta Psi fraternity, was named Trinity athlete of the year, and graduated in 1984 with a bachelor's degree in commerce.

Hired by blueblood Toronto accounting firm Clarkson, Gordon (now Ernst & Young) as the first employee in the newly created Entrepreneurial Services Group, he advised corporate clients on financings, mergers, and acquisitions. Unlike longer-serving members of the firm, Balsillie was familiar with all the elements of the newest computer technology, including the IBM XT and VisiCalc—the precursor to Lotus 1-2-3. "I just glommed onto this and could do spreadsheets that were input driven to the whole balance sheet, income statement, and cash flow. That really helped transform a lot of deals because you could run numbers. Before, you couldn't run numbers. It all sounds silly, but in the mid-80s that was huge. It was unbelievable because all the managers had to go and do photocopies for me because I was too busy on the computer. And then I'd have to bring them into the meeting and present the spreadsheets so it inverted the power structure."

After he'd received his chartered accountant designation in 1987, Balsillie immediately headed for Harvard Business School. By then he was married and his wife, Heidi, worked to help pay for their annual living expenses of $35,000, including $15,000 for tuition fees, by doing rehab therapy at health clinics. Balsillie took out student loans, obtained bursaries, and earned money by selling ads after winning the concession for a Harvard student guidebook. He also worked part-time at a boutique financial firm in Boston that was part of the Lexington Financial Group, running deal numbers as he had at Clarkson, Gordon.

In class, Balsillie was taught by the best: Jack Gabarro on power influence, Howard Raiffa on decision-making, and Michael Porter on competition strategy. Balsillie also undertook a project for Harvard's retail guru, Walter Salmon, on entrepreneurial distribution. His student partner on the study was Len Blavatnik, a Russian-American entrepreneur now worth £4.8 billion and ranked sixth on the *Sunday Times* Rich List. "You're a work in process at business school. A lot of people go into business school hoping it will show them the way and those tend to be lost lambs. If you see business school as a training ground for something then it really serves you well," said Balsillie.

Members of the Young Presidents' Organization, an elite group of individuals who can join only if they become corporate presidents before they turn forty, annually attend a week-long seminar at Harvard. Among other events, they mingle with that year's MBA graduating class at a reception. Balsillie attended the January 1989 gathering, inquired if there were any Canadians present, and met Rick Brock, part owner of Sutherland-Schultz. The two connected. Brock invited Balsillie to dinner, which turned into a night on the town that didn't end until 3 a.m. "In the course of the evening I was thinking, 'I should have one of these smart MBA guys working with me, that would really complement my skill set as an operating person,'" said Brock. "Over a few drinks, which turned into a lot of drinks, I offered Jim a job. He said yes and then we continued the night on."

When Brock awoke, he phoned Balsillie and asked, "Are you as hung over as I am?"

"Yeah."

"You know that job I offered you last night?"

"I was afraid you'd forget," said Balsillie.

"I just wanted to let you know I was serious."

"I was hoping you were, because I am, too," said Balsillie. After graduation in May 1989, Balsillie joined Sutherland–Schultz as a vice-president at an annual salary of $70,000. Balsillie soon became chief financial officer and took on major responsibilities, such as closing a plant and reorganizing one of the businesses. Most young executives want to move up and make money. Balsillie wanted more, including a high profile in the community. He joined the Kitchener Industrial Coalition, a local business group consisting of 125 companies employing 13,000 people. Rather than be a passive member, or use the organization simply for networking, he promoted himself and the coalition by writing numerous opinion pieces that were published in the Kitchener-Waterloo *Record*. His chosen topics included taxes, free trade, and how Canada could no longer rely on natural resources for its economic prosperity. "Whether we like it or not, the world is melding into a single economic entity, free of barriers both formal and informal. Our leaders wisely chose for us to face this reality with bold plans to compete and prosper in the new world economic order," Balsillie said in a commentary about free trade published in the *Record* on July 5, 1991.

Coincident with Balsillie's arrival, RIM was running hard to keep out of Sutherland–Schultz's clutches. After sales of RIM circuit boards to Sutherland–Schultz pushed RIM over the $1 million mark in annual revenue, Sutherland–Schultz expressed an interest in acquiring RIM. Lazaridis told them he was not interested in selling and hung tough even though Sutherland–Schultz threatened to stop ordering from RIM if he refused their embrace. Lazaridis concluded that the best way to repel the overture was to find another product, another customer, another big contract. "We were completely dependent on them at one point. I told Doug [Fregin] and Mike [Barnstijn], 'I've got to keep it up as long as we can until we get another contract,'" said Lazaridis. "It was a hand-to-mouth existence and that was the reason we were trying to get out of that, making sure it all works, that your bills are paid, and your employees are paid at the end of the month," said Fregin.

During the high-stakes standoff, Lazaridis came to know and respect Balsillie, who acted for Sutherland-Schultz as the "closer," the member of a negotiating team who joins talks already under way in order to finalize a deal. "When he walked in the door, you could just tell, he presented a unique personality. The thought that came to my mind was, 'You want this person on your team,'" said Lazaridis. He wanted Balsillie as a partner and he told Balsillie so.

There was no time, however, to pursue the matter. Balsillie and Sutherland-Schultz were soon caught up in more pressing personal concerns as the target of a takeover by Dutch conglomerate Stork NV. As part of the deal that was successfully concluded in 1992, Rick Brock bought the high-tech division of Sutherland-Schultz. Balsillie could see no future for himself under the new Dutch ownership, so he took a severance package and left. He looked into buying a division of Westinghouse, but when the deal fell through he called Lazaridis and asked, "Remember what you said about becoming partners?"

Indeed, Lazaridis did. "For me it was relief. I had seen so much serendipity in my life this made sense,'" said Lazaridis, who hired Balsillie in August 1992. "It's just asking too much of someone to have all the dimensions. Mike was the chief cook and bottle washer. It's pretty hard to do a deal by yourself. You need different people to play different roles," said Balsillie. "Mike Barnstijn and Doug Fregin were great guys, but very, very quiet. There were two or three people in production, in the lab, accounting, various coding and engineering guys. The technical power of the team was unambiguous. For me it was a pretty easy decision."

As RIM's new vice-president of finance and business development, Balsillie invested $125,000 that he assembled by using his severance pay and by increasing the mortgage on his house. In return, Balsillie received treasury shares issued by RIM giving him a one-third interest in the company. For the other two-thirds, the original 60-20-20 ownership ratio was maintained without Lazaridis, Fregin, or Barnstijn adding any new money. As a result, Lazaridis owned 40 per cent of RIM, Balsillie held 33 per cent, with Fregin and Barnstijn at 13 per cent each. "The arrival of Jim Balsillie was a turning point for the company in several respects," said Dale Brubacher-Cressman. "There was only so much Mike could do. He recognized the need to get business support into the company to get the company to grow. Prior to Jim's arrival was the only time in the history of my working for the company that there was one month I thought I might not get a paycheque. Jim's arrival brought some business expertise and some ability to focus on that side of the organization."

Balsillie's investment was quickly put to use. Two days after he joined, Balsillie asked accountant Mike Vasilliou to produce a balance sheet so he could see how much RIM's corporate health had been improved by his $125,000.

"Well, it's gone," said Vasilliou.

"What do you mean, 'it's gone'?"

"We had all these pent-up payables. It's all gone."

"At that moment, I thought this was certainly by definition a one-way door," recalled Balsillie. "I didn't realize how much financial duress the company was in." The tough slogging had only just begun.

It is August 1992 and Bill Frezza is sitting on the deck of the Staten Island ferry. The sun is shining brightly, the sky is blue, and the few clouds scudding above the Manhattan skyline look like mares' tails, a sign of changing weather. The director of marketing and business development at Ericsson-GE takes off his suit jacket, revealing wide suspenders, and hangs the jacket over a railing. Next, he rolls up the sleeves of his white dress shirt above the elbows, adjusts the tie bar on his three-inch-wide tie, and then settles down to work.

Unlike most commuters who are reading the morning paper, snoozing, or simply staring off into space, Frezza opens a 10 x 10-inch zippered case, turns on a Hewlett-Packard 95LX Palmtop, the smallest computer available, and begins tapping on the keys. Lurking beside the Palmtop is a brick-sized behemoth that weighs a pound: the Ericsson Mobidem, a radio modem complete with flip-up antenna that has been Velcroed to the inside of the case. Frezza is not composing a sales pitch or working on a spreadsheet. He is sending email messages on the Ericsson Viking Express, the first commercial wireless email device. "Bill Frezza was the first real visionary in the industry. He was the guy who saw the potential in us and took us over to Sweden," said Lazaridis. "Mike Lazaridis was years ahead of the folks at Ericsson. I had a real hard time getting them to pay attention to this 'nobody' Canadian entrepreneur. The he-men at Ericsson didn't want to think they were going to be out-innovated by some start-up guy," said Frezza, who tried to combine RIM, Ericsson, and RadioMail, of San Mateo, California. "There was all sorts of friction between RIM and RadioMail because each one was jockeying for leadership. Neither one was happy about working with the other. It was the typical start-up rivalry," said Frezza.

Frezza's consensus tactics failed. "Bill made a fatal contractual mistake. He tried to negotiate a three-way agreement while letting all three sides see all three sides of the agreement," said Lazaridis. "What bothered us was we were doing it all, but there was this third party involved that was resentful that we were doing any part of it. We were doing it because we saw a whole product opportunity. We solved all the problems. We made it work really well on a small computer and a big computer using a small portable Ericsson radio. We also did the gateway that made this all possible as well as the decompression software on the actual modem or the PC. We created Viking Express—but they decided to focus on the RadioMail product instead," said Lazaridis.

Losing out to competitor RadioMail turned out to be a minor setback. Email was still little more than a novelty in the marketplace. The unit itself was barely portable and the battery lasted only six hours. "We didn't see it as a big market opportunity yet. We saw it as a development opportunity," said Lazaridis. By then Ericsson had sold Mobitex to a U.S. carrier, RAM Mobile Data, of Woodbridge, New Jersey. RAM had built base stations in the fifty largest U.S. markets over which Viking Express was able to operate. Studies by consultants Arthur D. Little and Dittberner Associates predicted that by the year 2000 there would be four million mobile data users in the United

States as well as two million in the U.K., where RAM also operated Mobitex. "We could make money supporting Ericsson on their plans. We could make money supporting RAM Mobile Data on their plans. We could make money providing the early test equipment, pilot programs, early devices, and software. But there was no way this thing can go to mass scale because nobody knows what email is," said Lazaridis. "We're talking about a time when the fax machine was just starting to get on people's business cards, replacing telex. Not only that, but the hardware wasn't ready. The hardware was bigger than the cell phone at the time, which told you how bad it was."

There was so little interest that Viking Express users were left to compete with each other to see who could send an email from the most unlikely location. Bill Frezza sent a message from the ballot box while voting for Ross Perot. Jack Barse, who had worked at RadioMail and then RAM Mobile Data, lugged his Viking Express to Walt Disney World. When theme park staff wouldn't let him take the equipment inside Space Mountain, he had to settle for sending a message from Cinderella's Castle. "We just thought we were the coolest things, emailing each other. You know, who could send messages from the weirdest places, sitting in conferences in Silicon Valley, sending back live reports. It was a great time," said Jim Hobbs, of Bell-South's business development group in Atlanta.

As cellular phone sales increased, wireless email was supposed to follow, but enthusiasm waned. "You couldn't make a business case off email very well," said Hobbs. "A lot of RIM's business in the early days was Mike selling radio modems that were put into vehicular applications and, later, into laptops and other devices that people in field services and transportation were using." Moreover, opportunities for advancement were missed. At one point, AT&T was prepared to place an order with RAM Mobile Data for 11,500 messaging devices that could have meant research and development work for Research In Motion, but RAM held out for an exorbitant price and the deal fell through. "They lost probably the largest wireless enterprise contract of its day. All they had to do was take a purchase order," said Lazaridis. "It was a nascent industry. There didn't seem to be the discipline to put the stake in the ground and move on to the next thing. One of the mistakes that a lot of entrepreneurs make is that they think their current deal will be their last and they just negotiate it to death, not realizing that their next deal will be bigger and the sooner they get to it the better. These guys at RAM literally negotiated the deal to death."

As with any emerging technology, competitors took their own individual approach to wireless data transfer only to see all their efforts fizzle. Motorola produced Marco, a personal communicator running on ARDIS, a network competing with Mobitex. Launched in 1984 by Motorola and IBM for in-house use, Marco had been turned into a broader-use wireless data network by 1990. But since each network operated on a different frequency, a device made for ARDIS, for example, wouldn't run on Mobitex, thereby narrowing the market potential. General Magic offered Envoy, but the system required a stylus and tablet to enter messages and the machine's ability to recognize handwriting was poor. An application from RadioMail let a user look up news headlines, sports scores, and stock quotes, but the email-message capacity and memory were both limited. Software known as Graffiti, from Palm Computing, eased the problem somewhat, but there were too few users who were willing to buy bits and pieces from here and there to create their own personal system with or without email.

Consumers preferred a simple off-the-shelf solution, but none was available.

Even a wireless product launched with great fanfare by a president failed to find a market. In a July 22, 1993, demonstration on the south lawn of the White House, President Bill Clinton used AT&T's EO Personal Communicator to send an email to Vice-President Al Gore that said, "Al, stop the rain in the Midwest, thanks Bill." The device, intended to be the ultimate all-in-one appliance, consisted of a cell phone, fax, personal organizer, computer, *and* electronic mailbox. There was no keyboard. Clinton entered his message with a special pen on a screen that looked more like a child's Etch A Sketch than a technological step forward.

In a speech following the demo, Clinton announced that 200 megahertz of the electromagnetic spectrum used by federal agencies would be auctioned to the private sector, the equivalent of adding thirty-three television stations in every U.S. market, and four times the 50 megahertz made available to launch the cellular telephone industry a decade earlier. "This plan creates the infrastructure to develop the most advanced commercial wireless communication networks the world has ever known," Clinton told the assembled. "We have entered a new era of human communications where wireless technologies become information skyways, a new avenue to send ideas and masses of information to remote locations in ways most of us would never have imagined."

For all the ballyhoo, buyers were scarce. The AT&T EO Personal Communicator was discontinued a few months later because it was too expensive and too difficult to use. Other new products also floundered. Apple Newton, the PDA launched in August 1993, was more than just a disappointment; it was a disaster. The PDA's inability to recognize a user's writing became the butt of jokes in Garry Trudeau's *Doonesbury*. "Catching on?" wrote Mike Doonesbury on his Newton. "Egg freckles?" asked Newton. The Newton was finally killed in 1998, but not before Apple had spent $500 million on a lost cause. The lesson for Research In Motion was obvious. Be good out of the gate or go home. As Albert Einstein had once explained: "The wireless telegraph is not difficult to understand. The ordinary telegraph is like a very long cat. You pull the tail in New York, and it meows in Los Angeles. The wireless is the same, only without the cat." Wireless email hadn't yet been created in a way that could live up to Einstein's cat analogy.

CHAPTER FOUR

DIVIDING THE DUTIES

LOOKING BACK FROM A TIME when email is all-pervasive, it's easy to be mystified by the slow pace of development. Why didn't everyone realize the relevance of wireless email? Why weren't there more email adopters? The history of the telephone provides a helpful parallel. Both the cell phone and wireless email had their beginnings with Alexander Graham Bell's invention of the telephone in 1876 and the discovery of radio waves by German scientist Heinrich Hertz in 1887. Nobody knew what to make of Hertzian waves until 1901 when Guglielmo Marconi rigged up a kite with an aerial wire flying hundreds of feet in the air on the coast of Newfoundland. That first version of today's radio tower allowed him to hear a Morse code signal sent from Cornwall, England, proving that radio waves could bend and travel around the earth's curvature. Until then, everyone believed radio waves travelled in a straight line, so they could only be received for a certain distance before heading off into deep space.

Ship passengers sent the first commercial wireless messages to shore-based recipients. Police departments used wireless in the

1920s and troops conducted short-range two-way communications with Motorola's portable Handie-Talkie during the
Second World War. By 1946, comic-strip character Dick Tracy
had his famous 2-Way Wrist Radio but the first handheld
phone didn't arrive until 1973, again from Motorola, and commercial service took another decade. In the early going, the
number of frequencies available in large cities was so limited
that only a few dozen calls were possible at any one time.

Over the next few years, the Federal Communications
Commission (FCC) granted more licences to cellular operators for designated frequencies, a tale well told by James B.
Murray Jr. in his book, *Wireless Nation*. Canada's Department
of Communications began granting cellular licences in 1983,
with service in urban areas launched two years later. Initially,
car phones were the most popular consumer version in Canada
and the United States because the $2,000 systems required a
large box of electronics that could be stowed in the vehicle's
trunk. In 1986, phones weighed as much as 1.5 pounds. By
1995, they weighed less than seven ounces and there were 100
million worldwide. (In 2001, the number reached one billion,
hit two billion in 2006, and then they began selling at the rate
of one billion a year as cell phones became the globe's most
popular item of consumer electronics.) Cellular providers were
happy to focus on the bonanza; wireless email was less interesting, and, therefore, followed a slower path to popularity.

As a result, companies like RIM and futurists like Lazaridis
had to balance their long-term interest in wireless with short-
term money-making products. When Jim Balsillie arrived in
1992, half of RIM's fourteen employees worked on developing
wireless products for Mobitex, the other half on a succession
of more profitable engineering and manufacturing contracts.

As Balsillie settled into his role in charge of the sales side, Lazaridis took the unusual decision that both of them should carry the title of chief executive officer. Such executive role-sharing at any company was rare at that time and remains so today. For entrepreneurs, such sharing is even less likely; they frequently have trouble giving up responsibility and want to retain control, often to the detriment of the business. Most management textbooks say it's important to have just one leader. The dual arrangement didn't work when it was tried at firms such as Kraft and Citibank. The "two-in-a-box" organizational matrix has been used at Goldman Sachs and Intel, but only in middle management, not at the top.

Of course, RIM was much smaller; Lazaridis and Balsillie brought different skills to the roles and took on different tasks. As co-CEOs Lazaridis remained in charge of R&D and production; Balsillie handled business development and finance. In addition to being co-CEO, Lazaridis retained his other title of president. In 1993, Balsillie was appointed to the board and took on additional duties as chairman because he had board experience, having served as a director at Sutherland-Schultz. "I was classically trained and what I liked doing was technology and advanced problem-solving," said Lazaridis. "I also loved doing the business stuff; what I didn't enjoy doing was the finance stuff." Balsillie is the first to admit that everything he knows about technology he learns from Lazaridis. "I know I'm just a parrot," Balsillie is fond of saying, "but I'm a very good parrot."

One of the reasons that Lazaridis was so open to such role-sharing was that he had seen first-hand what can happen to an entrepreneur who moves away from his area of expertise to focus on financing. "John Corman was a micromanager who wanted to control everything. He was an excellent engineer and he just got more and more removed from the products, and more and more obsessed with the finances and banking. I didn't want that to happen. It was clear to me that if I didn't focus on what I did best, then eventually I'd get consumed. I'd seen it in Corman; I'd seen it in others. Whenever they got obsessed with financing, they took their eye off the ball. Being able to delegate the whole thing to Jim made a lot of sense," said Lazaridis. "Mike is very, very shrewd," said Balsillie, "even shrewder than people know, and very integrated. There's just elements that are not his strength. My job is to get the money; Mike's job is to spend it."

The practical benefits of having co-CEOs extend to the public face that the company presents to clients and the investment community. "If you want a speaker for your event and if Jim's available, he can do it, and if Mike's available, he can do it," said Jim Estill, former CEO of SYNNEX Canada and a director of Research In Motion since 1997. "They're both equally comfortable, and in both you've got the CEO title, so there is power in that. In a high-growth business, in particular, it works, and it works because they divide their areas and they're quite in sync. If they weren't in sync, it would break down quite quickly."

By the time of Balsillie's arrival RIM had outgrown the second office above the strip mall. The company moved to an industrial building at 170 Columbia Street West, a few blocks closer to the eastern edge of the University of Waterloo campus, feeding grounds for new recruits. Balsillie shared an office with Lazaridis until 1994 when RIM expanded again by adding the adjacent unit in the building. Mike Barnstijn relocated and Balsillie took over Barnstijn's former office across the hall from Lazaridis.

Despite the demands of his new role, Balsillie found time to continue writing pro-business commentaries in the local newspaper. At one point he defended the Brian Mulroney government, which was then on the outskirts of public esteem. "The federal Tories and Mulroney are far from perfect. Recent suggestions that it is time for a new generation of leaders in virtually all governments have merit. However, whatever transpires in 1993, the federal Tories deserve credit for nine years of overall fiscal and managerial responsibility," said Balsillie in a column that ran on January 12, 1993, a month before Mulroney announced his resignation.

In the federal election that followed in October, the Progressive Conservative majority government led by Kim Campbell was humiliated, winning just two seats. The Mulroney era left Canadians dispirited and depressed. The recession that began in 1989 after commercial real estate prices plunged by as much as 75 per cent led to high unemployment rates that peaked at 11 per cent in 1992. Because the U.S. came out of the recession more quickly, wireless development began to grow in the U.S. while languishing in Canada. RIM's extensive development work in the U.S. was beginning to pay off.

RIM's first big wireless sale, the result of all that pioneering work on Mobitex, came in 1993 when Ericsson ordered 2,500 Mobitex Protocol Converters (MPC), a modem that relays messages between corporate computers and Mobitex paging networks. "RIM had never built that many of anything that fast," said Steve Carkner, an electrical engineer hired that year who worked on MPC. He asked Lazaridis and Balsillie: "Do you understand how many units that is, just how hard it is going to be to package them?"

When the shipping date arrived, everyone, including the

co-CEOs, formed an assembly line to bag the units, tuck in the user manual, then box everything for delivery to Ericsson. "We shipped on time. It really opened our eyes to what we were up against. Everybody learned that day," said Carkner. At $1,000 for each unit, with engineering costs covered by Ericsson, MPC generated about $3 million in revenue, RIM's biggest deal to date.

With the wireless market at last beginning to show signs of life, Lazaridis decided that RIM should focus on the wireless business and phase out the contract and consulting work. In early 1994, Lazaridis called together all twenty RIM employees to tell them the company would move forward in a more targeted fashion. "We looked at the film-editing equipment and the paper-processing equipment and said, 'We're done with that. We're now going to be a wireless company.' That was to me the moment that changed RIM," said Carkner.

The change in strategy was necessary if RIM was to become a focused firm with a future. "We weren't hitched to the biggest wagons. Some of our prior deals involved a ton of work, a ton of risk, and small margins," said Balsillie. "The film bar-code reader was the same thing. Everybody loved it, but they all needed just one and it lasted forever. It was a nice time to jettison the fuel that got you to this orbit so that you could get to the next one."

Lazaridis aimed high; he wanted to be a major player. "Our goal was to get into the top five. We called it the MENS Club—Motorola, Ericsson, Nokia, and Siemens. Now it's Samsung, but the letters stayed the same. Our goal was to become the fifth letter." Getting there would take time and money, but he knew that such commitment would pay off handsomely. "I wanted to just keep investing, investing, investing, because you get to a point where you've just invested so much that it's very hard for anyone else to get in. I didn't know how long it was going to take, but I knew we had a real shot," said Lazaridis.

RIM's next contract for Ericsson was to make a mobile point-of-sale terminal built around Ericsson's radios. Called MPT, the terminal weighed just under two pounds and measured about eight inches high, six inches wide, and two inches deep. The battery-powered device unveiled in May 1994 had a flip-up antenna, numeric keypad, and magnetic card swipe that allowed merchants at outdoor events to complete credit card transactions wirelessly as they moved among spectators or worked on the floor of a busy trade show, rather than be tethered to a fixed location.

While the product was a technical success, it wasn't a big seller. "MPT was much bigger than it needed to be. We wanted to have a small keyboard, but the merchants wanted big keys and a big credit card swipe. They wanted it to look and feel like the existing terminal," said Carkner, who built one version with a see-through cover on the back in order to show that the mobile device could be shrunk by half. A December 1994 demo in Dallas at a Cowboys-Browns NFL game was successful, but few orders followed. The only major system in operation was at Toronto's SkyDome, where ten wireless handhelds connected to the VISA system at Canadian Imperial Bank of Commerce.

When it became apparent that further development of MPT would cost $1 million and might produce few sales, Lazaridis killed the product in 1995. "You have to create this whole world of applications and certifications. You needed different software for every type of merchant and every type of transaction," said Balsillie. "That's a case of trying to take on the world rather than enable the world. But it laid the direction of integration. It's all about evolving; there's no endgame."

A good entrepreneur learns more from failure than success. What might have been a setback became a springboard to the next product, much in the same way as Budgie led to the GM sign system. One-third of the radios shipped to RIM by Ericsson for inclusion in MPT did not work. "We've really got to build our own radios," Lazaridis told his colleagues. "We can do better than this."

The radios—the modems that wirelessly connect a device to the network—were basically old technology. "It was obvious to us that you couldn't rely on those radios. They were terrible. We figured we had a good chance of doing significantly better. We felt we could capture that market share," said Doug Fregin.

Over the years, any improvements made by Ericsson had simply been layered on top, thus rendering the radios unnecessarily large and power hungry. "Certain parts of the technology had been improved, but other parts had been left alone because radio frequency at the time was considered to be a bit of a black art. We took the attitude if we started with a clean slate we could do a heck of a lot better in a much smaller form factor and with a much lower power consumption," said Michael Barnstijn. "The evidence was there. Cell phones were getting smaller and less power hungry, so why not the data radio modems? They weren't transmitting nearly as much information. In hindsight it was a rather brash thing to say we were going to do, seeing as we had a very slight exposure to radio frequency design and certainly didn't have the corporate pockets of R&D departments at companies like Motorola and Ericsson."

The more he looked into it, the more excited Lazaridis became by the prospects. "Ericsson was distracted doing some very advanced cellular voice technology. But they didn't understand the future of data, so it was very easy for us to become quite sophisticated with data technology to the point where we knew that they wouldn't catch up. It was obvious; it was a transition point. I realized we could lead," Lazaridis said.

There was only one problem: RIM had no radio frequency expertise. Just as he'd done in the past, Lazaridis went looking for the specific talent he needed. Among the first respondents to an ad on Usenet was Peter Edmonson, an engineering professor at McMaster University in Hamilton. "I can't do this on my own," Edmonson told Lazaridis, "but I know where there is a team that's ready." Edmonson introduced Lazaridis to a group of graduate students at McMaster that included Perry Jarmuszewski, a doctoral candidate who had already built a working radar system with no moving parts. In February 1994, Lazaridis hired all six, including Edmonson and Jarmuszewski, to design and build an OEM (original equipment manufacturer) radio that was smaller and more powerful than the clunker made by Ericsson.

Another key employee hired for the same project was Matt Wandell, a talented writer of software code. Wandell was about to graduate from Waterloo but had been so caught up in his school projects that he had not looked for a job. Wandell heard about RIM, came by, and applied. As was his custom with all engineering applicants, Lazaridis quizzed Wandell in person to see whether he understood the core concepts or whether he'd merely memorized the course material. Lazaridis's technique was to ask questions orally and then observe how applicants jotted down the gist of the problem and how they set out to solve it.

"It's a whole different world when you get someone who understands the fundamentals as opposed to someone who just learned the fundamentals. Understanding becomes instinctive. You don't have to go look it up," said Lazaridis. "Matt was the only one who ever scored perfect on my test. I couldn't believe he was available."

Lazaridis continued to interview most recruits until 1999, by which time RIM had grown to four hundred employees. "Once it got to the point where we were hiring a person a day, I couldn't do every interview. By then, we had enough critical mass, the right people, the right culture," he said. "There's nothing more valuable than incredibly talented, gifted, trained, and motivated people. What you do is leverage that skill and that energy by giving them the best possible tools, whether it's laboratory equipment, labs, CAD tools, machinery, access to consultants, whatever, you leverage their skills as much as you can. I believe that one really capable person with the right tools is really hard to match. Their inventiveness, their insight, how do you scale up to compete against one gifted individual? Some people from Motorola even went so far as to tell me that they thought one RIM engineer could do the work of a group of one hundred Motorola engineers. We were technically fearless and completely focused on the realities of physics and technology."

Employees working on the OEM radio had to be technically fearless every time they gave Lazaridis an update on the project. "If people come into my office to present something to me, they better be prepared because I'll do a 'deep dive.' If there's anything in your plan, your design, your conversation, or your mannerism where I detect a hole, I'll just go as deep as I can into that hole. My management style is technical capability combined with incredible respect for people that are really bright."

That insistence on excellence meant employees working on the OEM radio tested out their ideas on each other to make sure they were headed in the right direction. Collaboration was a key part of RIM's corporate culture. "Some of our best meetings were held during lunch on the picnic table. What started out as lunch would continue as a design meeting, and we could blast through some major issues," said Edmonson. "It was a good environment for innovation because no reasonable idea was refused. The first one hundred engineers and techs at RIM all had great track records of design, experimentation, and troubleshooting. All of them were not afraid to work on the bench or crunch code."

With the companywide focus on radio frequency (RF), Lazaridis led by example, working late into the evening and learning along the way. "If Mike left before nine o'clock, he left with an armful of books. He didn't study RF, he *learned* RF so that he knew every component out there and what the specifications were," said Don McMurtry, who joined RIM as marketing manager in 1993. "In the early days the measure was producing cool technology that was absolutely out of this world amazing."

As Internet usage grew, email finally began attracting broad attention. In 1994 Seth Godin, creator of *The Internet White Pages*, published a book called *E-Mail Addresses of the Rich &*

Famous that revealed one thousand email addresses for the likes of Bill Gates, Ted Kennedy, Billy Idol, and Roger Ebert. Lazaridis's vision to invent and manufacture user-friendly technology that people could easily carry and use to send and receive email—just as they were using cell phones for voice— fit perfectly with the rising interest. After all, email offered a major improvement over pagers, most of which could only receive messages, not send them. Even then, some pagers just beeped; others displayed simple messages such as "Call home" or "Call the office." Senders couldn't always be sure their message arrived. If the signal acknowledging safe receipt happened to be weak, the same message might be sent to a single pager dozens of times.

The earliest wireless email adopters were road warriors who needed to keep in touch while travelling on business. In addition to making an OEM radio that could be sold to another company for inclusion in a product they were making, RIM also used its new-found radio frequency knowledge to build what was called a Type II PCMCIA card. The name came from the Personal Computer Memory Card International Association, the group that set the standards for three types of cards: Type I cards added memory to a computer; Type II served as modems; Type III was a portable disk drive. RIM's Type II PCMCIA card, called Freedom, consisted of a small box with an extendable aerial that fit into a slot on the side of a laptop so travellers could check their email from anywhere: airport lounges, hotel rooms, or client reception areas.

When Bill Gates introduced Windows CE, a Microsoft operating system developed for handheld computing devices, at Comdex 95, the major computer show held that year in Atlanta, he used a Cassiopeia E10 portable PC. One of the

Microsoft demonstrations involved a RIM Type II card that fared better than its competitors because of RIM's previous experience with similar technology in the MPT point-of-sale device. "Our power consumption allowed you to plug the card into a computer and it would last all day running off of a 9 volt battery that you could pick up anywhere. Motorola had a Type II card, but the battery life was a couple of hours. We were five to ten times better in terms of battery consumption," said McMurtry.

In 1995, RIM sold 33,000 PCMCIA cards to Megahertz Corp. that Megahertz planned to resell under its All Points brand. At $500 each, the order was worth $16.5 million, RIM's largest contract ever. RIM was just getting to know management at Megahertz, a group consisting largely of Mormons in Salt Lake City, when U.S. Robotics (USR), of Skokie, Illinois, acquired Megahertz in July 1995. "The executive team at Megahertz had incredible integrity. I really wanted to work with these people. We became really good friends. But of course, when USR got in, things changed," said Lazaridis.

USR next bought Palm Inc., which in turn put Lazaridis and Balsillie in contact with Palm founder Jeff Hawkins. Balsillie and Lazaridis had both seen a wooden prototype along with software running on a PC that emulated what would become the Palm Pilot, the personal organizer launched in 1996. They tried to convince Hawkins to include RIM's OEM radio in the Palm Pilot, but made no progress. "They were on their own trajectory. I think at that time Jeff wanted to build his own radio, but he was having trouble just building a PDA," said Lazaridis. RIM and Palm had other points of friction. Hawkins and Palm CEO Donna Dubinsky asked for a meeting in Waterloo, claiming to be interested in acquiring RIM.

Balsillie suspected the Palm executives were just on a fishing expedition to learn more about RIM's technology, but rather than reject the request for a meeting out of hand, he decided to go ahead while maintaining a healthy degree of caution.

At the meeting Balsillie purposely gave few direct answers to their questions. "I didn't have an obligation to give them any more than I gave them. They were quite frankly trying to extract information that they weren't entitled to, but I didn't give it up and, at the end of the day, I suspect they left feeling woefully unsatisfied," said Balsillie.

Such insincere meetings with masked motives were typical in the technology sector in those days, according to Balsillie. "Some of the bigger tech players in the early days played Lucy and Charlie Brown to the world for years before anyone got wise to it. They profited enormously." Balsillie says his style is very different. "It's fundamentally very forthright, but you always have a safety net that the other side doesn't see. I'm perfectly capable of letting you think you've got me duped if you are trying to play me. But mine is a legitimate and fair defensive strategy rather than a sneaky, disingenuous one. And people who play that disingenuous game are often so focused on duping you that they let their own guard down."

The apparent ruse with Palm was one thing, but allegations by U.S. Robotics that RIM's PCMCIA cards didn't work properly were far more unsettling. "We had some static problems. We fixed them quite early. But that was used as an excuse to get out of the deal," said Steve Carkner, who did the mechanical engineering on the card. When U.S. Robotics continued to balk at fulfilling its original order, RIM sought arbitration in August 1997. After a hearing involving ten witnesses, RIM won a $2 million settlement from U.S. Robotics in July 1998.

Undeterred by such hardball tactics as competitors tried to knock RIM out of contention, Lazaridis fought back from strength—his ideas. He brainstormed with his colleagues about a portable wireless device—"email on a belt" he called it—that could send and receive longer messages, not just the cryptic sentence or two permitted by pagers. Having seen the Palm Pilot prototype, he knew he didn't want any part of Palm's touch-screen and handwriting recognition technology. "For me, it was all about keyboards at the time because I could type very fast, very accurately, without ever looking at the keyboard. With a tactile system that's properly designed, within days your body memorizes where all the keys are without you having to look at them. So Jeff went off and did touch screens. I went off and tried to develop something with a keyboard."

Lazaridis's vision for a wireless email device, an idea he'd been musing about for half a dozen years, had at last met a need in the marketplace. "The wireless networks were going in. RAM Mobile Data was putting in a system straight across the United States, Rogers had expanded in Canada, and it was obvious to me that wireless data was the future. The big surprise was there were very few companies out there in this game," said Balsillie. Research In Motion, the tiny start-up from Waterloo, Ontario, was about to receive help getting into the game from two American giants: Intel and BellSouth.

CHAPTER FIVE

TUCSON AND SHOW LOW

THE TWO DESPONDENT INTEL EMPLOYEES sat slumped in an airport lounge in Calgary, Alberta. Terry West, a Toronto-based Intel field application engineer, and Graham Tubbs, of Intel's business development unit in Chandler, Arizona, had made numerous sales calls in the spring of 1995 with no success at selling the transistorized chips for which Intel was famous. As West racked his brains, he came up with one more possibility: Research In Motion, in Waterloo, Ontario, almost 2,000 miles east. "Those guys at RIM have some interesting product ideas. You should really consider visiting them," said West, who had worked at RIM from 1988 to 1993. Tubbs filed the idea away but wasn't able to get to Waterloo for another few weeks, when he and West finally met with Mike Lazaridis.

Initially, Tubbs was unimpressed. RIM shared the ground floor of a small office building with another tenant, Bell Canada. When Lazaridis took Tubbs on a tour, the whole process lasted about ten minutes, a far cry from Intel's empire with $10 billion in annual sales and a hundred thousand employees around the world. In Chandler alone there were ten thousand employees representing the breadth of Intel in research and development, assembly and testing, sales and marketing.

Then Lazaridis demonstrated some of RIM's application products running on the Mobitex wireless network. He also showed them prototypes for devices that would support email, a major improvement on pagers that could only send messages one way. "In a few years we're going to have something that will fit in the palm of your hand and you'll be able to receive and send email from it," claimed Lazaridis. But RIM had run into design difficulties with the circuit board. Engineers couldn't make it small enough to fit inside a handheld device that would appeal to a business user on the go. "Both sides of the board were crusted with parts. He'd stripped out everything he possibly could. It was as small as he could make it," recalled West. Tubbs and West told Lazaridis that Intel might be able to supply a more miniaturized solution by integrating the key semiconductor elements. "I was far more interested than I thought I would be," said Tubbs. "I could see that these guys were committed, but I could also see that they weren't going to go any further unless somebody took a risk on them."

Tubbs returned to Chandler where he recruited Terry Gillett, Intel division manager for microcontrollers, and the two men drew up a development plan to add extra memory and some peripherals to Intel's 80C186 microprocessor. The 186 had been around since 1982, prehistoric by technological standards. By 1995, Intel was making the far more powerful Pentium processor, Intel's first branded product, but a version of the 186 that was customized especially for RIM did offer potential. They estimated that the work involved would cost Intel $2.5 million with no guarantee that RIM would ever order the product, let alone achieve sufficient success to cover

Intel's engineering costs and yield a profit.

Such an expenditure required approval by Tom Franz, Intel's vice-president and general manager of embedded technology. But in the fall of 1995, when Gillett and Tubbs took their proposal to him, all of next year's development money had already been designated. Moreover, Franz was aghast at the idea of spending $2.5 million on an untested product destined for a no-name company in a city that he'd never heard of before. His questions became increasingly exasperated. "You want us to spend how much? Who the hell are these guys? Where are they from? Where the heck is that?"

Franz finally threw them a bone. "See what you can do with $100,000. We can afford that," he said. "That was like a slap in the face," recalled Gillett. "We went to the nearest bar and cried in our beer but then we said, 'We did get something. We didn't get what we wanted, but what can we do with this?'"

Many Intel products under development were given a code name based on an Arizona city, so the RIM project became known as Tucson. Beyond the meagre funding, the development team had another serious constraint. Intel usually produced chips for PCs or other products that could be plugged into a constant power source. RIM wanted to make a handheld that ran on one AA battery.

Intel co-founder Gordon Moore had declared in 1965 the number of transistors that could fit onto a computer chip would double every eighteen months. Moore's Law, as the statement became known, turned out to be accurate. As a result, engineers could design items that needed more chips than was currently possible in the full knowledge that by the time their concept was complete, the continuous miniaturization predicted by Moore's Law would have eliminated the problem. As a result, some household appliances have more computing power today than was available aboard the lunar module used by Neil Armstrong and Buzz Aldrin in 1969.

Batteries, however, follow no such path of automatic improvement. Manufacturers are lucky to increase battery life by 10 per cent a year. The multiple functions in the mobile device that RIM had in mind would drain one AA alkaline battery in mere hours rather than last the two to three weeks Lazaridis sought.

Intel first considered the silicon wafers that look like a network of tiny islands separated by streaks. The circuit board designed by Lazaridis had three such islands. What would happen, wondered the Intel engineering team, if those three were miniaturized and combined into one integrated package along with the other essential components, such as the multiplexer that combined electrical signals and the flash memory for storage and data transfer?

This concept, known as a "few chip package," meant a smaller circuit board that could fit into a handheld, give improved power, and fulfill all the functions RIM had in mind. When the Intel team added up the development costs using this approach, the total expenditure came to just under the $100,000 budget. "If we had got the full $2.5 million to develop a unique silicon die, it would probably have taken eighteen months to two years because silicon chip development is complex. By using the package-integration approach, the prototype was to RIM in March 1996, within three months of our proposal. Everything was accelerated," said Gillett.

Meanwhile, Lazaridis had his engineering team focused on

the rest of his demands for the first wireless handheld. "Mike had a little piece of paper on which he had written goals for this particular design. We were always to refer back to that one sheet of paper with its succinct set of goals: last a very long time on a single double AA battery, keep within the form factor of an existing Motorola one-way pager, be able to do the most common actions with a single hand," said Michael Barnstijn, who wrote the display driver, the software that managed the display on the screen and oversaw the other software developers. "If your design direction was taking you away from the goals then you were going the wrong way."

The location of the screen above the keyboard was crucial. "One of the first things we learned was that when you're typing and you're looking at the computer, your peripheral vision is actually seeing the keyboard. That's what keeps your fingers on the keys and gives you the confidence. It's all subliminal," said Lazaridis. "Your actual, active visual area is a very small spot. So that's tracking what's on the screen. The fact that your peripheral vision can really see the keyboard and where the thumbs are, that's what helps you build up the muscle memory because you have this confidence that you know where the keyboard is. Then after a while you don't even notice you're not paying attention to the keyboard."

In June, Intel delivered the production parts that became the basis of the Inter@ctive Pager 900, RIM's first portable two-way wireless messaging device. Flip the black clamshell lid and there was a full QWERTY keyboard, a four-line display screen allowing up to thirty characters per line, four rubber buttons for navigation—all running off two AA batteries. The one-battery handheld would have to wait. Lazaridis was scheduled to be at RAM Mobile Data headquarters in Woodbridge,

New Jersey, on a Friday in July to demonstrate the device on the Mobitex network owned jointly by RAM and the Atlanta-based carrier BellSouth.

RIM's development team—Dale Brubacher-Cressman, Michael Barnstijn, Mark Church, Steve Carkner, and Barry Linkert—worked around the clock to get the prototype ready. "Mike Lazaridis wasn't really a software guy, but in those early-morning hours he'd be sitting with us. He knew he had to get this thing done. Tuesday we did twenty hours, went home for about three hours; came back, did another twenty hours, home for another five hours, then came back until Friday morning at eight o'clock when we had everything done. It was *just* working," said Barry Linkert. "We were dead. Mike had left. He was pretty exhausted." They knew they were onto something when Lazaridis reported on how well their work had been received. "You should have seen their faces when I laid the device on the table, sent a message to their desktop, and they saw it arrive. The light bulb went on," he told the team at RIM.

While Intel called their end of the work Tucson, RIM had no internal name for the device when it was being developed. The official name resulted from another late-night session when RIM marketing manager Don McMurtry and director of business development John Latham were finalizing sales brochures. "We had a big whiteboard and we were throwing all kinds of names up on it," recalled Latham. "We tried to look at what it was trying to accomplish. It was interactive and I remember saying, 'Well, it's Internet related. Why don't we use the @ as the 'a' in Interactive to get the Internet connection?' We had about three different names with @ in the middle. We went to the legal department in the morning to see if these had already been copyrighted, to see which ones we could use, and found out that Inter@ctive Pager had not been used and that's how we got the name," said Latham.

Lazaridis was already looking ahead to RIM's next model, which was code-named Leapfrog because RIM wanted it to "leap" over whatever Motorola might be bringing out. Leapfrog would eventually become publicly known as the Inter@ctive Pager 950. Riffing off the sleekness of Leapfrog, the original Inter@ctive Pager 900 would be retroactively and jokingly nicknamed Bullfrog, given its comparatively large size and bulbous shape. At the time of its introduction, however, the Inter@ctive Pager 900 with its full QWERTY keyboard was, in fact, a significant technological achievement and a sign of things to come from RIM. Mark Guibert, who left Hewlett Packard to become RIM's director of marketing, recalls several friends in the tech industry questioning his decision to leave an established company like HP and ribbing him about the bulkiness of the Bullfrog and its niche opportunity. "I recall taking some friendly jabs at the time and telling them that they were looking at it the wrong way and saying that they were looking at it as the world's largest pager, but it was actually the world's smallest email terminal," said Guibert. "Of course, they weren't the only people who needed convincing. I spent a lot of time during my early years at RIM talking with skeptics about the potential of wireless email and RIM's ability to lead the industry."

The Inter@ctive Pager 900 aroused interest from competitors and others in buying the company. So pleased was Intel with the success of its work with RIM that Intel Capital, the company's venture capital arm, thought about, but rejected, the idea of acquiring Research In Motion. "The best thing that ever happened to Research In Motion was that Intel decided not to get them. Mike and Jim and their team have been so successful. I don't believe that could have happened in the Intel culture," said Intel's Gillett. BellSouth also considered buying RIM, but decided the company was not a fit with the BellSouth culture. "We passed on the idea because we weren't manufacturers," said Earle Mauldin, CEO of BellSouth Enterprises.

Consultant Andy Seybold, who wrote a monthly newsletter in collaboration with *Forbes*, also acted as an adviser to Motorola and Microsoft. At various times, Seybold urged both companies to acquire RIM.

As far as RIM was concerned, they allowed no one's interest in buying them to get very far. "There were people now and then taking runs at us, sure, but it just ultimately didn't seem to make sense for RIM," said Balsillie. "Palm, US Robotics, Ericsson took a good hard run at us. Intel took a sniff. You just play it out. You take the meeting, you hear them out, but you don't let them take advantage of you."

In no case did talks get far enough along that RIM opened its books for inspection by a possible acquisitor. "Somehow we were able to elude the grasp that each one of them thought they had," said Balsillie. "I don't think we'd be anywhere near where we are today if we'd slipped fully into their grasp because then you're really a puppet to somebody's agenda rather than have the ability to flourish. They were all part of the Indiana Jones movie that we lived. There were a lot of close calls."

By fall of 1996, RIM was producing working models of the Inter@ctive Pager 900 with Intel inside. At first, it sent and received messages only on a peer-to-peer basis—one Inter@ctive Pager owner could only talk to another Inter@ctive Pager owner—but then RIM engineers created a gateway so users could email anyone on the Mobitex network. "We knew that there was something special when our employees were taking home the early prototypes even though you couldn't put them in your pocket and they had to be charged every three hours," said Lazaridis. "We asked them, 'Why are you taking this home?' And they said, 'So we can keep working without coming back to the office.' Even then we were interacting with the rest of the world and you get conversations happening at different time zones. As time went on we realized that people were starting to use these things to message. We had turned email into instant messaging and that's what really drove it, because then people found email very productive."

But users were hampered by the unit's size and weight. At 3 x 4 x 1.4 inches and weighing three-quarters of a pound, the Inter@ctive Pager 900 (a.k.a. Bullfrog) was the size and weight of a double hamburger. Intel employees using Bullfrog at company locations in Arizona and Oregon complained, but no one would give them up. "People who were carrying them around started filing for workmen's comp," joked Gillett. "The implementation was horrible and the batteries didn't last very long, but everybody agreed that Research In Motion, at the conceptual level, had a winner on their hands."

On September 19, 1996, Lazaridis, Balsillie, and David Neale, of Toronto-based Rogers Wireless, attended a meeting in San Francisco of the pACT Vendor Forum. Founded in April, the pACT (personal air communications technology) group consisted of Ericsson, AT&T, Novatel, NEC, Casio, Sema Group UK, and Research In Motion. That morning, while panel members complained no one had been able to produce a wireless handheld device that actually worked, Lazaridis, Balsillie, and Neale were sitting at the back of the room with a Bullfrog, sending and receiving messages. "They were discussing how pACT would evolve, what would the terminals be used for. We were at the back, laughing," recalled Neale. One of the messages Lazaridis sent to Waterloo read, "I don't believe it—they don't know about this product."

The first Bullfrogs were built for RIM by a Toronto firm, Nikom, which is no longer in business. "Bullfrog was our first foray into low-volume mass production plastics. Almost everything we had built to that point was metal. MPT [Mobile point of sale terminal] was the first to have plastic housing, but the Inter@ctive Pager was at a different level in terms of complexity," said Dale Brubacher-Cressman. That crucial difference caused problems with the clamshell hinge. "The hinging was just a friction set. The more you opened and closed it, the more it wore the hinge off. Eventually there was no friction to it and it would just flop open," said John Latham, director of business development at RIM. Latham struck a replacement deal with carrier Bell Mobility as part of his Bullfrog sales pitch about how he would deal with hinge problems. "We came to an agreement that if it fell open more than three fingers, then I would take it back."

Lazaridis wanted more control over production, so he hired six people to assemble Bullfrogs in rented space and then began planning for a manufacturing facility where prototypes could be tested and produced with better quality control. In August 1996 he hired Rick Landry, who had worked at JRC Canada, a Lethbridge, Alberta, cellular manufacturer, and told him to prepare a larger and more suitable plant. RIM's seventy-two employees were used to working under tight conditions—Landry's first office was a closet—but the new plant on Shoemaker Drive in Kitchener (an adjacent city within Waterloo Region) was 36,000 square feet. The plant opened around January 1997. "At the time, I wasn't sure that going from contract manufacturing to your own manufacturing made a lot of sense, but when I started looking at the quality issues they were having, it did make sense," said consultant Andy Seybold. "They were having problems with batteries, screens, and what I would call 'infantile failures' in the field, where the thing lasts for a day and then quits working. Mike was adamant about the fact that these products were not run-of-the-mill, easy-to-build products. The way they had been designed, it took somebody who understood miniaturization and how to put these things together. He wasn't going to come out into the market with a product that wasn't as reliable as it possibly could be. They felt they had no choice but do what they did."

Reviews of the Bullfrog were muted. "The RIM Inter@ctive Pager is a good device, but it's a bit too heavy, bulky and expensive to attract many mobile professionals," declared *Wireless Internet and Mobile Computer Newsletter*, the industry bible, in its February 26, 1997, edition. Connectivity was also an issue. The pager might be worthy, but the article raised questions about the Mobitex network, a nationwide jumble of random access points, any one of which could be subject to problems ranging from interference to complete failure.

Fortunately, RIM also was making money selling its OEM radios for use in wireless operations such as ATMs, vending machines, and trucking fleets. Lipman USA Inc., Panasonic Personal Computers Co., Itronix Corp., and Symbol Technologies all used RIM's OEM radio in their handheld computing products and laptops. "OEM orders were small but gradually worked up to $1 million a year at a time when we weren't making a lot of sales. Rick Landry and his people in manufacturing loved it because basically there was very little hands-on assembly and essentially no returns, as opposed to the Bullfrog. The OEM was a nice little cash cow," said Latham.

While there was also revenue from wireless PC cards for use with laptops and PDAs, increasingly the Inter@ctive Pager 900 began to dominate RIM's production and profits. IBM ordered $10 million worth of Bullfrogs for use on its ARDIS/DataTAC network, where it was called the Inter@ctive Pager 800 to differentiate it from the 900 model used on the Mobitex network jointly owned by RAM Mobile Data and BellSouth. (ARDIS later merged with American Mobile Satellite to become Motient.)

In late 1996, Intel's Terry Gillett and Graham Tubbs were back in Waterloo, having learned some lessons from Bullfrog. "Taking a less than ideal product to market revealed much more information than either team could have imagined," said Tubbs. "The impact on the next stage of development was fundamental and profound." The Intel team believed the next obvious step was to move from the 16-bit 186 microprocessor used in the Bullfrog to the much more powerful 32-bit 386, first produced by Intel in 1985. Again, this was relatively old technology, but if RIM's handheld device were a car, this was the equivalent of putting a turbine in a Toyota. Moreover, gas consumption—power usage in the case of the handheld—would actually be lower and the unit would be better able to support new applications.

Lazaridis challenged the idea. "Are you nuts? Putting a 386 in a pager? That's insane. That's way over-powered." Gillett and Tubbs asked Lazaridis to at least consider the possibility, put their tails between their legs, and left. By the time Gillett and Tubbs returned to Waterloo in January 1997, Lazaridis had decided that they were right. "He was on the team. He'd thought about what he'd heard and he was really excited," said Gillett. "Mike's style is to challenge a viewpoint forcefully. He did not have much time for an individual who could not withstand such interrogation," said Tubbs.

Now that Lazaridis had agreed to use 386 technology in Leapfrog, he wanted to be certain that Intel was fully on board. "Commit," Lazaridis demanded. Tubbs and Gillett gave their personal commitment and shook hands with Lazaridis to seal the deal, even though they had no idea if Intel would approve. Back in Arizona, Tubbs and Gillett proposed a $5 million development project; Tom Franz agreed to a budget of half that amount. More troublesome, only three among the eighteen-member team assigned to the project had engineering or development experience. The rest were all recent college graduates. The previous project for RIM had been code-named Tucson, the second-largest city in the state of Arizona. As if to express the modest expectations of Intel brass, this project was named after Show Low, a town of 10,000 in the White Mountains of northeastern Arizona. According to local legend, the name Show Low was the result of a card game. The original settlement wasn't big enough for two hombres, Marion Clark and C. E. Cooley, so they played cards to see who would stay. "If you can show low, you win," said Clark. Cooley drew the two of clubs, saying, "Show low it is."

Intrigued by the code name given to the project, Lazaridis looked up Show Low on a map of Arizona and was surprised to see, beside the name for the town, the word "Rim," for the

Mogollon Rim, a regional escarpment 7,000 feet high and 400 miles long. Lazaridis regarded that geographic proximity as a good omen. Show Low and RIM were meant to be together.

Since so many Show Low team members were inexperienced, responsibilities were divided using a novel approach that Intel had never before tried. The three with solid backgrounds included Russ Chamberlain as program manager and Sandeep Shah as engineering manager. The third, Congquay Trieu, was appointed as a coach who wasn't expected to actually design anything. His sole role was to be a mentor who roamed from office to office helping the recent graduates solve their individual problems.

Lazaridis and Balsillie visited Chandler, met the development team, and kept abreast through weekly updates. At one point, Lazaridis gave a pep talk to the group, who had assembled to hear him in an empty cafeteria. He leaned against a table, holding a wooden model of the hoped-for device in one hand and an AA battery in the other. "Wireless is inherently constrained in terms of memory, power, and bandwidth. We develop from scarcity, so we have to be disciplined," he said. "Together, we're going to make a little device like this that runs for twenty days on this battery, twenty-four hours, seven days a week. I'm going to show you how to do that."

He urged them to abandon their usual reliance on Moore's Law. Instead, he told them to do something they'd never done before: decrease performance and go for lower power. Wowed by his speech, the group devised a slogan: "Have you saved a milliwatt today?" The slogan became a rallying cry printed on cards placed in every team member's cubicle and emblazoned on a banner hanging in the lab. "They got this massive improvement in power consumption because they had never optimized for power. It was all low-hanging fruit. Back then it was a big revelation because they didn't think they could do it," said Lazaridis.

The challenge by Lazaridis led to other fresh thinking by Intel. "The 386 was on .8 micron—these days they're doing .6 nanometer, one thousand times less—but .8 then was the leading technology in PCs in the late 1980s and early 1990s," recalled Terry West. "We said, what if we moved it forward two process generations to .35, what would happen to that chip? And instead of having 50 or 100 megahertz, what if we cranked it back to 10 megahertz? You'd have a ton of processing power, but pull a minuscule amount of battery power."

Show Low development at Intel took up most of 1997. At one point, Gillett sent a functioning version of a processor to Waterloo for testing. Lazaridis objected, saying he had no way of measuring the flow of electric current in anything that drew so little power. When Gillett insisted, Lazaridis bought from Hewlett Packard the necessary ammeter for testing, one that was so sensitive that the probes alone cost hundreds of dollars. He was stunned by the results. "I plug it in and I can't believe how little current this thing is drawing. It's minuscule. It was, like, twelve microamps, which is almost nothing. I mean, two pieces of wire put together with a little bit of saline would generate twelve microamps. I called him back and said, 'I don't know what you guys did, but this thing is drawing nothing,'" said Lazaridis.

Gillett then admitted that Intel had come up with similarly surprising results. "We got zero on our test equipment. We thought there was something wrong," Gillett said. Intel delivered prototype Show Lows early in 1998 and shipped the first production models later in the year. "It went from the team nobody wanted to be associated with to the team everybody wished they'd been on," said Tubbs. In June 1999, RIM and the Intel team won the Award for Canadian-American Business Achievement, presented by Canadian ambassador to the United States Raymond Chrétien, at a luncheon ceremony in the Canadian embassy on Pennsylvania Avenue in Washington, D.C., attended by Franz, Lazaridis, and Balsillie. In 2000 the team also won the Intel Achievement Award, the company's highest accolade.

The next step would have been to replace the 386 with either the 486 or Pentium. The new slogan among some people in Intel's business development unit became "Pentium in your hand," but development estimates ran to $25 million. This time, Intel balked at the expense. Intel continued to supply chips to RIM until 2002, when RIM turned to British microprocessor designer ARM Holdings to provide new technology for its first smartphone, the BlackBerry 5800, and then returned to Intel in 2005 to buy the firm's XScale technology designed for low-power consumption.

For Tubbs and Gillett, now retired from Intel and working together as consultants in Phoenix, the Tucson and Show Low projects stand out as career highlights. "I've managed a number of different projects at Intel," said Gillett. "I have never had one where the customer and Intel worked so closely together to bring about a positive result." Terry West, who still works at Intel, agrees. "You don't get to do many things like that in your life."

CHAPTER SIX

SUCCESS LIES IN PARADOX

WHILE INTEL'S INVOLVEMENT with the circuit board was crucial, serendipity also played a role. Lazaridis's young son had often seen his father slide a video into their home VCR player. The boy decided to stuff the same slot with a snack and the piece of entertainment equipment was rendered inoperable. "My wife and I had bought it and we were very proud of it. He fed it a banana, a sandwich, a piece of cheese—I can't remember what it was. It was so gummed up there was no hope," said Lazaridis. He purchased a new Panasonic VCR and was pleased with the picture quality, but what particularly fascinated him was a fat trackwheel on the remote control that he could operate with his thumb. "When I went to set the clock and use the features, the menu, I never saw anything so easy," he said. "You roll this thing, see the different features, then just press and click."

Menu settings on the Bullfrog were carried out using four rubber buttons, but Lazaridis could see that the trackwheel concept would be a vast improvement for Leapfrog. He took the remote to the office, gave it to Jason Griffin, mechanical engineer, and said, "Call these guys up and see if you can buy that wheel." The trackwheel was so new that Panasonic was still translating the technical specifications from Japanese to English. Panasonic sent Griffin the specs, half in Japanese, half in English, complete with handwritten scribbles. RIM then used high-speed photography to figure out why the original version broke down so often. RIM redesigned the trackwheel, made it slimmer, gave it a crisper feel, and added pull-down menus.

Concurrently, RIM was also developing a closer working arrangement with RAM Mobile Data, operators of the Mobitex network in the United States. During the early days of their association, RAM wanted to be in control and looked to RIM only for hardware, unaware of the amount of effort involved in creating the necessary software. But RAM kept changing its mind about strategic direction. RAM employees bickered so much over specifications on the first Inter@ctive Pager that development got mired. RAM finally admitted lack of progress, called an emergency meeting in Waterloo, and asked Research In Motion for help. "Could you do it? How much would it cost?"

Not wanting to get dragged into the same mire, Lazaridis agreed that RIM would write the required software, but, in return, he wanted creative control. "The only way I can get it done in time is with the freedom to do it myself," said Lazaridis. RAM Mobile countered by saying if that was the case they wouldn't pay for RIM's work. Lazaridis then made an unusual offer. "I'll do it for free." As far as he was concerned, he had nothing to lose. Without software the project was in jeopardy and RIM wouldn't get paid anyway. By working for free he still wouldn't be paid, but at least he had control and was certain there would be an end product. "If it's free," he said, "I own it."

RAM agreed. The project was headed by Dale Brubacher-Cressman, who wrote the software code with Michael Barnstijn and Louise MacCallum. "At the time, we didn't have the resources. We were a small company. We were already building the radio [modem], but I think it was the right thing the way it worked out. We retained ownership for the code that was on the device," said Lazaridis. "That was a turning point. That's when we became knowledgeable with an application that ran on one of these little devices. That application, of course, got rewritten over and over again, but it was the basic concept. The right things happened but at the time it was all just done out of necessity."

All these developmental threads were coming together nicely but still did not produce much revenue for either RIM or RAM Mobile Data. "We were relying on them and they were relying on us because we had the network that made their products work," said Bill Lenahan, president and CEO of RAM. "We didn't have any sales. There was a lot of talk, but nothing that was generating any revenue for anybody. Bell-South really didn't know what to do with the network. They liked the technology and thought it was great but they didn't have any idea of how to bring anything to market."

BellSouth, one of the original seven "Baby Bells" created in 1984 when the U.S. Department of Justice forced AT&T to sell off its regional phone companies, bought a 49 per cent share of RAM Mobile Data and Mobitex in 1991. Despite the ownership position, BellSouth's focus remained on the more traditional and very profitable phone business. Moreover, with $20 billion in annual revenue, BellSouth was huge in comparison to RIM. Big companies prefer dealing with other big companies, not tiny start-ups. As far as BellSouth was concerned, paging was just a monetary drain on the company with little to show for the capital outlay. "They just refused to believe that wireless email would be successful," said Don Mc-Murtry, who joined RIM in 1993 as marketing manager and was named vice-president, sales, in 1997. "Their culture wasn't an email culture, whereas I had an email address when I arrived at RIM." RIM had thoroughly embraced email as part of its communications culture and workflow ahead of many companies, and that undoubtedly helped it see the future for wireless email. "I had over a hundred emails on my first day at RIM," recalled Mark Guibert. "I hadn't even met most people before they were pulling me into the email communications flow on all the various projects. It was a really fast-paced environment, but people communicated as a team exceptionally well. It was a stark contrast to other companies where voice mail was far more common."

By the spring of 1997, BellSouth was on the verge of giving up on Mobitex. BellSouth had spent $300 million to build the Mobitex network and still had only 30,000 customers, nowhere near enough for a profitable business. With annual budget-setting due to take place in June, Jim Hobbs, vice-president, operations, BellSouth Mobile Data, was under increasing pressure from his president, Mike Harrell, as well as Earle Mauldin, Bell South Enterprises CEO, to find revenue-producing products for the network.

Bullfrog had been in production since January, but Hobbs wasn't impressed; he regarded the device as too big and too awkward. However, he knew RIM had another model under development, Leapfrog, so in mid-May he phoned Lazaridis to pass along the ultimatum he'd received from his superiors. "I've got to get rid of this business if we don't come up with something that's going to turn it around, put it on steroids, and jump-start it," said Hobbs.

Lazaridis was aghast. "You're so close, you've been at it so long, you've got a tremendous opportunity here," he said.

"OK, you think it's so great, you tell me exactly what you're going to do, and how you're going to do it. You've got a couple of weeks to get this stuff we've been talking about, this email on the belt concept, off the ground or I'm going to have to go to market and see what I can do to get rid of these assets," said Hobbs.

Lazaridis shared the bad news about BellSouth's ultimatum with Balsillie and then headed home around 9 p.m., only to find a distraught wife who had been unable to settle their two-year-old son all day. "I don't think people realize the stress you're under in these kinds of jobs" said Lazaridis. "You're just watching your whole life passing before your eyes, but you're just making it worse for everybody by saying, 'You think *you've* had a bad day.' You can't get mad at them. It's not their fault."

Ophelia handed over their boy, saying, "Your turn," then went to bed. Rather than see this as a duty to be endured, Lazaridis played with his son for more than two hours, enjoying some quality time together. After the lad was finally tucked in and had fallen asleep, Lazaridis went down to the basement at midnight, put on an album by rock guitarist Joe Satriani, and then fired up his computer. Playing with his son had cleared his head; the instrumental music created an inspirational mood. "I don't remember what happened, I just started typing, and typing, and typing. It just flowed and I put other music on and kept writing, writing, and writing for three hours." The end product was a white paper that brought together everything he knew about email and set out a business plan for Leapfrog, the next version of the Inter@ctive Pager.

The document began by outlining what Leapfrog was not. "Leapfrog is not a PDA, a general purpose PC, or a 'cute baby laptop.' Leapfrog is not a cellular phone, a high-speed portable link to the Internet, or a mini–web browser. Leapfrog is not just a piece of very advanced hardware," he wrote, then added, "If we attempt to make Leapfrog what it is not, then we will fail. If we forget what Leapfrog is not then we will design something that will be undesirable."

The device also had to take into account the strengths and weaknesses of Mobitex by squeezing every ounce of performance from the network. "Don't fight the network," he warned. "Make the most of it and get to market."

For Lazaridis the target market included 40 million existing one-way pager users in the United States, a number expected to more than double to 90 million within five years, as well as more than 125 million existing email users. To reach those users, Leapfrog required what Lazaridis called "the WOW factor." For him the WOW factor had multiple ingredients: brainlessly easy to use out of the box, fast, fun, and addictive.

Lazaridis then focused on what he regarded as the paradoxical aspects of Leapfrog. "We must revel in its limitations! We must turn its weaknesses into strengths. Less is More by definition in paging!" As an example of what he meant, Lazaridis cited the keyboard. "The tiny QWERTY keyboard is a ridiculous limitation to touch typing. Try putting the Leapfrog on a table and touch typing on it like you would on a large computer keyboard. Now realize that its tiny size allows Leapfrog to be cradled in both hands so that the thumbs can be used to 'touch type.' Notice that the small size of the keyboard has become its advantage."

Lazaridis was well aware there would be critics and doubters. "Don't believe me?" he wrote in the white paper. "Try cradling and typing on an HP200LX or [Microsoft's Pocket PC] WinCE device. By focusing on the new way that Leapfrog will actually be used we can further improve on its keyboard layout to take advantage of the 40-degree angle of the thumb tips and the curving sweep as the thumb is moved from the center of the palm to the outer edge. Notice that under these conditions the spacing between the keys is large enough to be practical.

"What is it about the tiny screen that makes it an advantage? Tough one, eh? A matter of fact, that tiny screen makes most applications and [user interfaces] appear restrictive, 'clunky,' and down-right 'absurd'! But if we remember that Leapfrog is NOT a PDA, but a pager, then the small screen's advantage becomes clear! The advantage of the small screen is that it focuses your attention on the notification! This is very important," he wrote, repeating the phrase in bold, italic print: *The small screen focuses your attention on a real-time event that needs attention.*

"This is the WHOLE of Leapfrog! This is all that it needs to do well to be successful! Stay out of the PDA 'no-mans' land! Don't try to be what you are not, become what you are! The simplest applications sell the most volume!

"Tens of millions of people pay for 'simple' notification [with their paging service]. Less than 100,000 people have paid for wireless data. People buy 'Benefits' not features! Software gives 'substance' to Hardware! Paging is a Service, not a product! Services are based on software not hardware! Hardware is the necessary evil. The least tangible things have the highest value! The most successful complexity is invisible. An advanced product is easy to use! The most sophisticated science and technology is indistinguishable from magic! The 'Application' Software is the magic!"

Having established the "why" of the device, Lazaridis then moved to another thorny issue: the established power of competitors such as Motorola. "David attacks and defeats the most fearsome warrior of his enemy with innovation, not brute strength. All successful strategies attack a competitor's strengths, NOT weaknesses! Paging is Motorola's strength, their most 'fearsome' warrior. RIM's innovation is turning an existing wireless data network into a two-way paging network by creating devices that 'look-and-feel' like pagers."

The best course is the simplest, according to Lazaridis, the one that changes the fewest things people already use. "We must not undertake strategies that require a complete rewrite of existing applications and servers. We must come up with a strategy that leverages the existing paradigm. We must minimize resistance by minimizing change. We must maximize adoption by minimizing complexity. Let's make email our transport and payload and beat them all to the punch!"

The paper concluded with a list describing how Leapfrog would look. Leapfrog would be "very small" and "wearable" on a belt. Leapfrog would be "two-way wireless data enabled ... always-on and always on-line" and run on existing nationwide wireless networks. Leapfrog would run on one AA battery that would last for a month. Leapfrog would have a backlit monochrome LCD display, clock, calendar, built-in antenna, vibrator, audio enunciator, a green LED to show wireless coverage, and a red LED to indicate when a message was waiting. RIM would create all the software applications and manufacture the device with a clearly displayed RIM logo. Finally, Leapfrog would sell for under $400.

Lazaridis entitled the document "Success Lies in Paradox!" to show the outside-the-box thinking that was required, and then emailed it to Balsillie at 3 a.m. with a message saying he might not make it into the office until mid-morning. When he arrived, Balsillie greeted him, saying, "This is great! This is great! I already turned it into a PowerPoint presentation!"

They sent a copy to Jim Hobbs who liked what he read well enough to set up a meeting a week later in a twentieth-floor executive conference room in Campanile, BellSouth's headquarters on Peachtree Street in Atlanta. The meeting, chaired by BellSouth Mobile Data president Mike Harrell, included Hobbs and Mauldin, as well as J. D. Gardner, CFO of BellSouth Mobile Data, Ron Dykes, CFO of BellSouth Enterprises, and Mark Fiedler, president of Interconnection Services. "This was a come-to-Jesus meeting. It was like going to the Supreme Court, let's plead the case," said Hobbs.

Lazaridis had just begun his presentation when he suddenly realized that he and Balsillie had been so nervous that they'd left behind in the taxi they took in from the airport the models of the handhelds they brought along to show the group. "What's really nasty about it is we're giving a presentation and *they're not believing* this is possible. We were losing credibility because we didn't have them." Lazaridis halted his talk to ask if someone could call the taxi company and retrieve the missing package.

Lazaridis spent thirty minutes telling the group about the

business opportunity for email, the market potential, and how the handheld actually would work. He told them about the development projects Intel had carried out for RIM and reminded them BellSouth had a significant head start over competitors because of the Mobitex network that would take several years and hundreds of millions of dollars for anyone else to replicate. Lazaridis urged BellSouth to change the focus of Mobitex away from service trucks carrying big boxes of electronics, and create a two-way paging network for corporate clients. He said he could help them fine-tune Mobitex and make it operate more efficiently in a way that could extend battery life in a device to as much as three weeks. "You need a device," he concluded. "Here's what one would look like."

By then, the errant package had arrived. The two devices Lazaridis passed around were far from working prototypes. They were wooden models that measured about 3 x 2 inches, the actual size and weight of Leapfrog, or the "Inter@ctive Pager 950," as it would eventually be named. Carved into each block was a rectangular recessed "screen," with half a dozen lines printed on plastic showing a list of email messages ready to be opened and read. Below was a pasted-on paper keyboard, with the letters arranged in an arc, and to the right, set into the surface, a trackwheel that could be rolled with the thumb to simulate the sensation of operating the menus.

So smitten were the grown men that as the models were passed around each excitedly waited his turn, just as if the inanimate objects were actual working handhelds that would allow them to check their email. "Mike was just awesome in his demeanor," said Hobbs. "He had those guys believing he could walk on water and he was going to do it. That sounds like I'm overstating it, but the guys walked in there thinking they were going to pull the plug, and they walked out going, 'Well, you know what? This is pretty cool if he can pull it off.' It was that significant."

Embracing the story was one thing; taking the plunge would be expensive. Saying yes to RIM meant that BellSouth would have to spend more money and expand the network beyond the current 1,200 base stations. As chair, Mike Harrell wrapped up the meeting by laying out a challenge. "If you put too many base stations out there, the financial case will not play. If you don't put enough base stations out there, the business will not fly," he said. "What's the number?"

BellSouth's marketing, operations, and engineering departments were all involved in the follow-on deliberations. They concluded that the number of base stations would need to double to 2,400 in order to cover at least 90 per cent of the top U.S. urban markets. BellSouth decided to proceed, but the business case was only part of the decision-making process. "We stayed in the game and rolled the dice one more time," said Hobbs. "We're usually pretty analytical. This decision was based on faith. It was more of a gut call. There was some element of being close, we've been pioneers, why give up now?"

Lazaridis's knowledge and enthusiasm also played a role. "The thing that I always liked about Mike was that no matter how crazy the business was, no matter how complicated his life got, he was always available when I called him," said Bell-South's Neale Hightower, who was involved in deciding the number of base stations needed. "And if you ask him about the nuts and bolts of the device, he usually had the answer. He did not become an executive, chief technology officer-type guy. He would up and build the blamed thing and make it work."

Back in Waterloo, Lazaridis met with RIM engineers on June 10, 1997, and gave them his own ultimatum: he wanted a working version of the Inter@ctive Pager 950 by January 1, 1998, less than six months away. It was just as well he issued those instructions when he did. In August, BellSouth ordered C$70 million worth of the Inter@ctive Pager 950 for delivery in 1998. The purchase order was a transforming event; RIM's order book suddenly ballooned from a relatively solid C$30 million to a far more substantial C$100 million.

The BellSouth deal almost didn't go through. Balsillie was in the midst of negotiations when he decided he needed a short break to clear his head, and so he left to buy himself a sandwich and be alone. Right before he was set to continue negotiations, he was in a collision while driving. After making sure the other driver was OK and while waiting for the police to arrive, he resumed negotiations on his cell phone. Ever the multi-tasker, he stayed on his phone for as long as possible, even after the police arrived, and went on mute intermittently while managing through the aftermath of the car accident. Once the police needed his undivided attention, Balsillie asked for a brief break in the negotiations and told the other party, "I'll call you right back." In the end, he resolved the situation at the accident scene and kept the deal moving without skipping a beat.

As new market entries go, RIM's deal with BellSouth was sweeping in its scope. BellSouth's expanded Mobitex network reached 93 per cent of the U.S. business population in 266 urban areas, thereby bringing millions of potential customers within wireless range of RIM's devices. RIM was so far ahead of its competitors that it was able to negotiate the $70 million order, which was a relatively large order for such a small company. "We needed the product and we needed RIM to be successful and we needed BellSouth Wireless to be successful. There weren't many other options for us at that point in time. The technology was so young on all fronts," said Bill Lenahan, president and CEO of RAM Mobile Data.

The initial order was just as significant a leap for BellSouth as it was for RIM. "A lot of kudos goes to BellSouth management for having the courage and the conviction to buy into some technology that I know a lot of the other RBOCs [Regional Bell Operating Companies] in those days would not have done," said Lenahan. "I believe that BellSouth had a lot to do with making this company successful," said Earle Mauldin, BellSouth Enterprises. "We certainly can take some credit for their foothold and their later building their business into a real successful company." (In March 1998, BellSouth bought the other half of RAM Mobile Data it did not own and then in 2000 merged with SBC Communications to create Cingular, the largest wireless carrier in the United States. In 2006, BellSouth Corp. and Cingular were acquired by AT&T Inc.)

With the BellSouth order in place, in September 1997, Intel invested $4,170,000 for 926,667 RIM shares at $4.50 each and received 139,000 warrants that could be exercised later for more shares at the same price. To keep an eye on its investment, Intel vice-president Tom Franz was given observer status on the RIM board. The money was less important to RIM than the strategic association with Intel. "Not to be cavalier, but at that time that wasn't that much money. There was a time that was an enormous amount of money. You want the credibility. RIM was a fledgling company entering the land of the giants where people said we'd be squashed," said Balsillie.

In addition to successfully selling BellSouth on the device, Lazaridis also convinced Ericsson, inventors of Mobitex, to let him make changes to the network that permitted longer battery life and reduced bandwidth use. "If you waste a lot of time listening for stuff that's not there you kill the battery. There were all sorts of tunable parameters in the base station that were initially under Ericsson's control. Mike convinced RAM to let him twiddle with those knobs and basically retuned the network to give the portables much longer life," said Bill Frezza of Ericsson-GE. "At certain points during the evolution, RIM knew as much about Mobitex as Ericsson. Mike appreciated what it was going to take to sell boxes to us and what it was going to take to be successful," said Hobbs. "Mike understood the nuances of packet data. He knew the limitations. He'd hold up a battery and say, 'There's only so many packets in this' and obviously you want the packets to be used for carrying a payload, not for forward error correction and all these other things. He was brilliant in that particular area," said Hobbs.

One of the changes Lazaridis made affected how a mobile device listens to the network. Since power in a wireless device does not come from a wall plug, a handheld can't be "on" all the time. If the modem in the handheld isn't doing anything, there's no point in transmitting or receiving. So the network sends what's called a "heartbeat" that triggers a brief response from the handheld that says it's on and gives a location. Adjusting that period between the heartbeat and the response ensured the handheld could be "always on, always connected" without being a constant drain on either the battery or the network.

Along with Intel's chips and BellSouth's network, the final piece of the Inter@ctive Pager puzzle fell into place with the release in 1997 of IMAP4 (Internet Message Access Protocol), which allowed access to email through Microsoft's Outlook Express. "Mike had the vision of this seamless push email being delivered to you so that whenever you picked the device up, the email was right there," said Robert O'Hara, wireless architect at Microsoft from 1992 to 2005. "He and his team had this clear grasp of boiling it down to the essentials. This is something that Microsoft could learn. RIM created this simple device that was incredibly usable. I was extremely impressed with the sophistication and the refinement of the user interface for their first device. This wasn't the fourth version, it was the first. Mike and Jim have the intuitive sense similar to Steve Jobs of being able to boil a concept down to its essence, define and state what that essence is, and then assemble and lead a team that follows through on that. I think that is absolutely part of their core strength."

After modest beginnings in 1984 as a hole-in-the-wall outfit on the second floor of a strip mall in Canada, Research In Motion had managed in a little more than a dozen years to create strategic alliances with two of the biggest corporate names of the American millennium: Intel and BellSouth. As news of the deal with BellSouth swept the industry, Lazaridis had a call from a competing carrier, ARDIS. "You're dealing with the crazy people," said ARDIS CEO Walt Purnell.

"Excuse me?"

"I'd never give you that big an order for this product."

"Why are you saying this to me?"

With that, the caller changed his tune and said, "You've got to build one for me."

"I really can't do that," said Lazaridis. "I have to honour my contract." Purnell hung up.

Lazaridis walked into Balsillie's office and said, "I think I made a big mistake. I just caused our second-biggest customer to hang up on me." The rift was not permanent. During the time RIM was building Leapfrog for BellSouth, there were persistent rumours that a competitor had an existing product. A few months later, Purnell called again, saying, "Lazaridis, this must be your lucky day. You know that competitor who was working on a competitive product? Well they just cancelled the project. How much do I have to order to get one of those units?"

CHAPTER SEVEN

GOING PUBLIC

TECHNOLOGICAL PROGRESS during the early 1990s was only part of what was happening at Research In Motion. If RIM were human, the company would have been the equivalent of a teenager: gawky, growing, getting some things right and others wrong, all the while needing more spending money for capital equipment, salaries, office space, and research and development in order to keep moving toward product maturity and more market share.

Jim Balsillie's investment in 1992 was welcome, but was only one among several sources of much-needed cash for such expansion. Additional amounts also came from Ontario Development Corp. (ODC) and Ericsson in 1993. "I remember Mike as a very enthusiastic entrepreneur. He was always out of money. He was trying to develop this wonderful machine for which the technology wasn't available yet," said Ake Persson, who worked at Ericsson in the 1980s, was vice-president, business development, at RAM Mobile Data from 1990–92, then returned to Ericsson, where he was in charge of their U.S. mobile data business. "When he was running out of gas we tried to help him out. We had to; we were obviously interested in driving Mobitex technology. Without devices, without consumer products in the market, there wouldn't be any more systems sold. He should take the credit for the growth of the mobile data industry. Without the BlackBerry, nothing would have happened."

The investments by ODC and Ericsson turned out to be more flexible than either Lazaridis or Balsillie expected. Immediately prior to joining RIM, when Balsillie had looked into acquiring a division of Westinghouse, he had gotten far enough along in the negotiations to have a partnership arrangement in place with ODC. When RIM set out to obtain seed money from ODC and Ericsson, Ericsson said it would be happy to replicate whatever documentation ODC used. As Balsillie read through the thick document drawn up by ODC, he came upon a key paragraph that was different from the paperwork he'd previously seen from the Ontario government agency. He handed the papers to Lazaridis and asked how he read the particular words. Both agreed that the phrasing meant that if within a year RIM paid back the $250,000 investment plus a modest amount of interest, neither ODC nor Ericsson would have any shares in RIM. What Ericsson and ODC may have hoped would ultimately result in ownership of the company could, in fact, result in just a short-term loan if RIM came up with alternate funding.

For Lazaridis, such a series of unlikely events was explicable. "If you're paying attention, there's always an opportunity. Cascade all the timing together. Sutherland–Schultz trying to buy us, we're dragging our feet for as long as we can trying to find another deal, Stork buys them, so they have to keep buying our cards so we still have cash flow until SS Tech gets butterflied out," said Lazaridis. "So, we don't lose the deal, I don't have to sell, Jim's deal with his mentor and friend collapses, he's now looking for a job, walks in the door, he's already done a draft for the deal, it's unilaterally changed by ODC to the point where it becomes a loan—the compound sequencing of all this stuff, you couldn't have planned it better. That one galvanized the company; we knew what we had to do. We had to raise enough money to pay them back within a year."

Outside ownership might have been kept at bay for the time being, but that did not end RIM's hunger to find fresh funds for equipment, research and development, or new staff. At crucial points in the history of every company there are three main choices for an entrepreneur seeking money: bank debt, selling a portion of the company to an outside investor, or taking the company public. RIM wasn't yet big enough for a public offering; banks demand stringent conditions while providing no strategic advice. The right investor can provide both cash and counsel.

Balsillie talked to his former boss at Sutherland-Schultz, Rick Brock, about investing in RIM. Brock was interested and brought in as a possible partner Brent Belzberg, CEO of Harrowston Inc., a Toronto-based holding company where Brock was a director. The discussions did not get beyond the preliminary stage.

RIM then turned to COM DEV International Ltd., makers of components for communications satellites, based in nearby Cambridge. Val O'Donovan, COM DEV chairman and CEO, agreed to invest C$2 million for four million shares of RIM, a 25 per cent interest, and became a director of RIM. At the press conference held in May 1994 at RIM's Phillip Street headquarters to announce the alliance, Lazaridis seized the opportunity to muse about a "wireless wallet." He predicted that by 2000, consumers would carry a handheld device that could send or receive email, conduct banking transactions, and even check whether they'd turned off the kitchen stove. "The world is poised at the perfect position to see the development of instantaneous information access, anywhere in the world at any time from the world's wireless data networks," he said.[1]

Getting the money is one thing; getting along with a new partner can be harder. The culture at COM DEV at the time was hierarchical in comparison to RIM. COM DEV was also much larger, with six hundred employees and annual sales of C$67 million compared to RIM's thirty employees and C$2 million in annual sales. In a speech in October 1994, O'Donovan tried to play down the cultural differences. "It was much more a partnership of equals than you could judge if you based it only on the number of people or the total revenue of the two companies. RIM has unique technology and a strategic vision of the future, which is not very normal among small companies or even among big companies," he said.[2]

In May 1994, RIM also tried another means for finding money by hiring John Latham as director of business development with a view to obtaining government grants. Latham had worked for three years at the Ontario Ministry of Industry, Trade and Technology, so he knew the system. Later that same year, he landed a C$4.7 million grant from the Ontario Technology Fund, a sizable sum that was greater than RIM's annual revenue at the time. In his written submission Latham focused on RIM's people more than their products. "I waxed poetic

---

[1] *Record*, May 12, 1994, p. B6.

[2] *Record*, October 26, 1994, p. E5.

about the dynamic duo. Mike had the technology expertise and Jim had the business and finance expertise. I think that was well received by the government," he said. "It wasn't as though we were really begging, but at the same time they could see that we needed a lot more money to do all the things we wanted to do and accelerate the development program."

As RIM moved on to a sounder financial footing, employees were granted stock options so they could eventually be shareholders, following Lazaridis's philosophy that employees with a vested interest work harder when they benefit from corporate success. In 1994, before RIM became a public company, a typical employee who'd been at RIM a year or two received 10,000 options with an exercise price of five cents, according to former employees who were at RIM in the mid-nineties. The same number of options was granted again in both 1995 and 1996, for a total of 30,000. Longer-term employees received more options, for a total of as many as 40,000. Employees who joined in 1995 or 1996 were granted fewer options, in the 5,000 range, on one or two occasions.

Exercising the options to hold the "nickel shares," as they were called internally, cost peanuts: $1,500 to cash in 30,000 options, or $2,000 for 40,000. RIM also promised to provide interest-free loans so employees could exercise the options and hold the shares, if they so chose, without dipping into their own pockets.

In 1996, prior to the company's IPO (initial public offering) and prior to any stock splits, there was another series of employee options priced at $3.40, with the actual number of options granted again dependent on years of service and effort expended. Engineers who clocked fifteen hours a day in the lab were given more options than nine-to-five office staff.

Although Lazaridis did not oversee the program, he would be aware who was still working hard when he regularly did his evening rounds. From time to time he'd be in the lab alongside engineers at 3 a.m., so he knew who was contributing the most and made certain they were rewarded accordingly.

In 1996, a typical employee who'd worked at RIM for two or three years received 8,000 options priced at $3.40. Longer-term employees received up to 40,000 of the $3.40 options that vested over five years at the rate of 20 per cent per year. In 1996, Lazaridis and Balsillie were each granted 250,000 options at $3.40 with a December 2006 expiry. Balsillie exercised 127,500 of those options (255,000 post-split) in 2005, the rest in 2006; Lazaridis exercised in 2006, by which time the shares were worth C$77 million.

Between 1996 and 2006, during the period of RIM's hyper growth, approximately two thousand RIM employees received options through a total of 3,200 separate grants. Ten years later, when granting of stock options in companies from all sectors became topical and began to attract the focus of securities regulators, RIM voluntarily looked into its own practices. A board committee review in 2006–07 that sifted through 900,000 paper and electronic documents found the company made errors in accounting for stock option awards made prior to August 8, 2006, and RIM restated its historical financial disclosures. The board committee also said that in some cases incorrect grant dates were used in pricing awards. RIM subsequently settled investigations by the Ontario Securities Commission and the U.S. Securities and Exchange Commission relating to its historical stock option granting practices.

RIM took a number of steps following its internal review

to enhance its governance processes and increased the number of independent directors on the board. Four new independent directors were elected: Barbara Stymiest, Group Head, Strategy, Treasury & Corporate Services at the Royal Bank of Canada; John Wetmore, former president and CEO of IBM Canada; Roger Martin, dean of the Rotman School of Management, University of Toronto; and David Kerr, managing partner of Edper Financial Group.

In 1996, the need persisted to find additional money for expansion. Revenue (sales, fees, and government investments) was doubling every year—C$4.2 million for the year ending February 28, 1995, C$8.4 million in the year ending February 1996, headed for C$13.5 million in February 1997—but there was trouble brewing on another front. The contract to build Type II cards that had caused problems with U.S. Robotics meant that by May 1996 Research In Motion had borrowed C$8 million from the Bank of Montreal so RIM could buy the parts to build the thousands of cards ordered. Because U.S. Robotics was not paying what they owed in a timely manner, RIM was falling behind in its loan with the bank.

Relations became so testy that bank officers Graham Parsons and Mike Moore threatened to convert a portion of RIM's debt into shares in the company. "The Bank of Montreal was trying to take over RIM. If they have leverage, they abuse it," said Balsillie, who found himself battling both U.S. Robotics and the Bank of Montreal to stave off financial disaster. "It was like an Indiana Jones movie and I'm sweating," he said.

In his search to replace bank financing, Balsillie was aided by Dennis Kavelman who had been hired the previous year. After graduating in 1993 in business administration from Wilfrid Laurier University in Waterloo, Kavelman joined accounting firm KPMG Peat Marwick Thorne in Waterloo. In 1994, he won the National Gold Medal and Governor General's Award for standing first in Canada among the 3,174 who wrote the Uniform Evaluation (UFE) conducted by the Canadian Institute of Chartered Accountants.[3]

Shortly after Kavelman arrived at RIM in 1995, the firm relocated from the Columbia Street offices to 295 Phillip Street, half a block away. Kavelman, accompanied by director of product development Steve Carkner, went to pick up a rental truck to move some of the larger items, only to discover that at twenty-four the new VP, finance, was too young to sign the rental agreement. Carkner, who met the twenty-five-years-or-older condition, signed instead and drove the vehicle.

At the time, RIM was still small, with twenty-five employees in 2,500 square feet of space. Kavelman distributed paycheques by hand. As is typical with private companies of that size, RIM had not had an outside audit. The firm's accounting system was being run on QuickBooks, a computer program more suited to household finances. Kavelman spent the first year setting up a more sophisticated system and making sure that RIM was receiving the appropriate tax credits from government R&D programs.

Everywhere Balsillie and Kavelman turned for fresh funding to replace the Bank of Montreal loan—other competing banks, the Federal Business Development Bank, venture capital funds—the terms were all unsuitable. Investment banking firms were little better. "Bankers started circling, knowing we

---

[3] Sarah Hadley, RIM's director of corporate taxation, was a gold medalist in 2002.

had to do this bridge financing first," said Kavelman. "They just wanted to lock you up for good. That didn't sit too well with us. We said, 'Look, we're just starting to go out [into the market]. If you do a good job on this financing, then, of course, we'll use you on the next one.'"

Out of the blue, RIM received a call from Rob Fraser of Griffiths McBurney Partners (GMP). The recently created investment banking firm in Toronto was so aggressive it was putting together a deal to finance the Cuban operations of Sherritt International Corp., a Canadian company run by Ian Delaney. Other U.S. and Canadian firms had refused to finance Sherritt for fear of running afoul of the Helms-Burton Act, which prohibited trade with Cuba and had just been passed by U.S. Congress a few months earlier in March 1996. GMP had no concerns about international repercussions and so was proceeding apace with the Sherritt deal.

Fraser met Balsillie and Kavelman at Fast Breaks, a restaurant near RIM headquarters. After several months of looking for funding, Balsillie and Kavelman had their corporate story polished to a brief fifteen minutes, after which they asked Fraser, "What do you think we should do?"

Fraser's reply was far different from anything they'd previously heard. "I don't know," he said. "I don't know what your company's worth. Why don't we have you come down to Toronto and put you in front of some of the biggest investors in Canada. You can tell them the story, no strings attached. We'll do up some slides and organize a day. Let's go see what people think."

In late May 1996, the day-long series of appointments arranged by GMP began with Adam Adamou at Working Ventures, a fund run by labour unions that invest in small- and medium-sized Canadian companies. Balsillie began by explaining circuit and packet switching in an easy, diagrammatic form. Circuit, one-way, is broadcast TV, he said. Circuit, two-way, is cellular and voice. Packet one-way is paging. Packet two-way is the future and nobody's there but RIM. There was no need to go any further. "We love it, we're in," said Adamou.

The next call on Frank Mersch at Altamira Investments, a mutual funds company, received an even more enthusiastic response. Mersch interrupted the presentation after three slides, pounded his desk and shouted, "I want the whole deal. I'll give you $50 million right now." Similar approval flowed at C.A. Delaney Capital Management, J. Zechner Associates, and Gluskin Sheff + Associates. By day's end, RIM had oral commitments for C$93 million. Balsillie phoned Lazaridis and said, "I think I can raise money here." Replied Lazaridis: "When somebody wants to give you money, take it."

Fraser had introduced Balsillie and Kavelman to one of the GMP founders, Brad Griffiths, who estimated RIM's market value at C$130 million. Griffiths said that given the high level of investor interest, his firm could help RIM raise C$30 to C$35 million by selling one-quarter of the company. The numbers made sense to Balsillie and Kavelman. Equally important, they liked GMP's style. "They fit exactly with what we were: small, start-up, trying to make it work. They didn't come in and put big corporate-bank pressure moves on us. They were just very practical," said Kavelman.

Griffiths suggested that Balsillie and Kavelman draw up a list showing how RIM would spend the money they raised. More than ten years later, Balsillie's enthusiasm remains as fresh as it was on that occasion as he replays the call-and-response conversation he had with the investment bankers. "We looked at every possible scenario. We're going to build a plant! Yeah! How much is that? Fifteen million. Marketing! Five million for marketing. Research and development, $5 million."

Asked GMP: "Can you get it up to $50 million?"

"We couldn't figure out a way."

"Do you guys want to sell some shares?" asked GMP, referring to holdings by Balsillie, Lazaridis, and other early-stage investors.

Replied Balsillie: "I can pay off the house! We gave little trust amounts to all our families. I think I sold $1 million. I had a couple hundred grand in the bank; I gave all my cousins and siblings fifty grand. I called the board. 'All in favor? Opposed, if any? Carried unanimously.'"

Under Ontario securities law the institutions investing in RIM were considered to be sophisticated, so the amount of corporate financial information revealed was modest. Once everyone agreed to the terms, a deal such as GMP was putting together could close in a matter of days rather than the several months taken by an offering to the general public. Unaware what RIM was doing, the Bank of Montreal continued to press the company to pay down its line of credit. Balsillie asked for a reprieve on the basis he was travelling. The bank agreed to wait one more week before seizing control of RIM. Without the GMP-led financing, said Balsillie, "he's got me. I'm not near dead, I'm gone."

Five days later, on June 10, 1996, RIM sold 10 million special warrants priced at C$3.40 each to five institutional investors: Altamira, C.A. Delaney Capital Management, Working Ventures, J. Zechner Associates, and Gluskin Sheff. The warrants would be converted to shares six months later when RIM filed a prospectus at which time the stock would begin

trading over the counter. (Over-the-counter trading is conducted between a specific buyer and a specific seller rather
than through a stock exchange with strict regulations.) GMP
brought in other investment banking firms to create a syndicate that included Midland Walwyn, TD Securities, Marleau
Lemire, and Yorkton Securities.

After fees were deducted, GMP issued RIM a cheque for
C$31.7 million. Kavelman and Eric Apps, RIM's lawyer from
Wildeboer Dellelce, took the cheque from GMP's offices
across the street to the main branch of the Bank of Montreal
at King and Bay in downtown Toronto. Kavelman deposited
the money in RIM's account then gave instructions to transfer
the full amount immediately to money manager TD Lancaster,
where the funds would go into an interest-bearing money
market account.

Kavelman and Apps then walked kitty-corner across the
King and Bay intersection to a restaurant named Jump, where
they joined Fraser and Griffiths of GMP and Rob Wildeboer
of law firm Wildeboer Dellelce in the restaurant's outdoor
patio, surrounded by the four towers that comprise Commerce
Court. The warm sun was shining down upon them, the wine
flowed freely, God was in his heaven, and all was right with
the world.

Kavelman's cell phone rang. Everyone stopped talking
because they knew exactly who was calling: Mike Moore from
the Bank of Montreal. "Hello, Mike, how're you doing? What's
up?"

"Good. Um, I just have a little question."

"What's that?"

"What was that $31 million that went in and out of your
account today?"

"Oh, we just did this special warrant offer. We didn't like the other things we'd been seeing. We're growing the business."

"OK, OK, take care."

As the group laughed and toasted their success, Balsillie's phone rang. This time, it was Bank of Montreal's Graham Parsons, a changed man from his earlier incarnation. "Can we offer any banking services? Would you like your line extended?"

"Nahh," said Balsillie, "I think we'll just pay it off, but sure, let's talk about a strategic relationship."

Some employees had been agitating to be permitted to buy shares in RIM, but Balsillie was reluctant. "He didn't want employees getting freaked out if the company tanked," said Don McMurtry. "I remember saying, 'I'm prepared to make an investment.' He said, 'No, Don, don't. Put it somewhere safe. This is a high-risk business and I don't want you losing your savings.'"

Once the special warrant deal had been completed, RIM employees were permitted to make purchases at $3.40 per share. Half of RIM's one hundred employees invested a total of $1 million for an average of 6,000 shares each. "It wasn't just Mike and Jim who were highly committed to the business. Half the company went out and begged, borrowed, and liquidated whatever they had to buy into the company, so you had a huge, broad base of employees who are highly confident of where the business is going," said McMurtry, who not only invested all his savings but also took out a bank loan.

By December 1996, RIM shares could be bought and sold on the over-the-counter market in Toronto, but trading was thin, pricing was erratic.

Nine months later, with Intel as an investor and production partner and BellSouth as a major customer, the time was ripe to take RIM public through an initial public offering (IPO). RIM was able to point to the specific areas where they'd spent the money they'd raised through the special warrants—half went to build a new manufacturing facility, while the rest was used to hire employees and purchase new R&D and lab equipment. "The plant gave us substance. It's one thing to be in a small office with a bunch of computer screens. As soon as people tour a plant it makes it seem all that much more real," said Kavelman. The plant was making PCMCIA cards, OEM radios, Bullfrogs and, of course, there were the famous wooden models of the Inter@ctive Pager 950 to show to potential investors.

Selling the warrants in 1996 had attracted interest from other Bay Street firms. "The banks smell blood in the water. They know an IPO is coming. As soon as the special warrant was done and we got a prospectus filed for it, the sharks started circling: 'When are we going to do an IPO?' They want to position themselves to lead it for the fees," said Kavelman. Sharks in the water worked for RIM, too. "We want to get as many people interested and get a feeding frenzy going to create a big awareness in the company."

As with all such IPOs, RIM, in conjunction with its investment bankers and lawyers, drafted a prospectus, a detailed fifty-eight-page document that described products, revealed financial information, and gave biographical details about management and the board. The action of releasing sales and profit figures is a life-altering event that not every young company survives. Never mind the fact that strangers need to be convinced to invest their savings, the job description of senior management changes forever. They have to publicly defend their strategy, announce financial results to thousands of share-holders in quarterly reports, reveal all at annual meetings, and regularly hold lengthy question-and-answer sessions with analysts working for investment banks.

The prospectus outlined RIM's plan to turn something familiar—one-way pagers—into something less familiar—two-way pagers—at a time when the market for two-way pagers appeared ready to take off. According to Yankee Group, the Boston-based research and technology consulting firm, of the forty million paging subscribers in the United States, only 390,000—less than one per cent—had two-way pagers, the market RIM was chasing. But Yankee Group forecast that by 2005 there would be 100 million pager users, 77 per cent of them with two-way devices.

Some investment bankers seeking to become involved in the IPO conducted their own due diligence to confirm RIM's self-described advantage. John Easson, managing partner at BMO Nesbitt Burns, attended an industry conference and trade show in San Francisco so he could compare RIM with its rivals. "The only one that was competitive, and talked about being competitive, was Motorola. Every device in the huge Motorola booth you could touch. They'd be on a cord. But the RIM device was in a glass case. You couldn't touch it because it didn't work yet. At least we knew RIM had the forwarding of emails working and a device that had a certain amount of battery life and Motorola did not," said Easson.

Easson concluded that RIM's prospects were excellent. "RIM was one of the few Canadian companies that actually had a great capital markets strategy, and that was to raise a lot of money early. They were going to play against the big boys, so they said we need to have a strong balance sheet. We can't be questioned by our very large clients, the global telecom players—are we going to be around to support our product three, four, five years down the road?" said Easson.

Prior to the IPO, the largest shareholder, with 10.3 million shares, was Technology Horizons Ltd., a holding company jointly owned by COM DEV and COM DEV CEO Val O'Donovan. Next largest shareholder was Lazaridis, with 9.8 million shares, followed by Balsillie, at 8.1 million shares; Michael Barnstijn and Doug Fregin each had 3.2 million shares. As a group, RIM directors and officers owned 35 million shares or 73 per cent of the company, a proportion that was reduced to 57 per cent after the offering, when the number of shares rose from 48 million to 64 million—an increase that's known as dilution. "Balsillie and Lazaridis have a reasonably small stake in the company today because of that, but I don't think anyone is crying because they diluted themselves early on. I think they were quite smart. They knew they were going to need a lot of capital and they weren't going to worry about dilution. They'd rather have a higher likelihood of being a success," Easson said.

RIM executives visited Toronto, Montreal, Winnipeg, Calgary, Vancouver, San Francisco, and Boston on what's known as a "road show," holding meetings to reveal their strategies and arouse interest among institutional investors and financial advisers with retail clients. Balsillie's props included a working Bullfrog and the same wooden models of Leapfrog he'd shown to BellSouth. The financial community was just as awed as the carrier executives had been a few months earlier. "It wasn't even a real deal, but Jim made you feel like it was an honour to hold it. It's like you're holding the royal jewels. He became incredibly good at selling the promise. He was very convincing," said analyst Barry Richards, of Paradigm Capital.

Expressions of interest during a road show, however, are no guarantee of success. Institutions and investment banks don't have to decide how many shares they want—if any—until the specific share price has been announced. The delicate balance for RIM was to set a price that raised the maximum amount of cash but left the market clamouring for more shares so that the price remained firm—or, better yet, went higher—once trading began. "We said you could price it at the top end of the range, $6.50 to $7.50. Jim said, 'Let's do it at $7.25 because I want to send a little message to everyone there's a free quarter.' It was good thinking because a bunch of things conspired to have the price be under water, but it was a message that was sent to the institutions that these guys are on our team," said Easson.

In addition to the price, another key decision for RIM was picking the firm that would lead the deal. The "lead" banker's name appears in the top left of the announcement notice, known as a tombstone. The second-ranking firm appears in the top right corner, with the rest arrayed below. Griffiths McBurney Partners (GMP) was an early favourite for lead because the firm had led the special warrant issue, but RIM worked hard to bring in some larger firms because any IPO will do better when backed by the powerhouse brokers. Canada's biggest investment banking firm, RBC Dominion Securities Inc., badly wanted to be lead banker. An RBC investment banker phoned Kavelman and leaned on him by saying, "There's no way RBC will be second to Griffiths McBurney. You have to put us top left otherwise we don't know if we can be in the deal."

When Kavelman told Balsillie about RBC's threat, Balsillie said, "This makes our decision very easy because now there's no way we can put them top left, or else it's clear that we bow to pressure in that they made us do it."

Kavelman called RBC and said, "Griffiths is getting top left. If you want, you can co-lead and you're top right. If not, let me know and I'll put someone else there." RBC acquiesced.

The IPO on the Toronto Stock Exchange on October 28, 1997, successfully sold 15,870,000 shares of RIM at C$7.25, thereby raising C$115 million, an amount that included C$6 million in underwriting fees for the members of the syndicate: GMP, RBC, CIBC Wood Gundy Securities Inc., BMO Nesbitt Burns Inc., Midland Walwyn Capital Inc., and one U.S. firm, NationsBanc Montgomery Securities. RIM's 64 million shares at C$7.25 meant the market capitalization—what the company was worth—was C$464 million, almost quadruple the firm's value a year earlier at the time of the private placement. Institutional investors such as mutual funds and pension managers purchased about three-quarters of the shares, with the rest going to individual investors. About 90 per cent of all shareholders were Canadian, the rest U.S.

Despite being top right on the deal, RBC's confidence soon reversed. Benn Mikula, RBC's bow-tie-wearing analyst, spoke positively about RIM throughout the sales period, but once shares began trading on the open market he recommended that clients sell the stock. After the shares briefly traded above the C$7.25 listing price, Mikula's negativity drove prices down into the C$6 range until April 1998, when they finally began rising again.

Despite that early weakness, those investors who had considered but decided against early-stage opportunities could have enjoyed a very high rate of return. For example, Mike Volker, who had been unsuccessful in his attempt to buy 15 per cent of RIM in 1988 for C$30,000, was in 1997 living in Vancouver where he worked with a group of local investors. Even if his holdings had been diluted to only 5 per cent, his investment would have been worth $23 million at the time of the IPO, and a lot more later. As Volker sat at breakfast reading a newspaper article about the initial public offering, he recalled thinking, "RIM...*RIM*....That sounds familiar." He had "completely forgotten about the company. It was like the guy finding the lottery ticket after it expired. That's the billion-dollar fish that got away."

CHAPTER EIGHT

MILLIONAIRES' ROW

RATHER THAN IMMEDIATELY DEPOSIT the proceeds from the initial public offering in the bank as they'd done with the special warrant deal, Balsillie and Kavelman brought the cheque for C$108,612,309 to Waterloo. They gathered as many employees as possible and passed the cheque around so everyone had a chance to feel their good fortune. Some employees had their picture taken with the document, all grinning and in the green. There was good reason to be gleeful. Their personal wealth was increasing along with the company's good fortune and many of them were even millionaires, at least on paper.

Balsillie gave a speech in which he said Research In Motion was not going to be one of those companies that followed the hourly ups and downs of the share price. Just as he and Kavelman had been educating investment bankers about RIM, Balsillie now tutored employees about the vicissitudes of the stock market. "We're public," he told them. "All that means is that we needed money to grow and this is the way we did it. The stock's going to go up; the stock's going to go down. You're going to work your ass off all day and the stock'll go down a buck. You could not show up for work one day and the stock'll go up two bucks. Over the long term, we're going to grow. Day to day don't pay attention to it. Let Dennis and I pay attention, you don't have to." Balsillie announced a new company rule: any RIM employee who so much as talked about the share price or was caught checking the share price while at work would buy donuts for everyone. "The donut rule sent a really important message to employees in a lighthearted manner," said Mark Guibert. "Don't let short-term stock fluctuations or the public spotlight shake *or* boost your confidence. Don't assume that external pundits know better than us. Don't worry about things outside your control. Stay focused on our customers, partners, and business plans to the best degree possible and, if we're successful at executing on those fronts, the stock will take care of itself over time."

When the special warrant deal was concluded the previous year, there was a celebratory dinner at Centro, a spiffy Toronto restaurant, attended by thirty key members of RIM management and the board of directors, as well as representatives from the investment banks and legal firms involved. Rather than limiting the celebration to the confines of a restaurant, RIM celebrated its IPO with a concert in Federation Hall on the University of Waterloo campus. The celebration included not only the usual bankers and lawyers, but all employees, as well as several hundred university students who received free tickets to hear Canadian rocker Tom Cochrane singing, among his other hits, "Life is a Highway."

RIM included students in the festivities as part of its ongoing efforts to attract the top UW graduates as future employees. "We built the refinery next to the gold mine," Lazaridis liked to say, commenting on the fact that RIM's office was located right next to the University of Waterloo and just down the street from Wilfrid Laurier University. As RIM executives went about their daily lives in the community, they constantly ran into hopeful interns, potential co-op students, and prospective employees in every pizza parlour and local pub. RIM hired as many students as practical through various programs and then offered many of them permanent positions after graduation in order to help fuel the company's steady growth. RIM has also tried to be careful when hiring engineers to make sure they understood a balance of goals. "Engineers are great for making sure their circuit works, but that can be very one-dimensional. You've got to be able to sell it, you've got to be able to make a profit. You've got to make sure you don't do a variety of things. The challenge is to realize that and realize that the optimizations that you make do not blur or dull the engineering sword," said Fregin. "So you shouldn't get discouraged if that component you really want to use is not assigned because for the overall good of the product it will actually maximize the return. That's the name of the game. I remember students at the University of Waterloo, all third-year engineering students, pretty sharp, and they asked me, 'How do you motivate people?' And I said, 'You're all motivated coming out. The trick is not to de-motivate you because you're going to have to make compromises for whatever reason, hopefully for the betterment of the overall product.'"

Although RIM continued to place a high priority on finding the "right" co-op students and new graduates, the company didn't rely on youthful enthusiasm alone. Unlike many entrepreneurs who foolishly think they can do it all, Mike Lazaridis was willing to share responsibility and had already begun recruiting experienced executives to build a stronger management team. Balsillie was the first in 1992, followed in 1995 by Mark Carragher who moved from COM DEV to RIM as vice-president, custom silicon. In 1996, Rick Landry, of JRC Canada, became vice-president, manufacturing, and Charles Meyer arrived from Compaq Computer as chief legal officer and corporate secretary. In 1997, RIM added David Werezak, from Hewlett Packard, as vice-president, marketing. Additional experienced management who were brought in from other companies during 1997 and 1998 to round out the team prior to the launch of BlackBerry and who continue to serve as vice-presidents in 2009 included Mark Guibert, vice-president, corporate marketing (from Hewlett-Packard); Hugh Hind, vice-president, protocol stack development (from the University of Waterloo); Benson Tendler, vice-president, hardware quality (from LG Medical Tech); and Elizabeth Roe Pfeifer, vice-president, organizational development (from Open Text). David Yach was hired from Sybase in 1999 to be vice-president, software.

Each of the final two executives recruited had more than twenty years' experience in related fields. At forty-seven, eight years older than either Lazaridis or Balsillie, Don Morrison was hired in 2000 as chief operating officer, BlackBerry. Morrison could see that Lazaridis was not as keen as Balsillie. "Jim was effusive and excited," recalled Morrison. "Mike was supportive and you could just see that mind working and he said, 'You know what, Don? You're not technical, but I'll hire you anyway.'"

Morrison, who'd held a variety of executive roles at Bell Canada and AT&T, including president of the consumer and small business division for Canada and regional vice-president for Europe, the Middle East, and Africa, had done his own due diligence. He talked to a fraternity brother of Balsillie's who'd worked with him at accounting firm Clarkson, Gordon fifteen years earlier. "I asked, are these guys straight up? I was leaving the security of an AT&T environment where you know the fundamentals are high integrity and very high service orientation and I'm going into the unknown, at least from my perspective," said Morrison. "That was table stakes for me."

Larry Conlee made a similar leap of faith when he joined RIM in January 2001 after twenty-nine years with Motorola's cellular and paging divisions, most recently in Chicago. Recruiting firm Heidrick & Struggles had been retained by RIM to find a vice-president, engineering, and turned up Conlee, who was born and educated in Texas. After meeting Conlee, Lazaridis decided to expand the scope of the role from vice-president to chief operating officer in charge of engineering and manufacturing. In November 2000, after Conlee flew to Waterloo for his initial interview, a snowstorm in Chicago closed O'Hare Airport, forcing him to stay overnight rather than return home the same day. The scheduled one-hour meeting with Lazaridis became a six-hour session that included dinner. "We got to know each other far beyond the usual first interview. We realized that we had a lot of common interests and a shared vision about where the world was headed in communications," said Conlee. "One of the pitches Mike gave me was, 'Larry, we've got a billion dollars, come and help me grow this company.' After twenty-nine years as a senior guy with Motorola, you're not interested in meeting with the bankers every week to make sure the bills are going to get paid. That was one of the things that attracted me to RIM. They were stable, they were publicly traded, they had money in the bank, and they had a vision," said Conlee. "Too often a technology company develops its technology and then says, 'Here it is. Someone figure out how to make some money out of it.' RIM had taken the steps to say, 'Here's the technology. The customer's CIO [chief information officer] is going to be happy because of the security; the CEO is going to be happy because he can use the device. He's going to have a good experience in terms of quality and battery life. It's going to be efficient through the network, the carriers are going to like it, and we can deliver the timeliness of data.' I thought that was different. I really liked that approach," said Conlee.

At fifty-three, thirteen years older than Balsillie and Lazaridis, Conlee also brought perspective. "Business goes through ups and downs. Some days you need to say, 'I've seen worse than this. We're going to find a way. We're going to invent a solution' or we're going to solve a customer problem. We just have to buckle down and work on it.' I did not come here to get promoted. My interest in RIM was a chance to come and build a company. The most fun I'd had in my various jobs at Motorola was helping build the cellular industry. To get a chance to do that again was very appealing to me and I thought RIM was well positioned to do that."

RIM was still relatively small compared with Motorola. "In those days, you had to look hard to find RIM on the radar screen," said Conlee, who told Lazaridis that Motorola had rejoiced when RIM landed that first order from BellSouth in 1997. "He said, 'You guys celebrated my order?' 'Sure, we'd been working so long trying to get wireless data and finally somebody got a big order, we thought it was time to celebrate.'"

The arrival of Conlee and Morrison demonstrated a new level of self-awareness at RIM. "One of the great things about Mike and Jim is that they didn't hire Larry and I in their image, which I think was a tremendous sign of maturity on their part. Each of us came here with an experience base, an approach, and a style," said Morrison. "If you survive here, it's actually an exercise in humility, because you find that the culture here is so very different from what it is you are bringing. It's actually the marriage of the best parts of a large company without all the inefficiencies and baggage that you might get from other places."

Morrison also became the highest-ranking delinquent ever nabbed by Balsillie's donut rule. A departmental manager had once let the share price slip in a conversation, only to have those with whom he was talking hold him to the rule, but Morrison's transgression was flagrant by comparison; he knew about the rule, but paid no attention. He even set up a "crawl" on his computer screen that showed real-time trades and prices on the stock exchanges. A colleague noticed this feature and reminded him of the decree, but he just waved off the warning.

Shortly after joining, Morrison listened in on the quarterly conference call with analysts at brokerage firms when Balsillie and Kavelman announced quarterly financial results and took questions. A friend emailed Morrison to say RIM must have posted good results because the share price was rising in after-hours trading. Morrison decided to pass along the good news, so he emailed Balsillie. "You guys are doing a great job. The stock's going up in after-hours trading."

Balsillie's email response was immediate and to the point: "You're buying donuts."

Balsillie copied his reply to Don McMurtry, Dennis Kavelman, and others, so all the recipients knew about the exchange that exposed Morrison's guilt and Balsillie's gotcha. "You are so guilty," McMurtry emailed Morrison. "Mine'll be a cruller," added Kavelman.

Morrison paid up the following Monday morning at Balsillie's regular 8 a.m. meeting that's attended by dozens of sales and marketing employees. Before the flurry of reports began, Morrison walked around the room doling out donuts to everyone. He also bought donuts for the other seven hundred employees in the three buildings then comprising RIM's Waterloo campus and sent money so employees in the U.K. office could buy the equivalent local fare. "This just shows you how egalitarian this place is. It's just a very different culture," said Morrison. "I might have been arrogant enough to say not all of this applies to me."

While RIM was adding senior officers, the company continued to develop Leapfrog, introduced in September 1998 as the Inter@ctive Pager 950 at the Personal Communications Showcase in Dallas. Curious Motorola engineers hid their name tags and visited the RIM booth to sneak a peek at the competition. "There was a notably different kind of buzz around RIM at that show," said Mark Guibert, vice-president, corporate marketing. "We didn't have a giant booth and the new 950 model was drawing such a crowd that people were spilling into the aisles all day long. It was an intense couple of days at the show and a solid launch for the product. Of course, our competitors noticed and I think that marked the beginning of a new competitive dynamic for RIM that has continued for over ten years."

Compared with the bulky Bullfrog, the Leapfrog was tiny, about the size of a deck of cards. It measured $2\frac{1}{2}$ x $3\frac{1}{2}$ inches, was less than one inch thick, and weighed only $4\frac{1}{2}$ ounces. The full three-row QWERTY keyboard was designed in a slight arc, higher in the middle than at the ends, just as Lazaridis had described in his early-morning manifesto, "Success Lies in Paradox!" Other advances had also been incorporated in the newest model. Bullfrog's keys were oblong, but after a redesign by Jason Griffin, Leapfrog's keys were oval. Bullfrog's four rubber directional arrows had been replaced by the trackwheel Lazaridis had admired in the Panasonic VCR. The 950 had only one AA battery, not two like Bullfrog, but could last three weeks, far longer than Bullfrog.

Leapfrog had indeed leapt ahead of Motorola's ReFlex technology, which was principally used to provide so-called "1.5-way paging," (allowing one-way paging with guaranteed message delivery) or "1.7-way paging" (allowing users to receive messages but send only canned replies). Latency, the length of time taken between sending a message and having it arrive at its destination, was quicker on Mobitex, too: six seconds versus as much as five minutes on some networks. "Two-way paging was viewed as a big deal with operators at that time since they faced commoditization and network capacity issues with one-way paging networks," explained Mark Guibert. "There were around 50 million paging customers in North America and the Inter@ctive Pager offered a higher-value user experience while also helping address a major network congestion problem."

RIM also made strides in high-volume manufacturing. Production of the Inter@ctive Pager 950 in RIM's Shoemaker Street plant ran far more smoothly than Bullfrog because Leapfrog was less complex, with only one circuit board and fewer components. "We could produce Leapfrog in volume. Bullfrog was almost handcrafted. The reliability was head and shoulders over Bullfrog because there were so many moving parts in Bullfrog. We outsourced the mechanical engineering of Bullfrog but Leapfrog was all done in-house and we learned a lot," said Rick Landry, vice-president, manufacturing.

Despite all the obvious advantages of Leapfrog over its predecessor, Lazaridis continued to educate BellSouth and RAM Mobile Data executives about the benefits of wireless email. Prior to the Leapfrog launch, Lazaridis met with a group headed by Janet Boudris, vice-president of RAM Mobile Data, who told him they wanted all users to have a PIN number rather than an email address. For Lazaridis, using PIN numbers was just so much backsliding to the bad old days of paging. He pointed out that everyone would soon have personalized email addresses and the whole process would be automated. He pointed to changes that had already taken place in paging, led by SkyTel, which allowed users to send messages directly from their computers rather than rely on operators to relay those messages as had previously been the case. Such automation caused costs to plummet and usage to skyrocket. Email addresses for the new subscribers buying RIM devices through BellSouth would permit the same kind of long-term savings, Lazaridis said.

Despite such conclusive evidence, the group insisted on PIN numbers. "People don't understand email," they said.

Lazaridis knew that most of the attendees at the meeting used email, so he asked, "How many of you have an email address?" Nearly everyone put up a hand.

Then he asked, "How many have a paging PIN number?" This time, only two or three raised a hand.

"Is it just me? Am I missing something? The trend is that most of you have an email address and very few of you use PIN numbers any more. We are witnessing a trend in this room," said Lazaridis.

RAM and BellSouth continued to insist on PIN numbers. In a follow-up phone call with Lazaridis, BellSouth developer Royce Jordan complained, "They're forcing me to convert all the email addresses to PIN numbers for the launch. I've got to change the whole data structure."

"Don't panic. Here's your answer. Use an alias. You've got an alias table, right? For the beta trial, just alias everyone to a PIN number. You can always switch back to email," said Lazaridis.

When Jordan expressed puzzlement at the strategy of running two systems in tandem, Lazaridis said, "Trust me. The first day they turn this on, the CEO of BellSouth is going to call them up and say, 'What the heck is it with all these numbers on my email screen?'"

After BellSouth conducted the trial run, Jordan phoned Lazaridis to say, "You were right. They called me up and asked me how quickly I could change PIN numbers back to email addresses."

"Royce," advised Lazaridis, "whatever you do, don't do it right away."

Despite that modest victory, Mike Lazaridis knew he couldn't count on BellSouth alone to properly market his invention. BellSouth's corporate background was all about voice communications and most of the buzz in the industry still surrounded voice communications; a wireless data product such as email simply did not arouse their enthusiasm in the same way. For many at BellSouth the thinking was, why go to the bother of emailing a message when you can make a quick phone call? Moreover, the data customers they did have were mostly service and delivery trucks. Lazaridis sought to reach an entirely new market: the Fortune 500. "The problem was that we had designed something that looked like a pager, worked like a pager, and we even called it a pager so that people would be comfortable with the new technology and relate to it. It was actually far more than that—it was a messaging terminal, it was almost a miniature computer," said Lazaridis. "These telecom companies were steeped in paging. When we started talking about email in 1997, email wasn't all that popular, it was just starting to become popular in much of corporate America. There was an opportunity there because we knew that's where it was going. We'd been using email for almost two decades."

Despite the massive order placed by BellSouth, relations with RIM were strained. Even before RIM delivered any units, BellSouth was pressuring RIM to cut manufacturing costs by $100 per unit. At the same time, BellSouth was proposing to charge subscribers $100 or more a month. Lazaridis was unhappy with such high fees, believing that a much lower flat rate made more sense as a business builder. Unable to change BellSouth's mind on so many fronts, Lazaridis began working on a business model that would eventually lead to the launch of the BlackBerry solution. It was decided that RIM would need to sell the complete package itself—device, airtime, software, and service. Lazaridis negotiated a deal for two years of unlimited network airtime with RAM Mobile Data for $5 million. He also struck a similar deal with Rogers Cantel, paying just under C$1 million, again for unlimited airtime, in a contract signed in 1998.

Those two deals made RIM one of the first mobile virtual network operators (MVNOs) in North America, a company without a licenced frequency reselling airtime from another company's network. "Selling the package ourselves was important because we believed in wireless corporate email. No one else really believed in it. Wireless corporate email required a lot more hand-holding and different marketing. We decided we were going to fund this ourselves, we were going to build our own sales force and support organization," said Lazaridis.

Although they were happy to sell the airtime, RAM and Rogers were surprised at Lazaridis's audacity. "He was persuading his board of directors to do something quite crazy, which was, 'I can't get these people to sell my product, so I'm going to do it myself.' That's kind of ballsy," said David Neale, of Rogers. "RIM was running around getting as many distributors as they possibly could. And you could have argued that they were competitors because we were both selling on the same network. It was contentious. As a network manager, I was saying, 'Some activity is better than no activity.'"

BellSouth agreed. "We had so few customers, and we had this big old network, that having somebody buy it from us wholesale and resell it was fine with us because at least we were making something," said Earle Mauldin, president of BellSouth Enterprises. "Our primary interest was the network usage. We never made a lot of money on the equipment because a lot of the times you had to price the equipment so cheap to get the customer that as far as the equipment [profit] margin was concerned, there wasn't any."

By the time BlackBerry had been developed, launched, and marketed by RIM for about nine months, Lazaridis's decision to put RIM directly into the wireless email business was proven correct. In September 1999, unsold Inter@ctive Pagers began piling up in BellSouth's warehouse. "It is amazing to look back and recall how hard it was to sell this stuff. The sales folks would tell people: 'There's something even better coming,'" said Mauldin. "That's always a problem," agreed Jim Hobbs of BellSouth Mobile Data. "We might have also have taken on too much stock. We were working with some of the other paging companies. There was the anticipation of being more successful with some of these other paging companies in terms of reselling off of our network. But that was emotionally very, very difficult for some of those old-timers to do, to sell a product that wasn't on their network."

Potential users were also slow to see the benefits of email. "This was still pretty early in the days of email," said consultant Andy Seybold. "I liken this whole thing to fax machines. When fax machines first started coming out, your first question to somebody was, 'Do you have a fax machine? OK, what's the number?' Then you made an assumption later on and you didn't ask if they had a fax machine. You said, 'What's your fax number?' When these things were coming out, it was still, 'Do you have an email address? ... OK, what is it?' It's very different from today when your assumption is that everybody has an email address."

RIM's management team was well aware of the industry skepticism. "The mainstream value of wireless email seems so obvious in hindsight, like many great inventions, I suppose, but the genius of it certainly wasn't intuitive to most people at the time. Looking back, it is really quite inspiring to think about how Mike and Jim instilled the necessary conviction throughout the company to go make this happen in the face of huge external skepticism," recalled Mark Guibert.

So great was marketplace uncertainty that on September 3, 1998, RIM's four-year-long investment deal with COM DEV

CEO Val O'Donovan unraveled. O'Donovan, through a firm called Technology Horizons, which was spun out of COM DEV, sold one-third of his shares without bothering to advise RIM in advance. The abrupt dumping of such a huge block of shares (approximately fifty times the normal daily volume at the time) sent RIM share price from C$5.40 to C$5, an all-time low, before recovering slightly to close at C$5.15.

RIM demanded and received the resignation of O'Donovan from the RIM board. Technology Horizons sold the rest of its RIM shares in 1999, explaining that the firm had decided to shift its investment into satellites. The RIM share price subsequently rose to C$10.25 by the end of 1998 and $60.70 by the end of 1999. While Technology Horizons realized proceeds of approximately $100 million from the divestiture, those same RIM shares they sold would have been worth $2 billion in recent years.

While Val O'Donovan was bailing out, some carriers were just coming aboard. Walt Purnell Jr., CEO of American Mobile Satellite Corp., waited for a year after the BellSouth announcement before he was able to buy Inter@ctive Pagers from RIM. He had IBM lined up to replace their Bullfrogs with the 850, as the new model was called on the ARDIS/DataTAC network operated by his firm. Purnell knew RIM had to sell to carriers in succession, first BellSouth and then American Mobile, because RIM was still small and could only develop and manufacture pagers at a certain pace, so he was delighted when Balsillie finally showed up in 1998 to make his pitch. "I saw that device, and that was it, that was what I was looking for. They are innovators that have no equal in the industry," said Purnell. "Jim and Mike both had a vision. History has proven them to be dead on. It's a perfect example of a couple of guys and a team of professionals that looked around the landscape and saw a market need for an inexpensive, powerful, lightweight device with a lot of capability."

In September 1998, American Mobile Satellite Corp. placed an order worth C$50 million for 75,000 pagers and 25,000 OEM radio modems, and then followed up in October 2000 with an order for another 50,000 pagers. (In 2000, American Satellite changed its name to Motient, spun off XM Satellite Radio, later went into Chapter 11, emerging successfully in 2002, and currently exists as TerreStar Corporation.) RIM also began selling to, among others, SkyTel, GoAmerica, PageNet, and Dell Computer. Rogers Cantel placed a C$3 million order for two-way pagers, in September 1998, almost ten years after the relationship between the two companies began. During that time, Rogers Cantel had developed what was then the only national wireless network in Canada at a cost of C$1 billion for capital equipment and operating losses. "We wouldn't be here if Rogers didn't invest in the data networks in the mid-to-late eighties that became our sandbox," said Balsillie in 2006.[1]

In an effort to spur sales in the investment community, RIM gave working prototypes of the Inter@ctive Pager 950 to financial analysts. Michael Urlocker, a former journalist who left the *Financial Post* in 1995 to join Gordon Capital as an analyst and then moved to Credit Suisse First Boston (CSFB),

---

[1] Canadian Club of Toronto, May 2, 2006.

was in Atlanta in June 1998 at SuperComm, the annual tele-com conference and trade show. Eager to learn the financial results of a particular company he followed, Urlocker bought an ice cream, sat down in a quiet corner of the exhibit hall, pulled out the Inter@ctive Pager 950 he'd been testing, and emailed a colleague in Toronto inquiring if the quarterly num-bers had been released.

Urlocker can no longer remember what company was on his mind, but he'll never forget receiving the emailed reply with the numbers he sought. "That was the moment when it [the 950] moved from being a toy to something that really provided information," he said. "RIM has the lead in this growing technology," Urlocker wrote in a CSFB research report dated February 2, 1999, when he initiated coverage of the company. "The popularity of and the amount that people rely on e-mail is rising, making this the right time for a prod-uct like RIM's. We see RIM as a high-risk, high-reward play on what could be the next Palm Pilot." Urlocker put a buy on the stock at C$14.25. A year later, RIM's share price was C$121.90.

The 950 was named one of the four hottest electronic gadgets of the year by *Profit* magazine, best pager by *Mobile Computing and Communications* magazine, and won CNET Editor's Choice for design and performance. The 950 was also ushered into the Smithsonian Institution's Permanent Re-search Collection of Information Technology.

But for all the growing acceptance and industry accolades, there remained a technical quandary. A 950 subscriber had one wireless address for email and another address on the com-puter at the office. Such a user might even have a third email address left over from some other company's earlier effort.

"The problem with wireless email was how many email boxes does this person have?" said BellSouth's Jack Barse, who had previously worked at MCI Mail and Sprint. "Many of us had used RadioMail. I had a RadioMail email box and a couple of others on various and sundry email services, so people had to figure out where I was. We called it 'the two-mailbox problem.'"

Wireless email had its beginnings in a series of products RIM devised in the early 1990s. Initially, messaging was peer-to-peer, device-to-device. RIM then devised RIMGate to provide Internet access; RAM Mobile Data set up its own gateway, called Ramparts. Both systems were excruciatingly slow. Users had to log in and verify their credentials before seeing any messages in a labour-intensive process that rapidly depleted battery life. Speed, power, and ease of access improved with the 950 operating on Intel's 386 chip and BellSouth's Mobitex network, but the problem of multiple addresses continued to impede usage. "We think the 950 is a gem and we have been forwarding our emails from our desk through the Ramparts gateway to these devices, so we know we can receive mail, but we can't reply because the reply path is broken," said Gary Mousseau, the X.25 specialist RIM hired in 1991.

During one of their many working sessions, Lazaridis told Mousseau, "'We've got to solve this two-mailbox problem. We've got to come up with a single-mailbox alternative.' Classic Mike, he's got this big vision," recalled Mousseau. "He would give out these mandates: 'It's got to have high security. You've got to have full encryption in there and we might as well use that compression stuff we developed all those years ago. We might as well take advantage of this growing expertise we have at RIM.' So I go off and put the meat to the bone, bring him back a spec and say, 'Is this kind of where you envisioned?'"

Lazaridis and Mousseau worked tirelessly on addressing the mailbox problem. "The more specs I write, the more we realize we could do in terms of mirroring the desktop experience: calendaring, tasks, to-dos, the global address list. And then Mike says, 'Stop. We'll never finish this product. Just stop right now,'" said Mousseau.

During the summer of 1997, a first draft was written of what became U.S. patent No. 6,219,694, on single-mailbox integration, filed May 29, 1998, and granted almost three years later on April 17, 2001. "We came up with this strategy of re-enveloping the data to get it to presume the original envelope and then off it goes to the destination with the new envelope," said Mousseau. "The outer envelope can be removed, in a sense, and the inner envelope preserves the addressing information. The reverse path is also re-enveloped. When it comes back to the desktop it is un-enveloped and there is the addressing information so it can keep on going to the proper destination." With the two-mailbox problem solved, Lazaridis was able to look further ahead than ever before. BlackBerry was in sight at last.

CHAPTER NINE

BIRTH OF BLACKBERRY

IN MARCH 1998, with the Inter@ctive Pager 950 gearing up for a fall launch with BellSouth, Mike Lazaridis sat down with the full list of all thirty-six RIM products and eliminated thirty of them in order to focus on what would become BlackBerry. Next, he created a steering committee headed by Dave Castell, hired two months earlier with a computer science degree from the University of Waterloo as well as an MBA and a law degree from the University of Toronto.

The other members of the committee, drawn from various disciplines across RIM included Dave Werezak, vice-president, marketing; Allan Lewis, vice-president, infrastructure group; Barry Gilhuly, senior software engineer; Barry Linkert, software developer; and Gary Mousseau, who served as acting vice-president, software, after Mike Barnstijn took a leave of absence in July 1998.

This new project led by Castell was ambitious because it encompassed so many elements: a new device, new software, a desktop component, a server, and infrastructure. "BlackBerry was not a hardware project. The hardware was already being built as a two-way wireless pager for BellSouth. BlackBerry was essentially a repositioning of the product as a wireless handheld or a personal digital assistant, but together with a range of new software and infrastructure to form an end-to-end wireless solution. We said, 'What you really have here is a 386 and a wireless modem. What it is, is all up to you,'" said Castell.

As a first step, the committee conducted surveys and found that what email subscribers wanted most was a means of dealing with the dozens of messages waiting in their desktop PC at the end of a busy day of meetings or travel. For RIM, the value proposition for the new device became the ability to deal with email whenever a few minutes became available: while travelling in a taxi, sitting in a reception area waiting to see someone, or standing in line at the bank. "You'd deal with them during your downtime during the day so by the time you come back to the office you're going home to your family," said Castell.

Two books were particularly helpful in setting the tone of the discussions and focusing RIM's thinking about what category the new device would occupy. The first was Geoffrey A. Moore's *Inside the Tornado*, which featured an account of Hewlett-Packard's spectacular failure with a new offering because nobody could figure out what it was, a PDA, an organizer, or something else. "You have to *be* something. People have to know where to find you, how to buy you," said Castell. The second book was Guy Kawasaki's *Rules for Revolutionaries*. A chapter called "Don't Worry, Be Crappy" described the 1984 launch of Macintosh and argued that revolutionary products can't be perfect; companies can't keep postponing the launch to make improvements. Another chapter, entitled "Churn,

Baby, Churn," argued that once a product was released, you fix the problems that show up as fast as possible. "This was a mantra with me. In an early marketplace, you just have to be better than the others, and work hard to solve your problems," said Castell.

Castell's steering committee met daily in Lazaridis's office to brainstorm about every movement, keystroke, menu choice, and icon on the new device. Among the team's early successes was rewriting the software in the 950 to create a full personal information manager with a calendar, address book, and memo pad. "The meetings had a positive effect of creating the ease of use you still see in BlackBerry today—uniformity across so many menu choices and so many sub-systems—that whole double-click action we came up with. 'Ease of use' became one of our catchphrases," said Mousseau. "There's no 'help' on this device. Mike wanted to keep 'help' off the device. He said, 'If it's that complicated, we're going to have to redo it. It's got to be easy to use.' That's his mantra and it survives to this day."

There were occasions when differing views blocked progress. For example, even though a user would not be able to read an email attachment on the handheld, Castell believed the recipient should still be able to forward the attachment to someone who *could* read it on a PC. A committee member disagreed, so while the dissenting individual was away on a one-week family holiday, Castell convinced a three-person team to build in the disputed feature in return for free dinners.

In mid-1998, when BellSouth's Jim Hobbs, Neale Hightower, and Jack Barse visited Waterloo, Lazaridis was able to demonstrate progress on the single-mailbox solution as well as several advancements on other fronts brought about by the committee. Lazaridis ushered the BellSouth trio into his office, turned on a monitor, and said, "I'm getting all of my Outlook messages on my pager."

"We were all thinking, 'That's a pretty big feat of magic there because you're synchronizing mailboxes,'" recalled Barse. "And here was Mike with a solution that was more than a redirect or an auto forward that's fairly simple. The hard part came in synchronizing what was going on in the handheld with what was going on in the server: marking the message as deleted or read. I can still see him holding a 950 in one hand and having Outlook running on his monitor. What I remember about that brief glimpse was his enthusiasm for the problem they had solved."

While Lazaridis's committee continued to meet to define and develop the BlackBerry solution, Balsillie assembled a business team, including David Werezak, Mark Guibert, Don McMurtry, and Justin Fabian to meet regularly and develop the sales and marketing plan. RIM had to initially take Black-Berry direct to customers rather than selling through carriers, and that meant assuming much more responsibility for sales, channel development, pricing, brand management, marketing communications, training, customer support, billing, and much more. It was a particularly big undertaking for a company that had principally been an OEM supplier.

One of the pressing marketing questions was what would RIM call this new solution that would revolutionize wireless email? In the search for an evocative name, in August 1998, RIM hired David Placek, founder and president of Lexicon Branding Inc., of Sausalito, California. Lexicon had come up with the name Pavilion for HP's line of desktop PCs, as well as other high-profile technology brand names such as Pentium for Intel and PowerBook for Apple. "Everyone thinks that developing a brand name is fun and relatively easy. It is fun, at least for a while, but it's really never easy, particularly when it comes to technology, because there are so many trademarks," said Placek, a former ad executive at Foote, Cone & Belding.

Lexicon began the assignment from RIM by conducting interviews with passengers arriving in Sausalito on the ferry from San Francisco. They soon discovered that the very mention of email made people nervous and sent their blood pressure soaring, offering further proof that the name for the device should be colourful and connotative rather than dull and descriptive. Lexicon set up three two-member teams: one team worked with a prototype of the actual device, while the other two teams saw neither the product nor the consumer research. Take risks with the name, the two latter teams were told; think about simple joys or satisfying pleasures.

The three teams worked in separate studios writing possible names on swatches of white butcher paper posted on the walls. Among the dozens of scrawled possibilities was "strawberry." When Will Leben, director of linguistics at Lexicon and a professor at Stanford University, walked through the studios and spotted that word, he saluted the concept but said the syllable "strawww" was too drawn out.

"Strawberry is too slow of a name," agreed Placek. "Email is instantaneous."

Unlike some of the participants in the naming exercise, Leben and Placek had seen the prototype of RIM's new handheld. Now that they thought about it, they realized that the oval keys looked like berry seeds. As Leben and Placek began considering other berries, Placek was struck by the simple fact that the handheld was black. Why not call it Blackberry? When a list of preliminary suggestions was passed along to RIM, Placek pointed to Blackberry. "You have to have something provocative and really different. There's no way that an AT&T or a South-Western Bell is going to have the flexibility to come out with a Blackberry. This gives you a very distinctive image of something that's fun and easy to use," he said. Placek also encouraged RIM to take their time to consider all the possibilities.

Coincident with the RIM project, Lexicon had just begun conducting its earliest research into sound symbolism, or consumer response to specific letters, and Blackberry scored very well based on the research. The letter B meant reliability, another affirming reason to adopt the name. If one B meant reliability, two Bs were even better, and gave rhythmic alliteration for the ear. Putting both Bs in capitals—BlackBerry— offered symmetry for the eye.

In November, Lexicon sent to Waterloo about forty names printed in black lettering on individual pieces of white card stock. With Placek on the phone, Werezak displayed the names on an easel for a group that included Lazaridis, Balsillie, Guibert, Castell, Fabian, and McMurtry. "It was just like a scene out of *Bewitched*. They put them up, one after another, just like Darrin Stephens used to do in front of the clients of his ad agency," said Lazaridis. "The names were all very technical, and some of them were just plain weird. I was getting upset because I didn't like any of the names. BlackBerry was the last name. I said in a very loud voice, 'I don't like any of the names.' And then I waited. There was total silence. I waited and I waited, and then I said, 'Except the last one.' When they started giggling at the other end of the phone, I knew I'd been set up."

Castell, Fabian, and McMurtry initially preferred another name—Blade—arguing that Blade captured their "road warrior" image of an email user. Their campaign collapsed after someone went online and discovered that one of the "Blade" Web domains led to an Internet porn site. A case was briefly made by Lexicon for two other possibilities, Byline and Outrigger, but everyone soon settled on BlackBerry. Lazaridis in particular liked BlackBerry because it echoed his 1984 thinking about Apple and Budgie as friendly trademarks that lowered high-tech intimidation levels. "Of all the naming work we've done, BlackBerry is the story most often told," said Placek of Lexicon, which has created two thousand brand names since the firm was founded in 1982. "Pentium, Dasani, BlackBerry, but BlackBerry's number one."

Mark Guibert credits Lexicon for providing solid knowledge on the technical aspects of naming, such as linguistics and trademarks, and a process that allowed RIM to be thoughtful and deliberate in choosing a name. But at the end of the day, it was the RIM team that had to decide which name, with each of its pros and cons, would best complement the product and business strategy that RIM was developing. Lexicon provided a long list of names that covered the spectrum from technical to fun and literal to abstract. The RIM team ultimately decided to go with a name that many perceived to be a risky choice.

"Dave Werezak and I talked a lot about the name and the risk of going with a connotative brand name like BlackBerry rather than a more conservative, descriptive name," explained Guibert. "We didn't have a big budget to promote the name in the early years either and that was a consideration. In the end, it came down to everyone's conviction in the product. Without that conviction and that belief that this product had the potential to be truly special, I don't think we would have gone with it. We would have likely gone the conservative route."

"Dave and I joked that it could prove to be a career-limiting move too," Guibert added. "If the product flopped, I suspect there would have been some suggestions that the name was dumb for a tech product and that those marketing guys killed the engineers' product. In fact, most people's instant reaction to the name inside the company was quite negative. There were a lot of people who were nervous about our decision. They almost couldn't believe it when we told them. We put together a presentation to walk them through the logic and present the name in its best light, but the silence was deafening in those meetings at the point when the name was unveiled. People were shocked. It wasn't something they expected from this company that sold OEM products and the Inter@ctive Pager. We even had certain individuals at our marketing agencies trying to convince us to abandon the name. But the name grew on people over time and we eventually won over their confidence. And all the hand-wringing quickly stopped as soon as we publicly launched. The name was a hit from the start."

BlackBerry was launched in a January 19, 1999, webcast featuring RIM executives as well as industry analyst Andy Seybold and representatives from Rogers and BellSouth. Both Intel and Microsoft also supported the launch with quotes in RIM's press release. It was a relatively modest launch by RIM's standards today, but it drew more attention than anything RIM had done before. The first BlackBerry leveraged the Inter@ctive Pager 950 hardware but came as part of a larger package from RIM that combined the hardware with new device software, PC software, server software, airtime, and a cradle linking the device to a PC.

As a secure extension of the Microsoft Exchange/Outlook email system, messages sent from the device maintained the user's Exchange-based email address and even showed up in the "sent items" folder of the user's email account. To the recipient, sending an email from the user's device was identical to sending it from the user's PC. Most important, the Black-Berry provided what was called an "end-to-end solution" for "pushing" email to and from a device that was "always on, always connected." Using Microsoft Exchange, proven software that worked well for email and could support large amounts of data storage, BlackBerry offered corporate users access to their own email without having to set up another email account or go through the hassle of remotely accessing Exchange. Black-Berry was priced at $399 for the hardware and RIM sold unlimited airtime for $39.99 a month per user over nationwide wireless networks in the United States and Canada.

The design was widely admired. "The keyboard, angling the buttons to your thumbs, worked so well. It had a magnetic switch so that when you put it in its holster it knew the difference between whether it was in the holster versus not. In the holster it could buzz you, but if you set it on the desk it could go silent. If you went into a meeting, you pulled it out of your holster, you didn't have to do a thing, you didn't have to fiddle with a thing, you just pulled it out of the holster, set it on the desk, and the thing would shut up. It wasn't buzzing you, it wasn't making any noise. It had little things like that that I wish I had in mobile phones today," said Robert O'Hara, wireless architect at Microsoft.

RIM created a network operations centre (NOC) that meant each device connected to the corporate server behind safe firewalls, which were in turn connected through a single secure line to the NOC so only legitimate traffic went either to or from a particular BlackBerry. RIM didn't store the data; it just encrypted the data and then moved it on what was in effect a private network that kept users more secure than the public Internet.

In the case of the previous models—Inter@ctive Pagers 850 and 950—RIM shipped the handhelds in bulk to Bell-South, ARDIS, Rogers, or Bell Mobility. The carriers then marketed and sold the devices, billed customers, and handled tech support. RIM initially had none of those administrative functions in place for selling BlackBerry. In the first few months following the launch in January 1999, RIM's primary means of promotion was through public relations and RIM sales reps known as "wireless email evangelists" who travelled extensively "spreading the word" and often provided free BlackBerry devices to influential business people in companies that were believed to have longer-term sales potential. "We probably gave away our first thousand and created addictive users in what was our first seeding to our target market," said Dave Castell. RIM was moving so fast that it didn't even al-ways·manage to keep records of individual recipients, just "ship to" reports. "It looked like Marriott and Red Roof Inn were our first customers. We weren't able to bill at the time, but we were sure they were leading to other sales," said Castell.

When RIM set up its billing system, the company charged subscribers a flat rate of $39.99 a month for unlimited service. RIM set up the flat-rate system not only because it would be popular with users but because it dramatically simplified billing. RIM didn't have to keep track of individual usage; one size fit all. Billing systems had been a nightmare for many other wireless companies and RIM eliminated this risk with its unlimited plan, while at the same time creating a competitive advantage in its pricing and also removing a potential barrier to adoption by users. With a flat-rate price, users didn't need to even think about how many emails they were sending and receiving and they had no surprises when the bill arrived. It proved to be a wise strategy. Behind the scenes, RIM scrambled to build up its business and technical systems. The relay infrastructure through which all BlackBerry messages passed—a precursor to today's network operations centres—initially ran on a single server. The customer-support function was augmented by outsourcing to a call centre. "It was an incredibly ambitious task for a company that had just raised money and was focused on designing, building, manufacturing, and shipping this two-way pager to BellSouth," said Castell. "*And* to do it as a 'side' business. The good news was we didn't have to be perfect."

Although it wasn't perfect and RIM was busy troubleshooting and fixing software glitches, BlackBerry was starting to be recognized for its innovation and substance. "The rest of the industry was building devices. Motorola was building two-way pagers for SkyTel and leaving it to the networks to put in the infrastructure. RIM was really the first company to understand they were selling an end-to-end solution, not a device. And they said it has to be encrypted," said wireless guru Andy Seybold. "They also realized that they had to offer not just a server version but a desktop version of the BlackBerry because in those days—it's not as true today—technology still got snuck into companies one device at a time, the way it had been with PCs, notebooks, pagers, and laptops. It was people sneaking technology in because it made their job easier."

Media reaction to BlackBerry was enthusiastic. "The RIM pager is the first wireless message device that I'd want to carry around," read a review titled "Close-to-Perfect Pocket E-Mail" in *Business Week* in May 1999. "The ultimate computing tool of 1999," said tech magazine *InfoWorld*. A lengthy feature in the *Wall Street Journal* on September 17, 1999, lamented the clunky nature of most technology items but then listed a series of new "information appliances" for people who wanted to get onto the Internet or use email. After listing nine possibilities, most of which are now long gone, BlackBerry was given a positive, if passing, mention in the last paragraph of the story: "One particularly good one is a pager with a teeny tiny keyboard, called BlackBerry, sold by a Canadian firm called Research In Motion. It has been a hit with corporate e-mail fanatics."

"It was especially important for us to get the positive media commentary because we didn't have a well-known brand or a big company name at the time," noted Mark Guibert. "We worked hard to establish our credibility with the media and, in turn, the credibility of someone like Steve Wildstrom from *Business Week* praising the product helped a lot."

That teeny, tiny keyboard came from a firm that was, in relative terms, still small at three hundred employees and revenue of $70.5 million for the twelve months ending in February 1999. But despite the modest corporate size and out-of-the-way location, the BlackBerry device had substantial advantages over its competitors. Motorola's PageWriter didn't have push email. AccessLink, a two-way pager from Glenayre Technologies, didn't have a full keyboard. The Palm VII was the only competing wireless handheld with any public profile, but it was a very different device. A Palm user had to turn on the network connection, raise the antenna, and then check for messages, unlike with RIM's always-on, always-connected push email solution.

As it turned out, the timing of the BlackBerry launch in 1999 was perfect. Email was finally becoming one of the main forces driving the growth of wireless Internet devices. By 1998, the Internet had become an indispensable network with 140 million users worldwide that would grow to 500 million by 2003, reported the International Data Corp. "Corporate email caught on much faster than we thought it would. It just hit at the right time in the right place. We were very controlled in our launches. We launched in New York, we launched in Silicon Valley, and then we launched in very targeted states because we didn't have the resources to go any further. Plus, they were the most receptive to the technology," said Lazaridis.

To tap into demand, RIM struck a deal to sell BlackBerry through Microsoft Exchange value-added resellers (VARs). Although there were thousands of VARs selling customized Microsoft products, RIM concentrated on only a few hundred outlets. The approach didn't work as well as RIM had originally hoped. VARs make their money customizing what they sell; BlackBerry could not be customized at the time. The software turned out to be so easy to install, VARs couldn't even charge for that service. What was more likely to happen was that one of the resellers would round up potential customers, a RIM sales rep would do a demo, and the reseller would collect commissions from any sales generated by the event.

RIM decided that the VAR route wasn't a fit at the time. Why not build its own sales force, just as it had launched its own network? In January 1998, a year before BlackBerry, there were only four full-time RIM employees in sales; by 2000, a year after BlackBerry, there were more than one hundred. Balsillie interviewed all new hires until the inflow grew too large. The new sales force targeted financial services and lawyers who needed to communicate with their clients and could afford the new technology. "There were hundreds of millions of email accounts out there, but our total addressable market when we first launched BlackBerry was a couple of hundred thousand," said RIM software engineer Dale Brubacher-Cressman. "We tackled that couple of hundred thousand by focusing on what would be compelling to those users, not by trying to take a small percentage of the hundred million–user market. Another major factor was just plain hard work. People would bust their butts to hit deadlines because we knew that deadline was strategically important to the company. Big companies like Microsoft and Motorola were constantly stretching out their delivery dates on products. We always hit our delivery dates."

Much of RIM's early sales success flowed from what can only be called guerrilla tactics used on the most likely prospects. "We had a unique approach to selling, which really got most of our leads. I would 'cold call' people on the street," said Justin Fabian, who opened the U.S. sales office. "We would also target trade shows and just go up and start talking to people. You could see their badges, see who they are. Another great place for targeting people was airport lounges where people are actually going online, checking their email."

At trade shows, rather than remain behind the table in the RIM booth, the evangelists would be out in the aisles, buttonholing attendees with open-ended questions designed to generate conversations. "What's the most exciting thing you've seen today?" "How do you get your email?" Then they'd demonstrate the RIM product and ask, "What if you could do this?" They disregarded strict exhibit times, preferring to be on the conference floor round the clock. On one memorable occasion, Fabian made a presentation to a law firm's chief information officer, who was so impressed that he swatted his Palm Pilot off the boardroom table, sending it crashing against the wall. Fabian took that as a sign he'd made a sale.

As part of the offering, RIM's evangelists gave potential corporate clients a thirty-day trial with free airtime and a money-back guarantee. "You can talk about technology all you want but until you actually use it you won't understand the benefits, the ROL, what we called the 'return on life,'" said Fabian. "ROL was being able to take control of your downtime and manage it more effectively so when you're in between meetings, if you've got some time in a cab, or even when you get home, to keep in touch." A survey conducted in 2004 by research firm Ipsos Reid confirmed that the average Black-Berry subscriber converted fifty-four minutes of daily down-time into productive use. On an annual basis, that conversion added up to 196 hours or $21,000 in productivity gains.

Key decision-makers made the difference between a prod-uct that flew off the shelves and one that flopped. "When RIM was first introducing their products they spent most of their marketing budget on giving people they identified as mavens or connectors samples of their product," said RIM director Jim Estill. "Most stockbrokers qualified. Because the product worked well, they evangelized it and eventually that led to more adoption and ultimate success."

Once prospects used BlackBerry for a few days they could see the advantage. It was not just the instant delivery, or the fact that they could deal with messages as they arrived. They also liked that they didn't have to go through assistants; they could send messages directly to the person they wanted to reach, just like having that individual's direct phone number. Even better, there was no wasted time talking about the weather, the weekend, or the worries of the day during every interaction. Sometimes, a few words in the subject area could be enough. Getting back speedily to a possible client could mean the difference between closing a deal and being scooped by a competitor.

Balsillie and Kavelman were an integral part of the early process to spread the word about RIM and its products. After RIM went public in Canada in 1997, both men began weekly visits to U.S. investment bankers, analysts, and potential investors with a view to eventually obtaining a U.S. listing on NASDAQ, the preferred exchange for technology companies. RIM needed the NASDAQ listing to create a broader market, but first the company had to generate wider interest beyond the one U.S. firm that participated in the IPO, Nationsbanc Montgomery Securities. To be traded on NASDAQ, RIM needed at least six different investment bankers who acted as market makers. "We knew our market was the U.S., we knew that was the logical place to be, where the sophisticated analysts were. Netscape had gone public, the Internet boom was just starting, we knew the U.S. was where we wanted to get," said Kavelman.

At first, getting anyone's attention was a tough slog. In 1998, Balsillie and Kavelman spoke in San Francisco at a tech conference sponsored by Montgomery. RIM's session has been scheduled at the same time as a presentation by Intel, obviously a much bigger draw, so the audience for RIM numbered exactly three people plus a sprinkling of Montgomery employees.

As time passed, individual movers and shakers became supportive and began telling their investment banking peers. SoundView, a boutique technology investment bank in San Francisco, was an early fan and would conduct trades on the Toronto Stock Exchange through Griffiths McBurney. Scott Morrison, who managed U.S. and technology funds for Toronto-based CI Mutual Funds, held RIM in his portfolio and spoke glowingly about BlackBerry to Steven Milunovich, global technology strategist with Merrill Lynch in New York, who in turn became interested.

By February 1999, a month after the BlackBerry launch, there was enough interest for Research In Motion to be listed on NASDAQ with the ticker symbol RIMM. By then, the market cap was a healthy $700 million, three times higher than it had been only eighteen months earlier at the time of the Canadian IPO. As Balsillie and Kavelman continued their visits to financiers, they began "seeding" either by giving away BlackBerry devices or collecting business cards to send one later. After a thirty-day free trial, the recipient was either billed the usual monthly subscriber charges or returned the handheld. Most kept the freebies and became subscribers. Patrick Spence, who now manages the RIM business unit that deals with Rogers and AT&T, got his start at RIM as a student whose desk happened to be near Kavelman's. Whenever Kavelman returned from a trip, he'd hand Spence a stack of cards and Spence would set up each of the prospects with trial devices.

Along with such seeding to individual users, RIM ran a pincer movement with information technology (IT) managers and chief information officers, convincing both groups that security would not be compromised with a wireless system. Higher encryption standards in the BlackBerry software and the unique security architecture of the overall system made it an ideal solution for corporate users worried about security of financial information, so sales staff focused on that portion of the potential corporate market. The BlackBerry 957, introduced in April 2000, operated from a BlackBerry Enterprise Server (BES) installed safely behind each company's firewall. There was only one outbound access line through the firm's firewall, so there was less likelihood of introducing a virus that would infect the system. The CIOs and IT managers learned they could recommend BlackBerry for use by key executives and managers, safe in the knowledge that their entire system would not crash or become infected by some rogue virus. "Security is the tail that wags the dog in IT. You have to go through a lot to convince IT managers," said Castell.

IT managers often said, in effect, this is a good system, but no one has asked for it, so we won't install it. That's where high-level seeding was helpful. "Once someone gets it, there's a dynamic that takes over. The instantaneous connection becomes something that you can't live without. The initial hook is about managing your incredible volume of email. Push is what keeps it in their hands, but it wasn't what put it in their hands. What's addictive is that it's so relevant to you because it is *your* email and it's immediate," said Castell.

"The desktop product was our stealth-mode product, it was our getting-our-foot-in-the-door product. If you could get email at your desktop, you could run BlackBerry because we piggybacked over an existing path in and out of the desktop. CEOs were our seed market. They would then tell the CIOs and IT managers to put the BlackBerry Enterprise Server in, saying, 'Because I want it,'" said Mousseau. Once the BES was installed, it automatically replaced any individual desktop redirectors. The IT department had taken control, but the CEO's service continued. Everybody was happy.

RIM's marketing methodology also included educating analysts at investment banking firms and getting them to use BlackBerry. "I'd be lying in bed at ten o'clock and I'd get six emails from Jim Balsillie. He was notorious for sending you stuff at midnight. In the normal course of business you wouldn't talk to Jim Balsillie more than once or twice a year. It was an unconventional type of communication; it was such a novel thing," said Barry Richards, an analyst with Paradigm Capital.

RIM would get devices into analysts' hands and invite them to Waterloo for tours and briefings. As a result, analysts wrote reports that reached both investors and RIM's target market. "BlackBerry became one of those products that got an awful lot of word of mouth. People started using Black-Berry and raving about it. If you had a BlackBerry in those days you were considered to be somebody who was a mover and a shaker, somebody who was important in their company. It very quickly became a status symbol," said Andy Seybold.

In the days before spam became more prevalent, every email was important, even urgent, giving BlackBerry—as well as the user—prestige. "If you got an email, someone you knew had sent you one and had something to say. I remember getting this high, this rush, every goddamned time the thing beeped," said Paradigm's Richards. "That lasted for years and years. It used to drive my wife crazy, but I remember feeling important. I liked being 'Always on, always connected.'"

RIM's lengthy efforts to educate and seed influential end users and win the confidence of investment bankers finally paid off in October 1999 when RIM was able to raise $172 million on NASDAQ by selling 5.6 million shares at $30.75, a price that was two and a half times greater than when the company had first listed its shares on NASDAQ only eight months earlier. Merrill Lynch led the U.S. investment banking syndicate that included SoundView, Banc of America Securities, SG Cowen, Piper Jaffray, CIBC Oppenheimer, and a number of smaller firms. The successful U.S. invasion called for a celebration.

CHAPTER TEN

TAKING MANHATTAN

THE SITE CHOSEN FOR JUBILATION was Lulu's, a famous Waterloo roadhouse with a stage, a 6,000-square-foot dance floor, and two oak bars, both 300 feet long, said to be the longest in the world. As had been the case with the previous concert featuring Tom Cochrane, the investment bankers joined RIM in paying for the event. This blast on January 13, 2000, was much bigger, however, with an audience of 1,800 that included RIM employees, suppliers, bankers, and invitations issued to many of the students (and potential future RIM employees) at the University of Waterloo.

The featured band was supposed to remain a secret until the last minute, but two days before the Thursday event word began to spread that Barenaked Ladies, one of Jim Balsillie's favourite groups, would provide the entertainment. "We are the Barenaked Ladies and who are you?" they rapped that night. "We are rockin' on the stage in Kitchener-Waterloo." Among the repertoire of the five-member Toronto-based indie band was one of their more popular tunes, "If I Had a Million Dollars." More than a few in the audience had that much and more given that the share price had risen tenfold from the time of the IPO three years earlier. In fact, Mike Lazaridis and Jim Balsillie were both billionaires.

In addition to being a concert sponsor and lead member of the NASDAQ syndicate, Merrill Lynch had agreed to buy 1,500 BlackBerry devices. RIM also signed large corporate orders with other Manhattan firms, including investment banker Credit Suisse First Boston, as well as law firms Gibson, Dunn & Crutcher and Holland & Knight. "The idea of lawyers carrying around a BlackBerry was insane. Lawyers had paralegals. Lawyers were technophobes. They let their assistants deal with things. Now BlackBerrys are very popular with lawyers. BlackBerrys helped take paging out of the blue-collar world," said Alan Reiter, president of Wireless Internet & Mobile Computing, of Chevy Chase, Maryland. In January 2000, Intel ordered 2,000 BlackBerry devices; the following month, Salomon Smith Barney bought 2,500. Other early adopters included IBM, Dell, and Oracle, as well as the U.S. Air Force, Navy, and Army.

BlackBerry was also becoming high profile in major business stories, a form of product placement that couldn't be purchased at any price. During the same week as the Lulu's concert, TV footage and photos of the press conference announcing the $160 billion merger between America Online Inc. and Time Warner Inc. showed CEOs Steve Case and Gerald Levin each checking their respective BlackBerry devices to see how the news had affected share prices.

Glowing reports were appearing in mass-market publications. "The screen is small, reflecting the device's heritage as a pager. It displays only six lines at a time, but the text is crisp and clear, and there's a backlight for use in dim light. The system retrieves only part of each e-mail message at first: the header and the first few screens of the body text. You can pull up the rest if you like, even if the message is very long," wrote Walter S. Mossberg, respected personal technology columnist in the *Wall Street Journal* on February 10, 2000. "At first glance, [the keyboard] seems impossibly tiny. But it actually works better than any small keyboard I've tried. I'm no great typist, but I was able to get good speed and accuracy on the thing. I found it easier to use than even the brilliant handwriting recognition system on the Palm Pilot and Handspring Visor."

At the time, a lot of people, including the media, were enamored of Palm's Graffiti handwriting recognition software and assumed it would continue to thrive in the market. "We spent a lot of time with tech and business journalists explaining our view that although the touch screen and stylus used in PDAs were popular, they were primarily used for application navigation and data 'retrieval,' but they were used much less frequently for data 'input,'" recalls Mark Guibert. "And as wireless email caught on and overtook the organizer as the killer app for these mobile devices, we argued that RIM's keyboards would become more and more popular. Most people were skeptical and we had to be persistent and keep chipping away at the market until we gained enough subscribers and momentum to attract broader attention."

In February 2000, the end of the first year of availability, there were 25,000 BlackBerry subscribers. While the number was relatively small, BlackBerry was gaining such a cult following that it acquired a nickname: CrackBerry. It's not clear when or where it was first used, but the term was cited during a CNBC interview on September 29, 2000. "I'm not sure if you guys use BlackBerry or have tried it, but it is pretty addictive," said Dennis Kavelman of RIM. Replied Geoff Colvin, *Fortune* senior editor-at-large: "Well, it is addictive and on Wall Street they call it CrackBerry for exactly that reason. Once you try it you can't live without it, so they say."

Usage of the word and the addiction metaphor soon spread. "The label on the little wireless e-mail gadget says BlackBerry, but users find it so addictive that it's known as the 'CrackBerry,'" said an article in *USA Today* on May 11, 2001. "It should be reported to the DEA—it's an addictive thing," Intel chairman Andy Grove was quoted as saying. "It is the heroin of mobile computing," agreed Marc Benioff, CEO of salesforce.com, in the same article. "I am serious. I had to stop. I'm now in BA: BlackBerry Anonymous."

With BlackBerry catching on, RIM now had a genuine product and real revenue, unlike some high-tech companies that were little more than a neat concept. During that high-flying time in the stock market, however, investors did not differentiate between those firms that actually produced results and those that only promised roses. From late 1999 to March 2000, the dot-com boom raised all boats. RIM shares on NASDAQ hit a high on February 28, 2000, of US$175.75. (On the Toronto Stock Exchange, the high was C$260 that same day.) At those prices, the market capitalization of RIM's 71 million shares— its total value—was $12.5 billion, greater than Canadian Pacific Railway Ltd. or some of Canada's national banks that had been in existence for more than a century.

As fast as new-found wealth had arrived, however, it evaporated even more quickly. In March 2000, the high-tech bubble burst and by the end of April RIM's share price had fallen, along with all the other recent darlings, by 75 per cent, to $42.50. Interest rates peaked and a recession arrived that lasted two years. Things got so bad that even Lulu's closed.

RIM was not only able to sail on, unlike some of the one-day wonders that sank without a trace, the company was able to bring new products to market because of the cash they'd raised. The BlackBerry 957 introduced in April 2000 came with a bigger, sharper screen that displayed twice as many lines of text as its predecessor, the 950. For many, the 957 was seen as "the Palm killer." The 7 in 957 was viewed to be a subtle reference and direct challenge to the Palm VII, introduced the previous year by the competitor company that at the time commanded about three-quarters of the $1 billion annual market for PDAs. RIM's press release announcing the 957 called the new device "palm-sized," as if RIM were taunting the competition to a duel.

The 957's larger size altered public perception about BlackBerry. "The solution, the software, everything, was the same, but it *looked* like a PDA. It shows you the value of optics in positioning your product. The headlines in April 2000 said 'RIM enters the PDA market.' Yet the only thing we did was change the look," said Dave Castell. The main invisible improvement was a mandatory password—a combination of numbers and letters—meant to further reassure IT managers that employees could use BlackBerry without compromising corporate security.

The original 950 remained on sale at $349, with the 957 priced at $499 ($699 in Canada). "When I look back at it, it was like cave painting, but at the time it was immensely exciting because you actually had the Internet," said David Neale. As Neale and his boss, Bob Bernard, criss-crossed Canada to promote the 957 on the Rogers network, they discovered that the speed of BlackBerry gave them an advantage on eBay. They could monitor the auctions while they were on the move, make a slightly higher bid in the dying seconds, and scoop items from other bidders who did not have the same ready access. Bernard greatly expanded his collection of English sterling-silver flatware. Neale's purchases were more mundane. "I was acquiring a large number of CDs I really didn't need over BlackBerry 957 in airplanes moving between these presentations just because you could," said Neale. "You get caught up in the moment."

A six-month multi-million dollar BlackBerry ad campaign was launched in April 2000 with two-page spreads in publications such as the *Wall Street Journal, Newsweek*, and *USA Today. PC World* named BlackBerry the best wireless communications device of the year and *Time* magazine included BlackBerry among the top ten technology gadgets on the planet. "It does e-mail like a whiz," declared a review in the *Washington Post* on June 9, 2000. "The steadily increasing accolades from journalists and the advertising campaign certainly helped fuel the brand, but Mike and Jim were always aiming the company higher and we all knew that we always had to be prepared to box above our weight class. We couldn't match the budgets of our bigger competitors, but we were nonetheless building a mainstream brand," said Mark Guibert.

In April 2001, *Forbes* designated BlackBerry as one of seven cult brands that had successfully evolved into a national brand name. Others on the list were L.L. Bean, Nike, Doc Martens, Peet's Coffee, White Castle, and Ben & Jerry's. In February 2001, there were 164,000 BlackBerry users worldwide, up from 25,000 the year before.

Unlike some new products that gain popularity by seamlessly insinuating themselves into people's lives, BlackBerry also made waves by creating business etiquette issues. Everyone knew it was poor form to take a cell phone call during a meeting, but what about email? Was it OK to respond quietly to a message by thumbing a few hasty words under the table in a way that didn't disturb the presentation or discussion? Could two people in the same room exchange messages? What if they were mocking the team leader? Was such interpersonal activity subversive, even mutinous, or no worse than two outfielders exchanging signals about how to play the next batter? It's perhaps better than leaving a meeting to deal with an urgent matter and certainly less offensive than the scores of people who mindlessly doodle on a piece of paper during a meeting.

And so was born the "BlackBerry Prayer," when a user sat quietly with head bowed, thumbing keys, while appearing to be listening to what was happening in the room around. "Everyone is content, the boring person talking is content, and the people using their BlackBerrys are content," joked Balsillie. "We like to think that we're the great liberators of the boring meeting."[1]

RIM's technological lead over its main competitor continued to grow even as Palm introduced a new model, the i705. "Palm says it plans to improve the i705 and its e-mail software. But it amazes me that the company took 18 months to develop this device and yet failed to match some of the key things that made the RIM so popular. They have become cult items among employees at some big companies," wrote Walter S. Mossberg in the January 31, 2002 issue of the *Wall Street Journal*.

---

[1] *Wireless Week*, March 1, 2003.

Palm finally added a keyboard later that year. "The day you knew RIM had made a major dent in the armor of Palm was the day that Palm announced they were going to a keyboard. I always thought that was an amazing concession," said Neale. "The key thing about Palm had always been the stylus. You were either a Palm user or you weren't. I could never be bothered using the Palm shorthand." According to Gartner, the research company, by 2005 RIM had replaced Palm as the world's biggest seller of handhelds.

As BlackBerry waxed in popularity, interest waned in the Inter@ctive Pager 950 offered by BellSouth. "They'd have all these sales reps trying to sell to Merrill Lynch and they'd sell to the paging group, and we'd walk into the investment bankers, hand them a couple of BlackBerrys and say, 'Try these out.' Within a couple of days you're totally addicted to Black-Berry. You can't live without it, especially if you live your life sending emails back and forth to colleagues and prospects," said Don McMurtry, RIM's vice-president, sales.

The sudden addition of several hundred new BlackBerry users at one corporate location in Manhattan would cause headaches for BellSouth. "They'd all turn them on and thought it was great fun but that base station would be exhausted, the next base station would get eaten up, the next thing we knew the chairman of Morgan Stanley is calling the chairman of BellSouth wanting to know, 'What the hell's wrong with the network?' And we'd say, 'Huh?'" said Jim Hobbs, of BellSouth Mobile Data. "We'd say, 'RIM, don't you think it would've been nice, given the nature of the network, to tell us that you were about to drop three hundred BlackBerrys in this building here in New York City so that we could have put some more radios in and been ready to handle the challenge?'"

But RIM simply couldn't provide sufficient warning. "We would give BellSouth as much notice as we could. As soon as we knew there was the potential of lighting up more than fifty, I'd call and say we're going to light up two hundred this weekend or a month from now, and they could just barely keep up. They'd say, 'We need months.' I'd say, 'I can't give you months.' Let's just say it was a trying time," said Lazaridis.

The BlackBerry 957 launch in April 2000 and growing subscriber sales caused a resurrection in the RIM share price that summer. Unlike some firms that had disappeared or went moribund after the March market crash, RIM continued to expand aggressively by announcing sales to carriers such as BT Cellnet, strategic alliances with firms like Compaq Computer Corp., and agreements such as the one with America Online offering wireless instant messaging to its 25 million members.

As a result of all this expansive activity, by October RIM share price had climbed above $100—more than halfway back to the February peak—while the rest of the market continued to fall or remained flat. The company decided to seize the moment and raise more money by selling 6 million shares on NASDAQ through an investment banking syndicate again led by Merrill Lynch. The window of opportunity wasn't open for long. RIM announced the plan on October 20 when shares were trading at $117. By the time the deal closed on November 1, prices had slipped to $102, but RIM was able to raise $580 million for continued research and development, marketing, and capital spending. "BMO [Nesbitt Burns] was the top Canadian firm involved in the deal, but we only had a tiny per cent," said John Easson, of BMO. "I remember complaining that only 14 per cent of that deal was allocated to Canadian investment bankers, and then when the final demand analysis was done, only 5 per cent of the demand was from Canada. It's amazing how RIM caught on outside Canada."

Share prices remained firm for a week, then started heading down again. By October 2002, RIM shares were worth $8 when NASDAQ and the Dow Jones World Technology Index both hit bottom after falling almost 80 per cent from their highs. "If we hadn't done that deal, we wouldn't be around today," said Kavelman. "At the time, we had no idea. The stock could have gone back to $200; $100 could have been a low point. You just didn't know. We said, 'Thank God we raised all the money.' It appears to be a shrewd move, but we just raised it when we could. Who knew how low the stock would go after that?"

What a ride it had been! On paper, the approximately 9 million RIM shares owned by Mike Lazaridis were worth $90 million in April 1999, hit $1.6 billion at the February 2000 peak, fell to $350 million in April 2000, and then bounced back briefly to $1 billion in November 2000, before sinking again. At the absolute bottom-scraping worst, when the NASDAQ share price was $8.37 on October 7, 2002, Lazaridis's RIM share holdings were worth $73 million, Balsillie about $60 million. The value of the entire company had fallen to only $600 million from a high of more than $12 billion. After that, share prices floated up for a while, then settled into a narrow range around $20 as RIM suffered back-to-back money-losing years. The glory days seemed long gone.

Repudiation by the stock market, however, did not deter RIM or BlackBerry sales. By 2002, demand had grown to such an extent that RIM moved production from its first 36,000-square-foot facility on Shoemaker Street to a new 125,000-square-foot plant on Phillip Street. "They were spending like crazy, running to South Africa, China, and Australia when everyone else was just trying to stay alive, and that was because they had $600 million of cash on the balance sheet," said John Easson. "Share price had done a dive, but that doesn't change cash balance. They were quite comfortable executing the strategy because they always knew that the winner was going to be the one that gets to the telcos [telecommunications companies] and gets them integrated on the products who then turn around and start selling."

Looking ahead, RIM would need much more office space and the market was tight in Waterloo. The University of Waterloo had been planning a new industrial park, but it wasn't coming together fast enough, so Balsillie set out to accumulate neighbouring properties. "We just went and got a bunch of buildings. They were all done very quietly. It was kind of a Duddy Kravitz move where nobody realized what he was doing until he bought the whole lake. Nobody knew what we were doing; they were all separate owners," Balsillie said.

When RIM's $100 million acquisition and construction program was complete, the company had eight buildings encompassing 600,000 square feet clustered on the northeast edge of the University of Waterloo campus, a substantial increase from 1999 when the company leased 91,000 square feet in three buildings. "It was not the opportunity that was the constraint, it was people and facilities. Even if you have this opportunity, if you can't find and house fifty people to hire into it, you can't pursue it. Ever since, we have a bias toward keeping a couple of steps ahead because the lack of facilities can really shut you down," said Balsillie.

Lazaridis insisted that the company's exterior signs in some cases be on the back of buildings so they pointed away from the main roads and toward the university instead. In fact, at the time when RIM had only one building next to the university and could only afford one sign, Lazaridis decided to put the one and only sign on the back of the building—facing the students as they walked on the university campus. "Of course, everyone initially recoiled, but I explained to them, 'I don't really care if anyone else knows where the building is. All I want is the students to know where the building is,'" he said.

Growth was aided by R&D money from the federal government. Technology Partnerships Canada, a Department of Industry program, contributed $5.7 million in 1998 to RIM's $19 million R&D project to create seventy new jobs and maintain ninety-five existing jobs at a time when RIM had 205 employees. In 2000, the same agency provided $34 million toward RIM's $113 million R&D program. The company's biggest-ever R&D project was carried out in new facilities in the Ottawa suburb of Kanata and at a new technology centre in Waterloo, as well as elsewhere in Canada. RIM also benefited from such government offerings as the Scientific Research and Development investment tax credits. In 2002, for example, that program put $12 million in RIM's coffers. Since 2004, RIM has sought no further government assistance.

While such expansion may cause local excitement and create

jobs, it's invisible to corporate users and individual subscribers. More obvious was the way BlackBerry began infiltrating the life of business and government. After the election of George W. Bush in 2000 to the American presidency, *New York Times* columnist Maureen Dowd gushed about how Bill Clinton and Al Gore had "tried so aggressively to be modern. There were gurus, facilitators, BlackBerrys."

Gore's presidential campaign relied on BlackBerry for internal communications and for sending messages to the media. An Associated Press story by Sandra Sobieraj describing how politicians survive on the road, separated for such long spells from spouse and family, opened with a scene-setter about Gore using his BlackBerry to send loving words to his wife, Tipper. On election night, when it became apparent that the results might depend on a few thousand hanging chads in Florida, Donna Brazile, Gore's campaign manager, sent the candidate (who was on his way to give a concession speech) a message to his BlackBerry, saying, "Never surrender. It's not over yet."

The Gore family enthusiasm for BlackBerry spread into the next generation. *Sammy's Hill*, a novel by Gore's daughter Kristin that was set on Capitol Hill and published in 2004, included an incident where the female protagonist hits the wrong button on her BlackBerry and mistakenly sends an email about video cameras and whipped cream to two hundred Washington movers and shakers.

In Hollywood, where "I'll call you," became "I'll Berry you," early BlackBerry fans included Pamela Anderson and Matt Damon. Business leaders like GE CEO Jack Welch were early adopters, as was First Lady Barbara Bush. For ordinary subscribers, BlackBerry was not just a quick way to keep in touch but also an equalizer, providing access they'd never before enjoyed. "You could send an email to Michael Dell [founder of Dell Computer Corp.] and get a reply back in three minutes. He wouldn't give you an endorsement of BlackBerry, but his actions alone were an endorsement," said analyst Mike Urlocker. "There was a great viral impact from having such influential customers. They talked openly and positively about BlackBerry to their peers and that is of course an incredible form of advertising," said Mark Guibert. "Jack Welch was like an honorary sales rep at one point. It was almost a weekly occurrence for a while in the early days that we would get a call from another CEO at a major company saying that they had been golfing with Jack Welch and he convinced them to get a BlackBerry."

A BlackBerry complete with free service was among the goodies given to performers and presenters at the Grammys held in Los Angeles in February 2002. (Such freebies continued. A BlackBerry 8700c was in the swag bag given to presenters at the 2006 Oscars.) As a marketing tool, the technique is tried and true. Jeweller Harry Winston and designer Oscar de la Renta battle to get their goods worn by stars on the red carpet at the Oscars.

Other deals were equally high profile, such as the one struck with the National Basketball Association in August 2002. RIM supplied the NBA with BlackBerry smartphones so league executives and officials could communicate with each other and also obtain details of games in progress, including box scores complete with a player's points, rebounds, and assists, as well as a leaderboard in each category. When Carlos Delgado played first base for the Toronto Blue Jays he had a BlackBerry to keep in touch with his family in Puerto Rico. Rogers, his carrier, decided to give BlackBerry smartphones to all team members. When they were distributed in the dressing room, players had already been assigned email addresses, so immediately they began sending each other messages. "Dave Neale and I were there to present each player with a BlackBerry, but the players didn't know why we were there and I think they were expecting some boring speech from a couple of corporate 'suits' and so we were standing in the dressing room surrounded by all these cold stares. Then we told them that everyone was getting a BlackBerry and suddenly it was all smiles and back-slaps," said Mark Guibert.

"It's fascinating watching how we went from the most ridiculously dry, boring data communications to watching people chatting," said David Neale, of Rogers. "When you think of the cumulative billions of dollars and the thousands of man-hours, you think, 'This is really cool.'"

Along the way, however, RIM's corporate costs became bloated. In the twelve months ended March 2, 2002, RIM lost $28.5 million as the company continued to add employees, rising from three hundred in 1999 to 2,200 by fall 2002. On November 12, 2002, the axe fell when RIM laid off over two hundred employees (approximately 10 per cent of the company), as many people as had been employed in the entire company only four years earlier. Other belt-tightening steps included an eighteen-month wage freeze and various cost controls. It was a difficult day for the whole company, but the management team believed it was the right thing to do. RIM had been investing ahead of the curve in order to pioneer the market, but it was time to show RIM's shareholders that the company could be profitable.

The harsh steps took some time to take effect. Losses continued until the quarter ending August 30, 2003, when RIM finally eked out a profit of $2.1 million or three cents a share. The share price immediately began to rise again in September after RIM reported it would exceed its initial revenue and earnings forecasts. The share price was also buttressed by other good news such as the number-one ranking of BlackBerry with the legal industry, release of the first models with colour screens, and a deal with Vodafone, the biggest carrier in the world outside China, for distribution of BlackBerry in France, Germany, Italy, Spain, the Netherlands, and the U.K.

It didn't hurt that celebrities like Donny Osmond praised BlackBerry on Conan O'Brien's *Late Night* show, but the celebrity endorsement that likely mattered most occurred in December 2003 when Oprah Winfrey, Queen of Daytime TV, held up the BlackBerry 7100, just launched by T-Mobile, and declared it to be one of her "favourite things." "It's wonderful. It's wonderful," she said to squeals from the studio audience. "It has literally changed my life." During the next week, T-Mobile's BlackBerry sales spiked.

RIM's earnings swoon abruptly ended on December 22, 2003, when the company announced profits of $16.2 million for the three-month period ending November 29, good enough for earnings of twenty cents a share. Moreover, the company predicted earnings per share would double in the next quarter to forty to fifty cents per share. The sizable profit and optimistic guidance caused the share price to jump 50 per cent in what was the biggest one-day increase in the company's six-year trading history.

Even analysts such as Barry Richards, who had been following RIM since the company went public, were astounded by the roarback. Fidelity, the mutual funds company and the largest institutional investor among the more than three hundred with holdings in RIM, had asked Richards a year earlier: What's the most RIM can ever generate in earnings per share? "I said fifty cents and that was for a year. If they put a thirty multiple on it, the share price could be fifteen dollars. The stock was then at six, seven dollars. Fidelity said, 'If that's the most, how do we ever get to one hundred dollars?' I was the biggest fan in the world, but I can remember thinking, 'I have no answer to that question.' Then suddenly RIM was saying we're going to do forty to fifty cents *in the next quarter*. They ended up crushing my numbers. That had never happened with any other tech company. Anybody who was watching should've known right there and then that any of the boundaries or limitations that we had imagined for RIM were truly not appropriate." As for RIM's co-CEOs, the boundaries and limitations that usually apply to business leaders at mid-career were equally inappropriate.

CHAPTER ELEVEN

DREAMS FULFILLED

IN THE SUMMER OF 1999, Howard Burton, recently graduated from the University of Waterloo with a PhD in physics, was looking for work. During the previous decade, many of his fellow physicists had been wooed away from science and academe by money managers who paid them to produce the mathematical models that lay behind derivatives and other exotic investment vehicles. Burton decided he didn't want to sit in a cubicle massaging numbers, so he wrote to twenty-five high-tech CEOs in the United States and Canada describing his education and aspirations. He ended each letter with the same plea: "Please help save me from a lucrative career on Wall Street."

Along with a few polite thank-yous there was a more pertinent reply from Mike Lazaridis, who emailed Burton on July 22, 1999, saying, "I just received your resumé and am intrigued." During a one-hour follow-up phone conversation, Lazaridis quizzed Burton about where he thought physics was headed, what new technology he envisioned in the future, and hinted at making millions of his own money available but didn't divulge any specifics. Lazaridis said he was attending a meeting in a few days' time at Nortel Networks, in Brampton, Ontario, halfway between Waterloo and Toronto, where Burton lived, so he proposed that the two men meet in the Nortel parking lot once his business was concluded. "I drive a silver BMW 540i, am six feet and have white hair," Lazaridis wrote. Feeling like he was part of a *Spy vs. Spy* drama, Burton replied, "I'm driving a beige Toyota Corolla, am five-feet-eleven with a beard and glasses, standard physicist attire."

The cloak-and-dagger rendezvous worked. Lazaridis suggested lunch, but neither knew Brampton very well so they ended up as the only customers at an Italian restaurant in a nearby mall. "Mike was passionate, charismatic, and capable. Some of the things he was saying were completely science fiction and some of it was completely reasonable," said Burton. "At one point, he held out his BlackBerry and said, 'Look at this. This is nineteenth-century physics. Imagine what we could do with twentieth-century physics or twenty-first-century physics.'"

Finally, Lazaridis said, "Are you interested?"

Burton, still baffled about where he fit in this wide-ranging monologue, replied, "Interested in what?"

Lazaridis scribbled $55,000 on a napkin and handed it to Burton. Realizing he'd just been offered a job, he asked, "So, what do you want me to do? Write reports on the importance of science?"

"I don't want you to do anything," said Lazaridis. "I want you to think."

"OK, I can do that. I've done that for years."

Four days later, a cheque from Mike Lazaridis arrived at Burton's house for his first two weeks' pay. Only then was he certain that the clandestine meeting and meandering conversations had actually resulted in a paying job. Burton lived with his wife and two children in the Beach area of Toronto where he regularly walked the boardwalk beside Lake Ontario. Now that he had full-time work, Burton followed his usual perambulatory pattern, but this time thought about what to do with the money Lazaridis wanted to spend.

On that very first day of employment, they concluded that Lazaridis should establish an institute for the study of theoretical physics. Playing on RIM and how the organization would work at the outer limits of science, Burton also devised a name: Perimeter Institute. Even the short form—PI—reverberated. Pi is both the mathematical ratio of a circle's circumference to its diameter as well as the sixteenth letter of the Greek alphabet, befitting a philanthropic engineer of Greek heritage. Burton emailed his thoughts to his new boss. "Sounds good," Lazaridis replied.

Later that month, Burton sent Lazaridis a longer email recommending he erect a building near to, but separate from, the University of Waterloo in a tranquil setting with working fireplaces and sufficient space for researchers to ponder such weighty topics as gravitational wave effects, cosmic strings, and black hole entropy. "I like everything so far," said Lazaridis.

Burton spent the next year finalizing his proposal and visiting other facilities, such as the Institute for Advanced Study, in Princeton, New Jersey, and the Institute for Theoretical Physics, in Santa Barbara, California, as well as research centres in Britain, Germany, France, and Italy. "The reason why I hit it off with Mike and why we always get along is that we think very much the same way," said Burton. "Some people do very strange things with their money or let it all go to their head. I was never interested in doing physics for anything other than the sake of curiosity. This stuff is glorious, it's exciting, it's cool, it's an expedition hunt you could be on for very altruistic motivations. It wasn't about making money."

But money made it happen. "My wealth has allowed me to do what I like doing, which is building stuff, investing in stuff, dreaming big. I was able to actually go out and implement things I wanted to accomplish. Creating something like Perimeter was a lifelong dream, but it was a back-of-the mind kind of dream where you were really passionate about it when you were younger and then, all of sudden, you find yourself in a position to do it," said Lazaridis.

On October 23, 2000, Lazaridis announced a C$100 million donation to create the Perimeter Institute for Theoretical Physics, with Howard Burton as executive director. Members of the Mobitex Operators Association (MOA) were meeting that day in Gothenburg, the second-largest city in Sweden and home to Ericsson and Mobitex. Because many of the North American attendees used RIM's wireless devices, Ericsson had set up a special base station in the Radisson hotel where the conference was being held so delegates could stay connected to their home networks. Jack Barse, executive director of the trade organization, was at the podium when David Neale, vice-president, new product development, at Rogers Wireless and chairman of MOA, suddenly shouted, "Holy cow."

Barse stopped in midsentence as everyone turned to Neale, who stood up, waved his BlackBerry, and said, "Mike Lazaridis has just given a $100 million donation." Neale read the entire announcement aloud to applause from the group who then sent their congratulations—via BlackBerry.

What Lazaridis had established, with help from Jim Balsillie and Doug Fregin, who each donated C$10 million, was the first such physics facility since the creation of the Institute for Advanced Study, at Princeton, more than seventy years earlier. "Technology has been so successful that it has distanced itself from everyday life to the point where it's invisible," said Lazaridis. "And what happens is that sometimes we can take it for granted. We can look around us and say, what else do we need? We have cars, homes, television; we have 5.1 Dolby theatres, food, medicines. One hundred years ago people thought they had everything they needed, too. So we need to be working on discoveries that will drive the next century and we need to be generous in funding education. Our public is not sufficiently aware of how crucial education and universities are to the world of business and progress."

Opened in 2004, the C$25 million 65,000-square-foot glass, steel, and wood Perimeter Institute was designed by Montreal architectural firm Saucier + Perrotte. On the other side of nearby Silver Lake sits a replica of Abraham Erb's gristmill, one of the earliest industries in Waterloo, named in 2007 as the world's most Intelligent Community. Sixty full-time scientists work at Perimeter in separate offices with woodlot views and individually controlled heating and air conditioning, as well as a crank window for fresh air. Every corridor is punctuated by sitting areas with leather couches, a working fireplace, and blackboards for collaborative thinking. There is even a blackboard outside in the courtyard. In addition to the permanent researchers, three hundred other scientists annually attend workshops or study on-site for anywhere from three days to three months. Facilities include billiards, a bistro, workout machines, library, seminar rooms, and a pile of hockey sticks for pickup games on a nearby rink. There is also a 205-seat auditorium (named the Mike Lazaridis Theatre of Ideas) for lectures, panels, and public recitals by musicians such as pianist Yefim Bronfman, baritone Sir Thomas Allen, and the Tokyo String Quartet.

While Mike Lazaridis may be the founder of Perimeter, in many ways Albert Einstein is the father. In 1905, when Einstein was twenty-six and toiling in the patent office in Berne, Switzerland, he wrote four papers in one year on arcane topics that included quantum physics and the theory of relativity. Theoretical physics, the focus of the Perimeter Institute, is all about the fundamental rules that govern the universe. "Mike would like to see the Perimeter Institute as the leading institute in the world for the study of theoretical physics and he'd like to see a breakthrough in theoretical physics to take it to the next stage. There hasn't been a major breakthrough in theoretical physics in over twenty years and there's been nothing hugely major since Einstein," said Don Campbell, senior strategy adviser at law firm Davis LLP, and a Perimeter director.

Lazaridis spoke about this dream while he was still a student at the University of Waterloo. "Young men on the make try my patience," said Larry Smith, the economics prof who counseled Lazaridis on his entrepreneurial plans. "If they've got staying power then I'm happy to talk with them. If they want a million bucks by Christmas, who cares? He [Lazaridis] described one of his goals by saying if he ever could make some serious money from his venture, he was going to start a not-for-profit research institute to free research from commercial constraint because some kinds of research could never have commercial application," said Smith. "Many rich people decide later in life that they must do philanthropy either because they've got more money than they know what to do with or they're doing it for PR points. Whatever Perimeter is, it's neither of those two things. Perimeter is the realization of the original vision. I suspect that was as important to him as anything that RIM was ever going to create," Smith continued. "Mike has a true passion for physics, which is somewhat unique as it is perhaps the most abstract of the sciences. He can show you in conversation how every advance has a basis in physics. Everything goes in cycles, and for long periods of time not much happens. Fifty years later you can look back and see the beginnings," said Robin Korthals, a Perimeter director. "It isn't as if he just wrote a cheque to create Perimeter. The institute is Mike. He is a very real presence and the institute is an extension of himself."

In December 2002, an overzealous journalist at the *Globe and Mail* wrote a story saying PI was in trouble because RIM share prices had tumbled and Lazaridis hadn't yet paid the full $100 million. Lazaridis had given the initial $20 million in the form of 105,262 RIM shares that were sold at C$190 a share (prior to a 2-for-1 stock split in 2004 and 3-for-1 split in 2007) to create the endowment. But if Lazaridis had given more right away, Perimeter would have been classified as a private foundation. Because he wanted others to support Perimeter and also receive tax credits, he extended the term of his gift to five years. The newspaper's speculation (that Lazaridis might not pay the full amount) was erroneous. "He took that very personally because for him there was a real sense that somehow he was all talk and no action and wouldn't be a man of his word. Mike is justifiably proud of the fact that when he says he's going to do something he goes ahead and does it," said Burton.

In fact, if Lazaridis had donated all the necessary shares up front and allowed Perimeter to be classified as a private foundation, the donation would have cost him considerably less since the RIM share price was significantly lower during much of the five-year term. Eventually, the government of Ontario and the government of Canada each gave Perimeter C$75 million. Lazaridis had been upset by the response of governments, which he regarded as laggardly and limited. "Based on what we've been able to accomplish so far, based on the promise of this kind of thing, based on the historical evidence that shows the values of these kinds of discoveries and these kinds of investments in a nation's sovereignty in the future, you'd think governments would be saying, 'Are you sure that's all you want?'" Lazaridis said. "They should be giving even more. These are drops in the bucket for governments. You'd think they'd be tripping over themselves to invest in something that had this calibre of people attracted to Canada. But it's been like pulling teeth. It takes a lot of work and I've been very consistent. I've been telling the same story for over five years. I put my money where my mouth is." Lazaridis has contributed a total of $150 million to the Perimeter Institute as of August 2009.

David Johnston, president of the University of Waterloo, had tried unsuccessfully to convince Lazaridis that Perimeter should be an on-campus part of the university. "He wanted freedom from the bureaucratic tendencies of the university. He wanted them to think rather than teach," said Johnston. However, Lazaridis had also told Johnston that he wanted to do something for UW, so in 2001 the president invited Lazaridis to Chatterbox Farm, his home near St. Clements outside Waterloo, for a brainstorming session with Dean of Engineering Sujeet

Chaudhuri, Dean of Mathematics Alan George, Dean of Science John Thompson, and Paul Guild, the university's vice-president of research. Lazaridis listened attentively to their ideas, including one from Dean Thompson about how he'd been able to stop tomatoes from rotting by turning off the aging gene and thought there might be human applications. Lazaridis wanted bolder ideas.

Rather than propose more ideas that fell flat, Dean Chaudhuri asked Lazaridis what his interests were. When he began talking excitedly about quantum mechanics, Guild said the university would also be interested in such a project.

"How much would you need?" asked Lazaridis.

"A hundred million dollars would do," said Dean Chaudhuri, the same amount as Lazaridis had already committed to the Perimeter Institute. "The lights went on with Mike," said Johnston.

In 2004, Lazaridis anchored the initiative with a C$33.3 million donation to the University of Waterloo for the Institute for Quantum Computing (IQC) based on the condition that it be matched two-to-one by funds from the university and the public sector for a total of $100 million. It was the largest private donation ever made to the University of Waterloo and was lauded by Prime Minister Paul Martin and Ontario premier Dalton McGuinty. Lazaridis later contributed additional amounts, bringing his total donation to C$100 million. By 2007, the institute was operating in temporary quarters in five different locations across campus. In 2010, when the new building opens there will be thirty faculty members, fifty postdoctoral fellows, and 125 graduate students. Among the first faculty members was Sir Anthony Leggett, winner of a Nobel Prize in 2003 for his work on superfluids. "Mike is responsible for the quantum computing thrust of this university. It's not simply his money, but his discipline," said Johnston. "He really pushes the provost and myself to be focused on this to be sure that not only is this our first priority but a priority that is much more than *primus inter pares*. As former president of the Natural Sciences and Engineering Research Council of Canada Tom Brzustowski says, 'This is Canada's greatest opportunity for gold.'"

Just as he personally recruited Howard Burton to run Perimeter, Lazaridis hired Raymond Laflamme, a Quebec-born quantum information theorist, from Los Alamos National Laboratory in New Mexico, to be executive director of IQC. "He's the only person to prove Stephen Hawking wrong. When he was a postgraduate student working for the legendary physicist, Hawking was so impressed he took Laflamme on as his personal assistant for two years," said Lazaridis. "I met him and we hit it off right away. IQC is built around him."

When Lazaridis announced Perimeter in 2000, Jim Balsillie had already begun planning his own endowed institute to study global affairs. Balsillie even had a site in mind, the former Seagram warehouse that served as a corporate museum until 1997. Seagram offered the building to the University of Waterloo and Wilfrid Laurier University, but both were so strapped for operating funds that they could not accept the warehouse, even as a gift. The city of Waterloo became the owner and found a tenant, software firm Waterloo Maple, by offering a lease with generous terms.

In 2000, Balsillie offered to buy the warehouse at a price to be determined and undertook to donate money for an institute that would be housed in the building. There were, however, so many other proposals floating about that municipal paralysis set in. Undeterred, Balsillie convened a weekend meeting at his Georgian Bay cottage in February 2001. Invitees, among others, included: Paul Heinbecker, a former Canadian ambassador to the United Nations; John English, a historian, author, and member of Parliament, 1993–97; *Globe and Mail* columnist Margaret Wente; University of Waterloo president David Johnston; Wilfrid Laurier University president Robert Roseheart; and then RIM directors Ken Cork and Doug Wright. Harry Swain, a former deputy minister of industry in the Canadian government, served as facilitator.

Balsillie told the group that the more he travelled the more he realized that an increasingly chaotic world required solutions on a range of issues from United Nations reform to nuclear proliferation. "We're making a stupid amount of money and we want to do something constructive with it," he told his guests. "What kind of a centre should I have?"

After a lengthy and freewheeling debate, Balsillie announced he was going for a run. Because it was snowing heavily, other joggers decided to stay inside, so Balsillie headed out alone. Two hours later, just about the time guests were beginning to worry, Balsillie burst through the cottage door looking like the abominable snowman, shouting: "I've got it. I've got the theme." As the group gathered to hear his idea, he told them, "If we can't get along with one another, if we can't govern ourselves, if we can't establish viable communities in each part of the world, then prosperity just goes to nothing."

And so was born the Centre for International Governance Innovation (CIGI). Balsillie initially donated C\$20 million and also paid C\$4.5 million to acquire the warehouse from the city and buy out the Waterloo Maple lease. Lazaridis contributed C$10 million, and Klaus Woerner, founder of Waterloo-based Automation Tooling Systems, donated a house for a country retreat. In 2007, Balsillie donated a further C$50 million: C$17 million to CIGI and another C$33 million to establish the Balsillie School of International Affairs in Waterloo for graduate programs in global governance and international public policy. The University of Waterloo and Wilfrid Laurier University each donated C$25 million to match Balsillie's second endowment. CIGI has also received C$30 million from the federal government, and the government of Ontario has given C$25 million.

Among the scholars and thinkers who joined founding executive director John English and began moving into the restored warehouse in 2003 were Paul Heinbecker, UW political scientist Andrew Cooper, former chief economist in the Department of Foreign Affairs John Curtis, and Louise Fréchette, former deputy secretary-general of the United Nations. "We're trying to create frameworks so we can break through these global impasses in trade, union reform, security, energy, health, you name it. CIGI is really building capacity at the university because they didn't have graduate programs," said Balsillie.

The donations from Lazaridis and Balsillie have done more than just create local institutions with global clout. "It's so different in Waterloo now than it used to be," said English. "We had to fight tooth and nail to get $10,000 out of some of the eminent people in our community. It's created a new standard. Jim [Balsillie] wants to make Waterloo a place where high-tech people want to work. Cities have to be edgy and creative and he knows that. We're attracting people now who want to come here that we couldn't get before. Both Mike and Jim were wise to really focus rather than just give to the traditional charities."

Balsillie has also made a wide range of donations of various sizes, a sampling of which includes C$5 million to the Grand River Regional Cancer Centre; C$3.5 million for academic chairs and student fellowships in public policy at Waterloo and Wilfrid Laurier universities; C$1 million to the Peterborough YMCA; C$500,000 to Trinity College, University of Toronto; and C$400,000 to create the Balsillie Roy Studio Collection consisting of 300,000 glass-plate and film negatives that represent work by three generations of the Roy family, documenting people, places and events from their downtown Peterborough studio.

Lazaridis and Balsillie weren't the only ones from RIM who took the unusual step of becoming philanthropists at mid-career. Michael Barnstijn, who'd been given a 20 per cent ownership after joining RIM in 1985, had three million shares when RIM went public in 1997. In July 1998, he took an unpaid leave and quit six months later. Barnstijn left because his father had cancer, he wanted to spend more time with his family, and he had ceased enjoying his job. "I'm happiest when I'm working on my own or with a very small group. You're thinking the same way, you're all in the same room, and there's that shared shorthand of experience. Some people can become really good managers. I don't think I was ever very good at it," he said.

Because Barnstijn was no longer a corporate insider who had to disclose his holdings, his share ownership after leaving RIM is not known. What is known is that in February 2000, he and his wife, Louise MacCallum, gave 60,000 shares of RIM to the Kitchener and Waterloo Community Foundation. The foundation immediately sold the shares for proceeds of C$12 million, an amount that doubled the size of the endowment. The couple has also given C$5 million to the Waterloo Regional Children's Museum; C$3.6 million to Rare, a 913-acre ecological research reserve in Cambridge; C$3.5 million to CIGI; C$2.5 million to the University of Waterloo's new school of architecture in Cambridge; C$1.3 million for a footbridge on a hiking trail across the Grand River; and smaller amounts to the Canadian War Museum in Ottawa, the Canadian Clay & Glass Gallery in Waterloo, and the Kitchener-Waterloo Art Gallery.

According to Barnstijn, working at RIM was never about the money. "It was more about the friendships between the people and working with state-of-the-art technology—or bleeding-edge technology in some cases—and just having fun. The money was incidental to a lot of us in the original group of thirty to fifty people," he said. Barnstijn sold his last RIM shares in 2004 not only because the volatile share price made financial planning difficult, but also because he wanted "to put some space between the past and the present." Complete withdrawal from RIM has been difficult. "I still say 'we.' You never really leave," he said.

The outpouring of philanthropy at such a relatively young age by Lazaridis, Balsillie, and Barnstijn has encouraged others at RIM to make donations to a wide variety of causes. Many donations have remained anonymous, but many others have become known in the community and beyond. Employees gave $2 million to help build a 500-acre local facility called RIM Park, with skating rinks, playing fields, and a golf course. Don and Debbie Morrison donated over 100,000 RIM shares to establish the Golden Thread Charitable Foundation, which invests in a variety of charitable programs for disadvantaged children in southern Ontario. The foundation is also funding an initiative focused on developing a better understanding of the link between ethical, proactive business practice among transnational corporations in the area of global peace and conflict resolution in conjunction with the Balsillie School of International Affairs. Sales VP Don McMurtry gave more than C$500,000 to the K-W Community Foundation; one year gave C$1 million to a range of charities such as World Wildlife Federation, the Nature Conservancy, and the David Suzuki Foundation; and participated in a 2006 fundraising climb of Kilimanjaro for Care. David Yach gave C$200,000 to the K-W Foundation and C$100,000 to the University of Waterloo. When Gary Mousseau won the Ernest Manning Award with Mike Lazaridis in 2002 for their patent covering single-mailbox integration, he shared his portion of the C$100,000 prize with the Integrated Centre for Optimal Learning as well as other organizations. Lazaridis bought science and engineering books for the Windsor library with his winnings.

Dennis Kavelman has given C$100,000 to the K-W Hospital Foundation and was the chair of a campaign that raised C$800,000 for a local initiative to woo family physicians to settle in the region. "One of the things I've learned from Jim and Mike is you've got to focus and decide where you want to make a difference, something you're passionate about," said Kavelman. "My wife and I are just getting to the stage where we're figuring out what we want to focus on. We want to make sure that when we do something that it makes a difference." Kavelman, and his wife Karen, have since started the Kavelman-Fonn Foundation, which focuses on children's welfare, education, and athletics.

In addition to personal wealth and praise for their beneficence, RIM's success has also brought honours to the co-CEOs. Balsillie has honorary degrees from Wilfrid Laurier University, Dalhousie, Trent, and Waterloo, and is an elected Fellow of the Institute of Chartered Accountants of Ontario (FCA). In April 2005, Lazaridis and Balsillie were listed among *Time* magazine's one hundred most influential people along with world leaders such as President George W. Bush and Hu Jintao, premier of the People's Republic of China, as well as Dan Brown, author of *The Da Vinci Code*; singer Melissa Etheridge; UN Secretary-General Kofi Annan; and actress Nicole Kidman. In 2008 they were both inducted into Canada's Telecommunications Hall of Fame and the Canadian Business Hall of Fame in 2009.

Lazaridis holds honorary doctoral degrees from the University of Waterloo (Engineering), McMaster University, the University of Windsor, and Université Laval. He served as chancellor of the University of Waterloo from 2003 to 2009, the first former UW student to occupy the role. In 2006, Lazaridis became an officer of the Order of Canada, and in 2007 he was named to the Order of Ontario.

But none of those honours, nor the fact that he has more than 450 patents issued or pending worldwide, gave Lazaridis the same celebratory status as being featured with actor Robert De Niro, comedian Ellen DeGeneres, and pro golfer Tiger Woods in a series of TV ads for American Express. Created by ad agency Ogilvy & Mather in 2005, the commercial was filmed at the Perimeter Institute and the photo for the print advertisement was shot by famed photographer Annie Leibovitz. In the "My life, my card" series, De Niro is shown walking the streets of New York City's Tribeca neighbourhood; DeGeneres dances from her bedroom to the TV studio. Lazaridis writes equations on a wall-sized blackboard as he talks about his life. "My life is about making ideas happen," he says. "I invented BlackBerry to improve the way people communicate. Its success helped me establish an international physics institute in Canada. Because when great minds come together, who knows what we can accomplish?"

The proposal from American Express had a personal impact as well. Before Lazaridis married, Ophelia made him promise he'd get an Amex card. He dutifully sent in an application but did not qualify and was rejected. When Lazaridis arrived home the night he'd learned about the ad campaign and told his wife the news, she said, "Hold that thought," went to the files, and produced the original Amex application. "Finally," she said, "I am getting my turn."

While accolades are important, Lazaridis can be equally passionate about RIM's manufacturing plant. "Most people would walk through and see it in ten minutes," said Andy Seybold. "But we spent an hour and a half because he had to tell me how the machines were designed so they could change production, and he showed me the little details with packing. He takes real pride in all of this stuff. Mike is as exuberant as they come."

For most of the early RIM employees, the money came as a surprise, like the first frost of fall. Lazaridis thought about the Porsche pictured in Ophelia's framed gift, but bought a BMW 540i instead. "The irony of this whole thing is that when I was finally able to afford that Porsche, I had two children and I couldn't actually use it," he told a chamber of commerce audience in 2006. It was left to Doug Fregin to buy a Porsche 996. For Lazaridis, his winter vehicle is a Range Rover. During summer he drives an Aston Martin Vanquish S with a V-12 engine capable of 200 mph.

Balsillie also says he is not inspired to work hard either by earning money or spending it. "The comfort-pleasure paradigm is an illusion," he said. "What I do is an honour, a privilege, a joy. What wouldn't motivate you about this job?" He has only one vehicle, an Acura SUV, but has acquired forty works by Canadian artists such as Homer Watson, Maurice Cullen, and Group of Seven members A.Y. Jackson, A.J. Casson, and Lawren Harris, as well as contemporary pieces by Cathy Daley.

In 2000, the sudden death of two friends at forty, the same age as Balsillie at the time, caused him to confront his own mortality and change his ways. "You grow up being active, you can eat whatever you want. All of a sudden work gets busier, you get kids, you're up all night. For the first time, you're really, really, really tired. You're eating more, and before you know it you've put on twenty pounds. Your muscle mass goes down, your metabolism slows a bit. It's so easy to get into and so hard to get out of it."

In response, Balsillie began a regime of daily one-hour workouts and watched his food intake by writing down everything he ate. He lost twenty pounds in three months and has since maintained his weight at 190 pounds. "I'll eat anything; I'm an omnivore, that's the problem. Give me a pie, I'll eat the whole thing. If I eat something now, I eat it very deliberately."

Life on the road causes particular problems that need to be kept at bay. "With time zones you can blink and have five or six meals," says Balsillie. "I'm not some saint, but you have to take responsibility for how you feel and what you do. For me to do what I do, it's important that I feel energized, that I feel good, feel connected. It's the only body I've got. I don't want to be one of those guys who drops at forty." To stay fit he plays golf and hockey at competitive levels, swims in a resistance pool at home, trains and competes in men's long-course triathlons, and coaches his son's basketball and soccer teams.

Those who knew Lazaridis and Balsillie before they became rich and famous agree that neither man has been much altered by the money or the fame. Balsillie considers his family at every opportunity. UW president David Johnston attended a conference at CIGI one afternoon, listened to Balsillie's welcoming remarks, and then tried to slip away, only to come upon Balsillie, who was also leaving early. Balsillie put his fingers to his lips, said, "Shhh," and explained that he was taking his son's basketball team to the Toronto Raptors game and wanted to be there for the 7 p.m. tipoff. "This is the consummate multi-tasking Jim. He discharged his emcee duties beautifully and put family first, where it belongs, by getting the boys to the game on time," said Johnston. "As an individual, he's grounded, down-to-earth. Jim and his wife try and instill modest living in their kids as best they can," said venture capitalist and friend John Albright. "He would prefer to be respected for his intellect, not his wealth."

To Lazaridis, family orientation and learning opportunities are paramount, just as they were when he was a boy. At home, Lazaridis, his wife, and two children often sit, each reading a book of their choice, with no TV, video games, or other interruptions to spoil their quiet time together.

"Mike handles his ego very well and he hasn't changed dramatically," said Jim Estill, a RIM director. "He's one of the most successful business people in Canada, and he's successful on a world scale. Some people, if they are that type, might forget where they came from, might have huge, huge egos. Mike has remained humble." "Mike is a mixture of attributes," said Robin

Korthals. "You get the idea that if this all went away he could do it one more time." For many business leaders, once is more than enough. Add the element of strong family values and the combination is unique.

CHAPTER TWELVE

FAMILY VALUES

ON A FRIDAY NIGHT IN DECEMBER 2003, the board of directors of the Perimeter Institute gathered for their annual Christmas dinner at the home of Mike and Ophelia Lazaridis. The couple's two young children, then eight and six, entertained during cocktails by singing a few seasonal songs from the stairs leading to the second floor, and then the guests and their spouses took their seats around the dining-room table.

The full complement of directors doesn't always attend, but the festive group can include John Reid, chief operating officer, KPMG Canadian Region; Ken Cork, a former Noranda executive and now managing director of Sentinel Associates; Robin Korthals, ex-president of TD Bank and former chair of the Ontario Teachers' Pension Plan; former Canadian ambassador to Japan Don Campbell; Cosimo Fiorenza, a tax partner in the Toronto office of law firm Bennett Jones and an expert on non-profit organizations; Lynn Watt, professor emeritus in electrical engineering at Waterloo; and Doug Wright, president at the University of Waterloo when Lazaridis left in 1984.

The wine was poured, but the soup was not yet served as the guests turned toward their host, who had on the table in front of him a small lectern holding a Bible. Lazaridis read a selected passage, picked out some key words, and then wove them into a five-minute homily to the assembled about physics and faith. "He is a sincere Christian and not afraid to show his Christianity," said Ken Cork. "He's a Christian in the sense of the instruction in the Bible—love one another—and he does. That's part of why RIM's such a great company. When he reads the Bible he's not a politician trying to make a point. He's trying to raise up his audience by reading something to them that's uplifting. He's pursuing the high road to get to the high goal. To him, religion is practical and that's quite different from the politically activist type of religion."

In this regard, Lazaridis—the engineer who is fascinated by physics—follows in famous footsteps. Einstein argued that nature could not possibly be a random place; there must be an underlying reality that causes the particles that make up our world to have defined positions and known speeds. "God does not play dice with the universe," Einstein famously said, a concept with which countless others have been wrestling ever since.

While neither Lazaridis nor Balsillie hail from the Kitchener-Waterloo area, they have come under its spell and have created a corporate culture at Research In Motion that matches the area's Mennonite roots. The first Mennonites arrived from Pennsylvania in the early nineteenth century, and today some Old Order Mennonites can still be seen in their horse-drawn buggies on the rural roads in Waterloo County. Mennonites are pacifists who have built strong communities based on family values, where the watchword is helping each other. Unlike some religious groups, who have had little influence on others, Mennonites and their beliefs have had a lasting impact on the regions where they settled. The twin cities of Kitchener-Waterloo, along with Winnipeg and southern Manitoba—another part of Canada that was also settled by Mennonites—have the highest per capita charitable-giving levels in Canada, a testament to times past.

Family values were relevant in the lives of Lazaridis and Balsillie when they were growing up. So was the freedom of movement and the independence offered by smaller centres as they learned personal responsibility and the work ethic early. They are proud of their small-town heritage and staunchly reject the notion that world-class high-tech companies can only thrive in Silicon Valley. For much of the company's first twenty-five years, small-town values mattered as much as professional skills when they interviewed new recruits. When Balsillie first met David Castell in 1998, he specifically asked Castell how he liked Waterloo. Castell replied that he'd gone to school in Waterloo, met his wife in Waterloo, and had probably lived in Waterloo longer than any other place except Peterborough, not knowing Balsillie had also grown up there. "Peterborough!" exclaimed Balsillie, who now had two reasons to see Castell as a kindred spirit and make some assumptions about the nature of his character.

Not every Waterloo graduate can be a candidate for RIM. Many of Waterloo's top grads have been lured away by the siren call of U.S. companies. In October 2005, Waterloo was the only Canadian stop on Microsoft founder Bill Gates's three-day tour of six campuses that also included the University of Wisconsin, Columbia, Princeton, the University of Michigan, and Howard University in Washington, D.C. The overflow Waterloo audience watched via closed-circuit television in several rooms as Gates predicted interactive computers that also functioned as furniture would replace email. "Waterloo is a special relationship for us," he said. "Most years, we hire more students out of Waterloo than any university in the world, typically fifty or even more."[1] Gates returned in 2008 on another recruiting mission.

Canada's first technology cluster was in Ottawa. Bell Northern Research and the National Research Council, as well as two universities, Carleton and Ottawa, caused private sector spinoffs. Key to commercial success in the National Capital Region were entrepreneurial individuals such as Denzil Doyle, Terry Matthews, and Michael Cowpland. Matthews, for example, founded Mitel, which he sold to British Telecom, and Newbridge Networks, bought by Alcatel. The Welsh-born investor, now Sir Terence, continues to finance high-tech ventures such as Sandvine Corporation (also based in Waterloo, Ontario). Another Canadian technology cluster is in British Columbia, where the biggest homegrown success was Creo Inc., acquired by Eastman Kodak in 2005 for $980 million.

Although Waterloo has become the biggest high-tech centre in Canada, and some like to call it Silicon Valley North, it is still relatively small compared to the original Silicon Valley and its anchor institution, Stanford University. "Stanford is a place where students have always dreamed of starting their own companies or going to work for a pre-IPO startup," writes John Battelle in *The Search*.[2] Stanford has been the midwife for such high-profile tech start-ups as Hewlett-Packard, Excite, Yahoo!, and Google—far bigger names than most associated with Waterloo.

---

[1] http://www.ctv.ca/servlet/ArticleNews/story/CTVNews/20051013/
billgates_waterloo_20051013/20051013?hub=Canada

[2] Battelle, John, *The Search: How Google and Its Rivals Rewrote the Rules of Business and Transformed Our Culture.* New York: Portfolio, 2005, p. 60.

To be sure, Stanford has also been around since 1891, a lot longer than Waterloo. Stanford engineering professor Fred Terman encouraged Dave Packard and Bill Hewlett to start the first major success, Hewlett-Packard, in the 1930s. Today there are 23,000 employees at 120 companies in the Stanford Research Park. UW's 120-acre Research and Technology Park opened in 2002 and has far fewer high-tech companies, but who knows what it will look like in fifty years. In addition to the fifty-year head start, some would argue the weather is to Waterloo's disadvantage. Waterloo gets an average of 158 centimetres of snow a year and the average temperature is about 12°C; Silicon Valley has no snow and an average temperature of 22°C. On the bright side, the median house price in Waterloo is C$245,000 versus $682,000 in Silicon Valley. Moreover, Nokia, the largest mobile phone company in the world, is headquartered in Finland, which has its share of snow.

For its part, RIM has spawned few start-ups; satisfied employees remain on the job rather than take an idea and launch their own business. "Entrepreneurship often starts with the grads in universities rather than the employees of existing companies," said Dennis Kavelman. "If there are no choices around among small companies, you can see four or five people graduating from school, working with the prof and starting their own thing. But given the abundance of opportunities in Waterloo, you don't have as many entrepreneurs. We are still on a trajectory that every employee here strongly believes in. If RIM wasn't exciting any more, wasn't going anywhere, sales were flat, people had made their money, and Mike and Jim were not spending as much time around here, and if the company had matured and waned, then I'd see people go off everywhere, but we're still hiring a lot of people, and Mike and Jim are as engaged as ever."

Among local high-tech companies with a University of Waterloo connection, there have been more start-ups by professors than students. Academic entrepreneurs include Scott Vanstone and Gordon Agnew, Certicom; Savvas Chamberlain, Dalsa; Keith Geddes and Gaston Gonnet, Maplesoft; and Otman Basir, IMS. In 1984, Oxford University Press selected the University of Waterloo to computerize the *Oxford English Dictionary*'s 600,000 words on 21,000 pages. Completed in 1991, the electronic version was made available on CDs and on the Web. Open Text was created that same year as a spinoff of the dictionary project to do search-related projects for university libraries. The company went public in 1996, and now has 3,000 employees and US$725 million in revenue. Waterloo grads who have gone on to do well in the United States include Calvin Ayre, the billionaire founder of Bodog.com, and David Cheriton, who obtained his doctorate at Waterloo in 1978, became a professor of computer science at Stanford and was an early investor in Google. In 2005, Cheriton gave C$25 million to Waterloo, which named the School of Computer Science after him.

While the University of Waterloo's policy permitting professors to retain ownership of their inventions means that the university does not directly benefit from commercialization, there is another advantage. "In something like RIM, very little money is received by the university in the technology transfer office but huge donations are received, not only from Mike, but from a wide number of RIM employees who are Waterloo grads through the donations office. How do you put a value on that in terms of giving back to the university?" said Gerry Sullivan, a former member of faculty at the University of Waterloo who served as CEO of the Accelerator Centre, which opened in 2006 in Waterloo's Research + Technology

Park. About two dozen early-stage companies that are mentored by more seasoned business leaders populate the centre. "These guys have got a lot of scar tissue on them and they can tell entrepreneurs very quickly what they're doing right and what they're doing wrong," said Sullivan, himself a former professor who has started up half a dozen companies.

Unlike the approach of some business leaders, who encourage individual employees to leave and launch their own companies, Lazaridis's philosophy is to attract the best people and give them interesting work. He has filled Perimeter with researchers who decide what they want to do and feel valued by society. In turn, such researchers attract the brightest students who go on to invent commercial products that create wealth, which is then plowed back into research. "In the history of Research In Motion, I have licenced exactly two technologies from university research teams. Over that same period I have hired more than 5,000 students as co-ops, interns, and full-time employees. I've even hired some of their professors," Lazaridis said in a speech delivered in 2004 to the Re$earch Money Conference. "When I decided to build radios and introduce CAD [computer-aided design] into our engineering process, I went looking for great people and found them in our universities. Together we have built a successful global company with an enviable intellectual property portfolio."

Lazaridis has also talked about "receptor capacity," the term he uses to describe how the rest of the world needs to listen to what students are saying and realize how wise they are. "Universities today are leading industry, not the other way around. And that's precisely how it should be," Lazaridis said in a speech delivered in Pittsburgh in 2005. "Industry needs to build up our receptor capacity to understand the research that top university students are doing today. Often we don't understand it, and we somehow make that the students' problem. But maybe the reason we don't understand it is that these students are decades ahead of us, and it's not their problem that we don't understand what they're telling us. But students have a sense of something very different—of what will be needed. And we need to have the courage and wisdom to invest in them, to invest in the future."

For Mike Lazaridis, innovation is not just his forte, it's the very fibre of his being. When his wife, Ophelia, gave birth to the couple's second child, Lazaridis took some time off work. His mind, however, did not take a holiday. He established the best placement for the components of his home entertainment system by using a series of algorithms. As breakthroughs go, this one might not have been earth-shattering, but it was practical. Those who have listened to the results claim it's the best sound system they've ever heard.

"Innovation and entrepreneurship are largely misunderstood," said Lazaridis. "Innovation and entrepreneurship is a process, a discipline. It's one you either want to do or you don't. It doesn't just happen. You don't have a eureka moment. It's like any art—you have to train for it and you have to get experience for it. You have to discipline yourself. It's hard work, and it pays off if you stick to it. It took RIM a long time. We started in 1984 and took a long time to get success, but all along we were innovative. It's a journey."[3]

---

[3] Case study #7, Innovation in Canada, Government of Canada, July 29, 2003.

Joining the journey today are RIM's more than twelve thousand employees. Two-thirds of them work in Waterloo, with the rest spread throughout Canada, the United States, the U.K., and more than forty other countries. "Fundamentally our culture hasn't changed. What has changed is the process, the business surroundings. We're a culture of heroes, but they're realistic heroes. We're very, very proud of the fact that we're a Canadian success story. We are driven to be successful," said Elizabeth Roe Pfeifer, vice-president, organizational development, who joined RIM in 1998, when the company had less than two hundred employees.

Space was at a premium so her desk was squeezed into a hallway between and across from the office doors of Lazaridis and Balsillie. "Talk about pressure! But it was a great spot because I got to meet everybody. There was a flow coming in and out of those offices. There was also the opportunity to know when they were free so that I could pop in with the two or three things that I was working on," said Roe Pfeifer.

Competitors must be monitored, but never mimicked. "We are always reminded to think, yes, what you've learned at school, what you've learned at other corporations is important, but take those learnings and really look at what we're trying to do," she said. "We don't need to be the same as others. We're pushed to go that extra mile, to think outside of the box." RIM has kept hierarchy to a minimum, so communication is easy across the flat structure. Directors who report to Roe Pfeifer, for example, are told they can speak freely to senior executives without checking with her first. "They're the experts. I'm there to help with the direction. I don't want them to put a nice little

PowerPoint together for me so that I stand up and look like the queen. It's all about teamwork; it's all about them being involved. They're the ones that should see the expressions and hear the feedback. That's the only way they're going to learn; that's the only way my team's going to be successful."

Chief Operating Officer Don Morrison describes RIM's senior officers as a Venn diagram, a series of overlapping circles each with its own separate portion but all sharing a central section. "It's a wonderful collection. We all have things that are unique to us and then there's a common ground that is the soft-skill stuff, your approach to life, and how you treat people," he said. As a result, RIM has an unusual corporate culture that rewards individualism but requires a willingness to build consensus. "Everybody is so transparent and egalitarian," said Morrison. "This is not an image place and I think maybe in that sense it's very Canadian, strong in its humility."

Email, the reason for RIM's very existence, has also had a pronounced impact on corporate culture ever since the early days of the Bullfrog. "One hundred per cent of the employees have BlackBerry, so you can always depend on reaching them. I get people who say, 'We emailed you something for approval an hour ago and you haven't responded.' You get productivity because it becomes ingrained," said David Yach. At RIM, 'twas ever thus. "If I had something that needed doing, and I blasted an email out, nobody had an excuse for not giving me a quick response. Jobs got done faster, answers came quicker, there was a new trust level in communication with someone," said Gary Mousseau. "I'm working late, trying to make a decision, and okay, there's my answer. If I was at home, and someone needed my help, five minutes later I'm back with the kids and there's their answer."

RIM's corporate culture has also been fuelled by the one thousand fresh-faced co-op students from ten universities—eight in Canada and two in the United States—who every year spend four-month work terms at RIM. Their presence not only supplies bright sparks throughout the organization, they leave behind new applications they've written, and have a lasting impact on the place by keeping everyone abreast of technological trends that otherwise might escape an older generation, even one that's only ten years out of school itself. Each co-op student is given a free BlackBerry, which they get to keep when they go back to school if they're returning to RIM for another work term or as a full-time employee. RIM also welcomes about fifty interns annually from universities with programs that allow a student to spend a full year with an employer before returning to classes for a final term.

"You need to be excited every day when you come to work. There's always going to be components of your job, including my job, that are administrative and not so interesting, but what drives me to come in every day is all the exciting things that we're doing," said Elizabeth Roe Pfeifer. "That's what we try to ensure happens across the organization, including the co-op students. We don't want them to just come in and be an assistant to our engineers. They are deeply engaged in our projects. When they go back to university they can pull out their BlackBerry and say, 'I helped develop that,' and they're very proud of that."

While the University of Waterloo and Wilfrid Laurier have supplied RIM with a significant number of its employees over the years, RIM has also hired from 350 universities around the world. Among those Lazaridis personally recruited was a German student who in turn told Lazaridis about a student he knew at Shanghai University. Lazaridis not only hired that student, but also the student's primary professor. When the professor met Lazaridis for the first time, he asked, "'Do you know who you've hired?' He had the highest mark in engineering in all of China," said Lazaridis in recounting the story. "We really focused on hiring the best and the brightest and supporting the institutions that produced them. They're what made RIM successful and they're the ones that are going to make the regions successful. We need that because it's all part of the virtuous cycle."

Lazaridis expanded on this theme of the virtuous cycle in a speech to the Empire Club of Canada in 2006. Talking about the innovation that has been driven as a result of war, he said, "Mankind has this ability under stress to exceed our expectations. Why don't we carry through what we've learned in times of peace? Imagine what we could accomplish if we take that and make it our culture. Our natural resources will only carry us so far and it isn't just knowledge creation that creates future wealth. It's the students and researchers that graduate that start their own companies with their talent, with that information, and with that connection to the research community. Those students are the most efficient commercialization machine ever invented. I believe in that cycle and I've done it myself."

CHAPTER THIRTEEN

POSTER CHILD FOR PATENT REFORM

CHARLES MEYER DIDN'T KNOW QUITE WHAT to make of the cryptic letter he received from NTP Inc., dated January 27, 2000. The document looked like a form letter, came from a firm he'd never heard of before, and declared that RIM was guilty of infringing on patents. The letter referred to a "distinct commercial advantage" if RIM entered into a licencing agreement with NTP. There was no proof offered of the allegations. There were only seemingly random excerpts of marketing material from RIM's own Web pages and a BlackBerry "Getting Started" guide that was typically included in a BlackBerry smartphone box.

Such letters are common in the high-tech industry and, as RIM's chief legal officer and corporate secretary, Meyer regularly received such demands. Over the next few weeks, he diligently sought information on NTP and consulted in-house patent attorney Krishna Pathiyal. Meyer, an American everyone called Chuck, saw little need to fret. After all, RIM had undoubtedly invented BlackBerry, held several dozen patents, had never heard of NTP or seen its patents before, and had not copied any technology from anyone (NTP or otherwise). Meyer, who had joined RIM in 1996 with degrees in engineering and law, investigated NTP's claims and as a former patent attorney himself, he concluded that RIM did not infringe the patents and NTP's claims were meritless. As an extra precaution, Meyer even wrote a letter to NTP asking for an explanation of why NTP thought its patents would apply to RIM. Meyer did not hear anything back from NTP.

At the time of NTP's letter, BlackBerry had only been on the market for a year, but it had achieved a small foothold of 40,000 subscribers in the United States and a growing reputation as a highly promising technology for enterprise customers. NTP looked like nothing more than a so-called "patent troll," a company with no product and no payroll that holds on to vaguely defined and potentially invalid patents. Many such companies do so in the hopes of being able to successfully threaten litigation to wheedle a licencing fee somewhere down the road after a "real" company invests the effort and takes the entrepreneurial risk to develop a product or service that satisfies customer needs and generates revenue for the risk-takers. "These are paper companies," says Philip Swain, a patent lawyer in the Montreal office of Fasken Martineau, "that never built a product, never built a business, and never really did any good for anyone." Swain, who wrote a brief supporting RIM's position on behalf of the Canadian Chamber of Commerce, says such outfits use patents to hold up legitimate, successful companies, "just like the trolls in mythology who hid under bridges they didn't build themselves."

Patent cases, whether brought by a company that commercializes its own technology or a patent holder that owns a patent with no actual products or services, can be crucial to corporate success or failure. A patent infringement lawsuit brought by Polaroid in 1976 took nine years to resolve and put Kodak out of the instant-camera business. Licencing can also be lucrative. Two-thirds of Dolby Laboratory's annual revenue of more than $300 million comes from licencing deals for its audio and surround sound.

Contrary to Kodak, Polaroid, and Dolby, which have actual products and customers, Meyer found that NTP essentially consisted of one man, Donald Stout, a lawyer in the Arlington, Virginia, firm of Antonelli, Terry, Stout & Kraus. Stout represented patents obtained by Thomas Campana Jr., an electrical engineer from Chicago. In the mid-1980s, Campana started Telefind Corp., and he and others, in the course of co-development work with AT&T, pursued a different way of sending messages via existing email systems using wireless communications networks. Even though the fundamental idea and innovation of sending a message wirelessly had already existed and had previously been implemented by other companies such as TekNow, Campana nonetheless filed for various patents. And, as is too often the case with an overworked United States Patent and Trademark Office (USPTO)—the Patent Office—where patent examiners are sometimes simply unable to thoroughly research each patent application, he was granted the patents. When Telefind went bankrupt in 1991, Campana asked Stout, himself a former examiner with the Patent Office, to form a holding company, New Technologies Products Inc. (NTP), for the portfolio of pending and issued patents held by Telefind.

RIM was just one among forty-seven companies to receive the form letter from NTP in January 2000. The forty-six other companies included 3Com, AT&T, BellSouth, Ericsson, Iridium, Microsoft, Motorola, PageMart, Qualcomm, SkyTel, and Sprint. A common tactic by patent trolls is to put a wide number of companies on notice, oftentimes without regard to the merits, and then wait to see which company becomes most successful and perhaps willing to pay down the road. It's effectively like printing your own postdated lottery ticket for the meagre cost of a registered letter. In the case of RIM, Lazaridis and Balsillie had laboured away and built a successful business and when they were finally starting to see the fruits of their labour, that's when NTP reappeared.

NTP had previously been unable to line up legal representation but, once Stout decided to proceed, Jim Wallace, of Wiley, Rein & Fielding, in Washington, D.C., agreed to take on the case in return for one-third of any court-awarded settlement. NTP also raised a campaign war chest from twenty-two other investors, including some members of Stout's law firm. NTP filed its lawsuit on November 13, 2001, in the U.S. District Court for the Eastern District of Virginia, also known as the "rocket docket" because it moved matters along so quickly.

This was hardly the first time a Canadian invention had come under attack by a foreigner. Florentine-born Antonio Meucci claimed that he, not Alexander Graham Bell, had invented the telephone before Bell. In 1871, Meucci filed what was called a patent caveat, a one-year renewable notice that required less information and was cheaper to file but did not mean a patent would be issued. Meucci did not renew his patent caveat after 1874. Bell obtained his patent in 1876, and then was charged by the U.S. government a year later with fraud and misrepresentation. A trial date was set, but Meucci died in 1889 and the case didn't proceed, proving that patent matters are fraught with peril, are fought with vigour, and can drag on for years.

RIM responded promptly to NTP's lawsuit and issued a press release on November 21, 2001, explaining that NTP's "documentation did not readily demonstrate any support for potential patent infringement." RIM also said it had previously written to NTP requesting more information but had received no reply.

Cleveland-based law firm Jones Day, where Chuck Meyer had worked before joining RIM, was retained to act for RIM. Founded in 1893, Jones Day opened a Washington office in 1946 and employed more than 2,200 lawyers in thirty cities around the world.

Less than a year after NTP's initial filing, the trial began on November 4, 2002, in Richmond, Virginia. Compared to slower-paced jurisdictions, that was like running the four-minute mile. Thomas Winland, author of an article titled "A Whirlwind Ride on the Rocket Docket" and a partner at Finnegan, one of the world's largest IP law firms, said that "when sued in the Eastern District, the defendant often must make a mad dash just to keep up with the fevered pace that litigation in this federal court invariably entails. As a result, detailed analysis of complex issues of patent infringement or invalidity ... becomes nearly impossible."

The lawsuit fell on the docket of Judge James R. Spencer. Born in South Carolina in 1949, Judge Spencer was the first in his family to attend college. His father worked as a mechanic, his mother was a domestic worker and cook. He graduated Harvard Law cum laude in 1974 and received his master's in divinity from Howard University in 1985, standing first in his class. Appointed by President Ronald Reagan in 1986, Judge Spencer was the first African-American judge in the U.S. District Court for the Eastern District of Virginia.

RIM's case was largely damaged when a key piece of evidence was excluded from the case due to a technical error. The evidence was software from a company called TekNow that existed prior to NTP's patent filings and could have proven to the jury that NTP's patents were invalid. RIM argued that NTP had no claim because TekNow, of Phoenix, had an automated message system that could deliver wireless email in 1989— well before Campana's 1991 patents. When TekNow founder David Kenney demonstrated the system to the court by typing into a computer, "Tommy, the deal is closed," the message was duly received on a nearby printer.

A team comprising RIM's technical staff, a paging consultant, and a former TekNow technical-staff member under the careful supervision of Jones Day had spent weeks building the demonstration wireless network system that used software, modems, and laptops from the late 1980s to simulate the TekNow system as it existed in the pre-Campana days. Unfortunately, due to a technical error, the file date on some of the software files had been automatically updated when the software was transferred to a disk and brought to the courthouse to be presented to the jury. During a recess in the midst of Kenney's cross-examination, NTP lawyers spotted the recent dates and argued that the more recent file dates meant that the software was not actually as old as originally thought.

When the jury returned, Judge Spencer instructed them to disregard the entire TekNow demonstration. RIM asked for permission to show jurors another demonstration created with the software files that had the earlier, correct file dates, but Judge Spencer denied the request. It was a technicality, but NTP lawyers managed to get this key evidence thrown out of court. The lack of a simple real-life example of pre-existing prior art technology only further burdened the ability of the jury to appreciate the many legal and technical complexities in this case.

"The U.S. is the only country in the world that burdens lay jurors with the complex task of applying complex patent law to complex technology to decide infringement and invalidity, and they are usually given a few days to make the determination," says David Long, of Howrey LLP, counsel to RIM. "For example, the NTP jury only had a few days to consider infringement, validity, damages, and other issues in that case. In contrast, NTP's technical expert, who had a team of patent attorneys at his disposal, took the position that he would need months to consider and respond to issues of patent validity in the re-examination proceedings."

The twelve jurors took less than five hours to arrive at a verdict, found in favour of NTP, and awarded NTP damages of $23.1 million based on an extraordinarily high royalty rate of 5.7 per cent of RIM sales. In a ruling issued August 5, 2003, Judge Spencer enhanced the damages based on the fact that NTP had notified RIM years earlier (through its cryptically written form letter) and that RIM could not provide evidence that it took enough steps in response. The law actually allows for damages to be tripled in such circumstances, but the judge only opted to enhance the damages by half the original jury award. The full award equaled $53.7 million, an amount that included interest, legal fees, and damages to account for products sold between the time of the jury verdict and the judgment that followed about nine months later. Judge Spencer also issued a permanent injunction against RIM to prevent any further manufacture, use, importation, or sale of the BlackBerry in the United States. Such a stoppage would have been fatal. By then, three years after that letter from NTP, more than two-thirds of the 500,000 BlackBerry subscribers worldwide lived in the United States. RIM filed an appeal with the U.S. Court of Appeals for the Federal Circuit, and the injunction was stayed pending the outcome of the appeal.

So, what happened at the trial? *NTP Inc. v. Research In Motion Limited* was not about RIM stealing NTP's secrets. NTP never claimed that RIM copied NTP's patents. In the world of patent law, that's not what matters. As long as NTP was the first to be granted a patent, if RIM comes along later and produces a popular product that somehow infringes on the claims of the patent—even though the company developed its product independently and even though the patent may have been improperly granted in the first place—RIM can be found guilty of infringing.

Patent disputes hinge on the offended party, in this case NTP, being able to show that their patent existed before the defendant, RIM, launched BlackBerry. In response, RIM must show there was "prior art" or another similar product in existence before the NTP patents were granted. Again, the question is not did NTP know about or copy that prior art; RIM just has to uncover such prior art and present it to the court in order to show that NTP was not the first even if RIM was unaware of either NTP or the prior art. To heighten the drama, patent law places a higher burden of proof on the defendant to demonstrate that the claims of the patent are invalid than on the party claiming to be offended. RIM expected to present the TekNow demonstration as the "prior art" needed to invalidate NTP's patents before the court, but the evidence was not allowed to be considered by the jury due to the technical error that caused the file dates to be updated when transferring the files to a disk.

RIM replaced the Jones Day law firm with the Washington-based Howrey LLP, and pursued three courses of action following the jury verdict and judgment. First, the U.S. Patent and Trademark Office on their own prerogative ordered what was called a "Director-initiated" set of re-examinations of the NTP patents on December 26, 2002, to revisit whether the patents should have been issued in the first instance. RIM, in turn, then filed its own set of re-examinations requests to also actively participate in this review of the NTP patents before the U.S. Patent and Trademark Office. In effect, if the patents were invalidated through the re-examination process, the Patent Office would formally acknowledge that they should have never been issued in the first place and hence NTP's lawsuit would be moot. Second, RIM appealed the jury verdict. Third, RIM entered into settlement talks with NTP.

The first course of action received backing from the Cellular Telecommunications and Internet Association, a trade group with scores of corporate members, such as Cingular, Verizon, Ericsson, Cisco Systems, Intel, and Lucent Technologies, that supported a re-examination of NTP's patents.

Political encouragement soon followed. On January 16, 2003, James Eagen, chief administrative officer of the U.S. House of Representatives, declared in a letter to both sides that losing BlackBerry service because of a court injunction would have a "severe impact" on House operations. The House began

using BlackBerry in the summer of 2000 and had expanded
the service to include all newly elected members in January
2001. By the following summer, there were five hundred users
and Eagen said the system proved to be "a vital communication mechanism" during the terrorist attack on September 11,
2001, as well as during the anthrax scare the following month.
By the time Eagen wrote his supportive letter the House had
supplied more than three thousand BlackBerry devices to
members and staff and had spent $6 million on BlackBerry
technology. "Because the BlackBerry system has proven to
function effectively when other communications do not, the
BlackBerry service is essential to the House's operations," he
wrote. In addition, RIM and other companies lobbied for new
legislation so companies such as NTP, which did not manufacture products, would not be entitled to obtain an injunction
that would prevent manufacturers, such as RIM, from putting
innovative technologies into the hands of the public.

Strategy number two, appealing the lower-court ruling,
played out at the Federal Circuit in Washington, D.C. The fifteen Federal Circuit judges, who are presidential appointments
confirmed by the Senate, have national jurisdiction in a number of areas, including government contracts, patents, and
trademarks. On December 14, 2004, a three-member panel,
which included Chief Judge Paul Michel, released a fifty-
seven-page ruling that upheld the lower court's verdict but did
reduce NTP's sixteen claims to eleven and sent the case back
to Judge Spencer. RIM asked the appeals court to reconsider
its ruling and, on August 2, 2005, the same three-member
panel delivered a seventy-four-page ruling that further reduced
to seven the number of NTP's claims. The court also altered
some of its views and the case was again referred to Judge

Spencer to determine how the new finding would affect the jury verdict, damages, and the injunction.

The third strategy of pursuing a settlement almost succeeded. On March 16, 2005, RIM announced an agreement to pay NTP $450 million for a perpetual fully paid licence to all of NTP's patents. The deal, described in a joint press release by RIM and NTP as "a binding term sheet that resolves all current litigation," would have been one of the largest payments ever made for patent infringement, but the deal collapsed three months later due to an impasse in finalizing the definitive agreement. RIM said that it had negotiated in good faith to complete the agreement, but NTP refused to honour its obligations outlined in the term sheet. The word on the street was that NTP now wanted $1 billion. RIM took court action to attempt to enforce the term sheet that NTP had previously acknowledged to be binding, but NTP fought, and six months later convinced Judge Spencer to find that the term sheet was not an enforceable agreement. And so the fight continued.

A patent is a grant of property rights by the U.S. government that excludes anyone else from making, using, or selling the invention in the United States unless there is some kind of licencing agreement. Hank Morgan, one of Mark Twain's characters in *A Connecticut Yankee in King Arthur's Court*, declared the importance of patents when he said, "The very first official thing I did in my administration—and it was on the very first day of it too—was to start a patent office; for I knew that a country without a patent office and good patent laws was just a crab, and couldn't travel any way but sideways or backways."

Still, there have been doubters, even within the system. In 1899, Charles H. Duell, commissioner of U.S. Patents, recommended the Patent Office be abolished, saying, "Everything that can be invented has been invented."

In fact, the number of patents is huge and growing. It took seventy-five years after the U.S. Patent and Trademark Office opened in 1790 to grant one million patents. The most recent million, from patent #6,000,000 to #7,000,000, reached on February 14, 2006, took only six years. U.S. commissioner of patents and trademarks Bruce Lehman offered some insight into the process in 1992 when he said, "We are the patent office, not the rejection office."

James Rogan, director of the Patent and Trademark Office and a former Representative from California, ordered a director-initiated re-examination of NTP's patents. Director-initiated is the rarest type of re-examination, accounting for only about 2 per cent of the seven thousand re-examinations conducted since re-examinations were instituted in 1981, and typically indicates that there are strong reasons to believe that the patents are invalid and should not have been issued in the first place. None of this patent activity convinced Judge Spencer to put the lawsuit on hold until the Patent Office completed its re-examination of the patents. The judge also made it clear that he wanted the case resolved soon. "I have spent enough of my time and life involved with NTP and RIM," he said at a hearing on November 9, 2005. That same month RIM announced a software "workaround" that was designed to avoid the remaining patent claims in the case and allow the Black-Berry service to continue in the event that the injunction was imposed. At the same time, RIM received further official support when the U.S. Department of Justice filed a ten-page brief with the Virginia court describing the U.S. federal government as "a major user of BlackBerry" and asked for an exemption from any injunction, calling BlackBerry "essential" for federal, state, and local governments.

By 2005, the number of U.S. subscribers had reached 3.5 million of the 5 million worldwide. With public fear continuing to rise about the possibility of an injunction that would interrupt service, RIM's co-CEO, Jim Balsillie, published a lengthy op-ed piece entitled "Patent Abuse" in the *Wall Street Journal* that pulled no punches in describing NTP's behaviour during the protracted battle and explaining how NTP was "trying to exploit the [patent] system by leveraging the relative speed of the judicial system while obstructing the deliberateness of the USPTO." He also assured his customers that RIM would continue to "innovate, re-invest and service its customers" and would implement the software workaround if necessary to maintain the BlackBerry service. The op-ed also made a compelling case for patent reform. "Few contest that the U.S. patent system is overburdened," wrote Balsillie. "Only a few weeks ago, Patent and Trademark Commissioner John Doll was reported saying: 'When you've got 1.3 million cases in the backlog, and it's taking [four to six] years to take a first office action, you've got to ask the question: Is the patent system still actually working, or are we just stamping numbers on the applications as they come through?'

"Commissioner Doll is not alone," noted Balsillie. "In a survey by the Intellectual Property Owners Association of the nation's top patent lawyers, over half rated the quality of patents issued in the U.S. today as less than satisfactory or poor. The future doesn't look much better. According to the survey, over two-thirds of respondents said they thought the patent process would get longer, not shorter, over the next three years. And nearly three-quarters said they would be spending more, not less, on patent litigation."

Balsillie argued that the patent process should be allowed to work and said that RIM was prepared to "provide reasonable and substantial compensation" even though the Patent Office was in the process of rejecting NTP's patents one after another. RIM was already paying royalties to many other patent holders, but at rates that were usually significantly less and nothing like the 5.7 per cent awarded by the jury. "No one (including NTP) disputes that RIM invented BlackBerry independent of NTP's patents. Moreover, unlike NTP, RIM actually created something—a company and a new market segment through over twenty years of innovation, risk-taking, partnering, customer service, growth and re-investment," said Balsillie.

After all that effort, RIM didn't bring about any immediate changes to the system and didn't send NTP packing, but RIM still had another hearing to go.

By 7:30 a.m., ninety minutes before the hearing began on February 24, 2006, more than sixty people were already waiting outside the Italianate courthouse in Richmond, Virginia, to assure themselves of a seat in Judge Spencer's wood-panelled third-floor courtroom. Cameras on tripods bloomed on the far sidewalk. Down the street, TV trucks sprouted satellite dishes. When everyone had filed in, all eyes were on Balsillie, who had a front-row seat immediately behind his legal team, which had been expanded to include Henry Bunsow, an intellectual property specialist and managing partner in the San

Francisco office of Howrey LLP; Marty Glick, also from San Francisco, senior litigator and intellectual property specialist from Howard, Rice, Nemerovski, Canady, Falk & Rabkin; and former U.S. ambassador to Canada Gordon Giffin. James Blanchard, another former U.S. envoy to Canada, had also advised RIM, as had the law firm of McKenna Long & Aldridge, of Atlanta and Washington.

In court, RIM's Henry Bunsow argued against an injunction. "It will frustrate the public interest. There are more than three million BlackBerry users, many of whom are embedded in the infrastructure." Bunsow cited support for BlackBerry from, among others, the Florida Department of Health, Harvard Medical School, and the American Gas Association.

As if the case weren't already unusual enough, the U.S. government had requested status as an intervenor. The U.S. Department of Justice was represented by John Fargo, who told the court that government users must be exempted from any injunction. "We do not want the carriers to shut off our service," he said. "The carriers want to make sure they are not held in contempt of an injunction."

At the end of the hearing, Judge Spencer said he'd wait to rule on both questions—damages and an injunction—but his comments seemed to indicate that he would rule in favour of NTP. He expressed surprise that the parties had "left this incredibly important and significant decision to the court. I've always thought that this, in the end, was really a business decision. And yet you have left the decision in the legal arena, and that's what you're going to get, a legal decision." Of course, RIM had long contended that it had no choice but to keep fighting since NTP was not offering a settlement deal that would protect RIM's carrier partners, and RIM could not consider paying NTP such a large sum of money without also securing protection for RIM's partners. It would have been ridiculous for RIM to settle the lawsuit only to have NTP sue RIM's carrier partners the next day over the same BlackBerry products and services. The judge could not, however, impose a settlement, and NTP, after hearing the judge's comments in court, seemed confident that it would get an injunction and therefore could negotiate an even higher payoff.

Judge Spencer was also unmoved by the fact that the U.S. Patent and Trademark Office had that very morning completed its lengthy review by finally rejecting the last of NTP's patent in re-examination. "It was like a judge in a murder case pondering execution while ignoring new DNA evidence that exculpates the defendant," wrote Steven Levy in *Newsweek*.[1] But this was not a murder trial. A patent is not considered invalidated until all available appeals have been exhausted, and the judge was not willing to postpone the lawsuit in the meantime. Despite the view of many experts that the rejections were sound and would never be overturned, those rejections suffered by NTP's patents could nonetheless be appealed to the USPTO's Board of Patent Appeals and Interferences. That ruling could then in turn be appealed to the federal Appeals Court. Patent law and case law only come together once all appeal possibilities have been concluded, and NTP had shown significant expertise in bogging down the USPTO's re-examination process so that it could not be completed before the completion of the lawsuit. That was the core of the problem for RIM. The patent system and the court system were out of sync and RIM was caught in the gap.

---

[1] *Newsweek*, March 13, 2006.

In the meantime, the uncertainty about service was beginning to affect BlackBerry sales despite RIM's technical and business leadership. That fact, together with Judge Spencer's ominous comments at the end of the hearing and NTP's eventual willingness to include protections for RIM's partners, caused RIM to settle for an even larger amount. On March 3, 2006, RIM paid NTP $612.5 million, more than the $450 million deal that was negotiated a year earlier, but far less than the $1 billion payoff that some had predicted. "It's not a good feeling to write this kind of a cheque," Balsillie told financial analysts in a conference call a few minutes after the settlement was announced. "We took one for the team," he said, referring to the fact that RIM protected its partners in the settlement and removed the uncertainty that was causing so much angst amongst its customer base. RIM's shareholders certainly seemed to agree with the merit of RIM's decision. Following the announcement of the settlement, RIM's stock price surged by 15%, adding $2 billion to RIM's market capitalization. It was a tough pill to swallow, especially since the USPTO indicated that the patents were invalid, but the uncertainty had been removed from customers' minds and RIM and its partners were now free and clear to pursue the giant opportunity that lay ahead.

On the Tuesday following the Friday settlement, RIM posted an open letter on its website and ran full-page ads in eight U.S. newspapers including the *Wall Street Journal, Washington Post*, and *San Francisco Chronicle* that declared, "You can rest assured the BlackBerry is here to stay." The statement by Balsillie and Lazaridis drew attention to the vagaries of the patent system, saying, "As to the lingering question of why the patent system should allow such a bizarre set of circumstances to threaten millions of American customers in the first place, we share your concern. The good news is that this topic is currently receiving much more attention from policymakers and the Supreme Court and we hope the patent system will evolve to close the loopholes and become more balanced."

Carriers, relieved to see the end of the issue, fell in behind RIM. "There was obviously concern: would the product have to go dark? I never for one second even imagined that would be the case. They had a workaround," said David Neale. "Was there any change in the user experience? Not that you would have seen. Did it solve their problem? Apparently. Anyway, it all got sorted out. Rumours of their demise were greatly exaggerated."

While none of RIM's 60,000 corporate clients cancelled service because of the fight with NTP, Balsillie did admit that the battle had consumed a lot of his time. However, he also saw a positive side. "For us, it really consolidated our capacity to withstand stuff. We realized that you just can't let these things get to you. Plus, customers paid huge attention and Black-Berry's technical leadership was reinforced in the market in a major way. And on a broader scale, I think a lot of good reform will come to the system as a result of the incredibly unfair circumstances we endured in a very public manner."

True to Balsillie's words, the entire patent system is now coming under closer scrutiny by legislators and others. RIM received support for its position in a report entitled *Reforming U.S. Patent Policy* commissioned by the Council on Foreign Relations that was released in November 2006. "The burdens of the U.S. system stand in sharp contrast with the more balanced systems of its major competitors. Other patent regimes in the developed world, such as those of Canada and the European Union, are more supportive of dynamic competition and the diffusion of technologies," said Keith Maskus, author of the report and professor of economics at the University of Colorado, Boulder. Maskus also castigated the U.S. Patent and Trademark Office as "underfunded ... [with] increasingly diluted patent standards, and a legislative and judicial presumption of patent validity."

Since the NTP case, there have already been a number of changes in the patent system, the most significant of which is the Supreme Court's decision in the eBay case. In that case, the court took away the automatic right to an injunction and stated that courts must apply a standard reasonableness test to determine if an injunction is warranted. Jessica Holzer, writing in *Forbes* magazine about the eBay case, concludes: "The high court's decision deals a blow to patent trolls, which are notorious for using the threat of permanent injunction to extort hefty fees in licensing negotiations as well as huge settlements from companies they have accused of infringing. Often, those settlements can be far greater than the value of the infringing technology: Recall the $612.5 million that Canada's Research in [*sic*] Motion forked over to patent-holding company NTP to avoid the shutting down of its popular BlackBerry service."

Another significant change is the willingness of courts to grant a stay when re-examination proceedings are pending. In fact, in recent suits started by NTP against Palm and certain wireless carriers, Judge James R. Spencer granted a stay pending re-examination of the same patents that were the subject of the RIM/NTP lawsuit.

RIM's case was certainly one of the most publicized patent cases ever in the United States and the high stakes drama drew the interest of millions of people around the world. "We obviously didn't seek it, but RIM clearly became the poster child for patent reform," said Balsillie.

CHAPTER FOURTEEN

GLOBAL REACH

"BIG WTC EXPLOSION. I'M GOING TO STREET. I'm scared," Lynne Federman frantically typed into her BlackBerry on the morning of September 11, 2001, then sent the message to her husband, Joseph Korb, who was on jury duty in Newark.

"What??" he wrote back on his BlackBerry.

"Seems helicopter crashed into WTC," she replied. "Going to street now. Very scary."[1]

Federman, a corporate lawyer at J. P. Morgan Chase, three blocks from the World Trade Center, survived. But nearly three thousand others died that morning when two aircraft, hijacked by terrorists, crashed into the Twin Towers. For everyone else, the world forever changed.

Regular telephone service, cellular phone systems, and some two-way paging networks were damaged, disrupted, or didn't work at all. In stark contrast, BlackBerry service continued unimpeded, creating lifelines for emergency services and frantic families. Cingular Wireless, the carrier with the

---

[1] *New York Times*, September 20, 2001.

most BlackBerry subscribers at the time, noticed a massive surge in use immediately after the attack. Rather than trumpet the success of its technology on that awful day, RIM took a low profile but did quietly donate more than one thousand BlackBerry devices for use by those who searched for survivors in the rubble at Ground Zero, and sent a truckload of Black-Berry chargers and batteries so that those emergency workers who already had a BlackBerry could stay charged and connected during the days that followed.

RIM also worked with Cingular and emergency services teams, using a special transmitter to send a wireless signal containing an emergency broadcast message directly into the rubble at Ground Zero, in an effort to try to reach potential survivors who were trapped and could possibly provide information about their location. Given that many BlackBerry users worked inside the World Trade Center and their company's BlackBerry Enterprise Server would no longer be functioning after the towers fell, a trapped user would not have been able to send or receive an email through the normal method, so the idea was to broadcast a special type of message that could reach anyone within range and allow them to communicate back to people at RIM's headquarters who were given a direct line to the New York City Fire Department. Guibert explained, "The transmitter couldn't perfectly contain the signal to the area of the Twin Towers location and so we received a bunch of replies from people standing on the streets nearby. Our hearts all skipped a beat every time a response came in, but we unfortunately didn't find any survivors. It was probably a long shot, but initially there was a widespread sense of hope that more people would be found alive, and the emergency teams were pursuing every possibility."

RIM received emails and letters from people for months afterwards, citing examples of how BlackBerry had impacted their lives on that terrible day. For some, they received their last communication from a loved one who sent a message from their BlackBerry before the towers collapsed. For many more, BlackBerry served as the only means to communicate and confirm their safety to their family, friends, and colleagues.

The value of the BlackBerry was again demonstrated soon after the 9/11 tragedy when sensitivities about unresponsive aircraft remained high. Florida governor Jeb Bush told a packed room in 2006 at RIM's annual conference in Orlando that he was in the air when the pilot told him he'd lost contact with the control tower due to a failed communications system on board. "They were concerned that F-16s could be deployed to shoot them down," explained Lazaridis. "So Governor Bush took his BlackBerry and, once they were at a low enough altitude to connect to the network, he sent a message to his assistant to contact the airport to tell them who was in the plane and that they had simply lost their communications system." Bush used his BlackBerry to such an extent as a means of communicating with voters that he became known as the e-governor. Among the iconic items that appear in his official portrait hanging in the capitol in Tallahassee are a Bible, a family photo, and a BlackBerry.

For the carriers, RIM's success may not have been expected, but it wasn't going unnoticed. RIM's achievements as a mobile virtual network operator (MVNO) that dealt directly with customers concerned some carriers who wanted to control the subscriber's commercial relationship while RIM looked after tech support. In fact, RIM had come to a similar conclusion on its own. "If you want to grow and be big you either do it yourself or you rely on other people who are already there doing it. To do it ourselves was not scalable," said RIM's COO Don Morrison. "We were walking around back in 2000, 2001, saying 'We're going to 10X this business.' That's a nice slogan, but how are you going to do that? The simple truth is if you had thirty salespeople doing 30,000 net activations a quarter, how are you going to get that to 300,000? The answer is you're not going to do it by multiplying your sales force. From a cost standpoint I just think it's unmanageable." Because there were those within RIM who wanted to continue the MVNO arrangement, there was a vigorous debate. "Jim always encourages that we argue things through," said Morrison. "You separate personal conflict from what are the different views on this subject. There were people that had a very different view that had a lot more tenure than I did. They thought we should carry on."

Once Balsillie concluded that working with carriers would be the right path, then the question arose, how would RIM organize itself to do so? With his two decades of big-business experience Morrison favoured the traditional approach of geographic units, where one vice-president was responsible for, say, Europe, while another vice-president might oversee operations in Southeast Asia. Balsillie disagreed, saying that would only add an unnecessary layer of management.

Balsillie decided that RIM's relationship would be on a carrier-by-carrier basis with one person assigned to each carrier. Starting in 2001, RIM signed separate contracts with many of the world's biggest carriers, including AT&T Wireless, VoiceStream (which became T-Mobile), Nextel and Verizon in the U.S., Rogers and Bell Mobility in Canada, O_2 and

Vodafone in the U.K. and Europe, and Hutchison Telecom in Hong Kong. "Jim Balsillie has scratched, and grinded, and created a lot from nothing. Carriers weren't begging for the product," said Barry Richards, of Paradigm Capital.

Some deals were relatively small but they did help create international momentum. In February 2001, RIM issued a press release saying that U.K. mobile telecom operator O$_2$ (formerly BT Cellnet) had ordered 175,000 wireless handhelds. "The next most competitive market after the United States is the U.K. Balsillie went there and said, 'You've got to be the first guy or I'm going to these other guys.' It was two years later before they actually started to ship the products. But we had the buzz," said Richards.

But many carriers, not just O$_2$, were not as ready for email as RIM might have liked. "You've got an industry that has its genesis in voice that goes back to 1982–83 and has learned through trial and error what makes success. In the voice business, it evolved to being a game of scale. It's not knowledge intensive, it's price, advertising, call centres, and retail presence eventually gravitating toward a commodity-type business," said Morrison.

By contrast, BlackBerry was about more than just price and availability. "Now the carrier has to learn a lot," he said. "When the customer wants to strap on the tanks and go deep you have to go deep with him, which is not typically where carriers were. Even though executives are buying in, you have to deal with all that inertia in the organization." Carriers had also begun to realize that BlackBerry was more profitable than a cell phone with no email plan. "The profit of one customer for BlackBerry is much greater than the customer without it. The margins that you get on this customer and the length of time—which is called 'customer lifetime value'—is much greater, it's three times greater with BlackBerry than it is without," said Morrison.

Despite the success of the new carrier strategy, Balsillie was not satisfied. It was all well and good to sign up twenty-one carriers in a year, thereby bringing the total to fifty carriers for the fiscal year ending February 2003, but, said Balsillie, "Do you realize how many people we're upsetting by not going fast enough?" We'll hire more sales staff, said Morrison. "No, change the process. Make it easier, cookie-cut it, so that you can accommodate a greater number simultaneously," said Balsillie.

A new, streamlined process was in place just in time for increased demand. Balsillie, Conlee, and Morrison noticed the difference in February 2003 when they attended the annual 3GSM conference in Barcelona, the world's biggest annual wireless conference. "In 2002, the image I have of us is chasing these carriers down the hall. They'd bat us away, saying, 'I'm not interested.' GPRS [General Packet Radio Service] came along and the family of products—the 6210, the 7210, which was in colour—started to take off and one year later the carriers were chasing us down the hall," said Morrison. By the end of 2004, BlackBerry was available in forty countries through eighty carriers as RIM became more efficient at the carrier set-up process by reducing the time taken from six months to six weeks. BlackBerry sales soared 47 per cent year over year, outstripping growth of 19 per cent in the overall market. That year, BlackBerry sold 3.2 million units out of a worldwide total of 14.9 million PDAs, replacing Palm as the top-selling company. Using the same streamlined process, RIM added one hundred new carriers in each of 2006 and 2007. By mid-2009, BlackBerry was available through 530 carriers and distribution partners in 170 countries.

Changing from the MVNO strategy and signing more carriers accelerated subscriber growth. During the first few years of BlackBerry, the majority of subscribers were in New York City and Washington, D.C., with Toronto running third among big cities. By February 2004, there were one million subscribers. Finding that first million had taken five years from the 1999 launch. The second million took only ten months, until November 2004. A year later, in November 2005, the number of subscribers had doubled to four million, and then doubled again to eight million in February 2007. By then, RIM had signed up 270 carriers, a list that included China Mobile and DoCoMo in Japan, with their access to huge markets, and was adding new subscribers at the rate of one million every three months. At the end of 2009, there were more than 35 million subscribers and the number of subscribers outside the original home base of North America grew to 35 per cent of the total. "I was in New York on 9/11 and on 9/11 the only way you could communicate was with a BlackBerry. Four years later, the U.S. government was saying that the BlackBerry was essential to the national interest. That's warp time—even in communications technology these days," said Paul Heinbecker, a career diplomat who served as Canada's ambassador to Germany and to the United Nations. "It was only five years ago when you used to have to check when you were travelling in Ontario where the BlackBerry would work. Now you can get off a plane in 150 countries and it's going to work."

As the number of customers grew, the demographics expanded beyond corporations and governments. Beginning in 2003, in addition to the BlackBerry Enterprise Server for corporate accounts, RIM also offered BlackBerry Internet Service (BIS) for smaller businesses and individuals. To make its services even more widely available, RIM struck a deal with Yahoo! so that an individual BlackBerry user could have push email just the same as an investment banker. Eight out of ten people on the Internet use Yahoo! and eight out of ten Yahoo! users use Yahoo! Mail, so Yahoo! Mail users constitute 64 per cent of all Internet users—a huge group RIM was now able to tap into.

Similar tie-ins were created with AOL, MSN, and Google that increased the number of subscribers and produced service revenue just as if the individual were part of a corporate system. By 2006, fully 25 per cent of the seven million BlackBerry subscriber base was made up of small businesses and individual consumers who wanted the unique BlackBerry service—push email, always on—and were willing to pay for it out of their own pocket. "I don't think it will be too long before consumers outstrip enterprise," said Balsillie at the time.

Among smartphones with calling, email, and organizers, BlackBerry now dominates with 75 per cent of the market share; Palm has 20 per cent, Nokia and Motorola 1 per cent each. Such leadership constitutes high-tech success, as measured by Geoffrey A. Moore in his seminal book about high-tech marketing, *Crossing the Chasm*. "This is what Oracle has achieved in the area of relational databases, Microsoft in PC operating systems, Hewlett-Packard in PC laser and inkjet printers, and IBM in mainframe computers," wrote Moore. "Each of these companies hold market share in excess of 50 per cent in its prime market."[2]

---

[2] Moore, p. 15.

Historically, BlackBerry made the deepest penetration in the high-end market—governments and corporations that can afford the initial outlay for the handhelds, the monthly contracts, and upgrades when new models come along. All branches of the U.S. government taken together make up well over one million subscribers, making the U.S. government the biggest single user of BlackBerry. In addition to governments, RIM originally focused on targeting financial services companies and law firms, but has since broadened its reach to virtually every industry segment.

Citigroup was one of the earliest companies to deploy BlackBerry broadly to tens of thousands of employees, and its relevance to RIM went far beyond the numbers. Salomon Smith Barney was among the early adopters of RIM two-way pagers by the time the investment banker's parent company, Citicorp, merged with Travelers Group in 1998 to form Citigroup, now the largest financial services firm in the world. When BlackBerry was launched in 1999 it became such an important communications tool that Citi set up its own monitoring system, one that was so sensitive it could spot trouble on the network and occasionally let RIM know before it was even aware. So impressed was RIM that they hired Ken LeVine, who had run the system for Citi, to work at RIM and help deploy large user groups.

The growing popularity of BlackBerry dramatically changed RIM's revenue profile, or where the money comes from. In the fiscal quarter ending May 1999, RIM's total revenues amounted to $24.1 million, almost none of it from BlackBerry. For the fiscal quarter ending February 2002, only three years after its commercial launch, BlackBerry produced 82 per cent of the $66.1 million RIM generated in revenue, a proportion that continued to grow in the years since. "The BlackBerry products, the 950, 957, and all of those product lines started to explode and dwarf the OEM business even though the OEM products were growing at a nice little clip," said John Latham, director of business development at RIM. "Any other company would've loved to have had that kind of product, but it dropped very precipitously in terms of its percentage of sales." RIM was producing a line of OEM radio modems compatible with the next generation of GSM/GPRS wireless equipment, but then stopped making the product as end prices fell and profit margins shrank.

RIM's monthly service fee from every subscriber that is collected by the carriers is not typical in the business, but RIM provides value to the carriers by offsetting much of the technical and operational burden through its BlackBerry infrastructure and carrier and customer support teams. RIM has also modeled its business plans to support the carriers in the belief that RIM will be successful if the carrier is successful.

After carriers became the main sales point, RIM gave up the majority of the service-revenue stream in exchange for the opportunity to increase its overall sales dramatically, but it continued to share in that monthly fee in return for the service provided by RIM's network operating centre (NOC) in Waterloo through which all data passed. (Today, RIM has multiple NOCs around the world.) The NOCs give RIM an advantage over other device manufacturers by providing carriers and customers a whole solution, including the comprehensive network infrastructure that is managed by RIM to improve the performance and security of the wireless service.

BlackBerry has more security certifications with countries, defence systems, and world organizations than any of its competitors. As part of the certification process with the United States, U.K., Canada, the Netherlands, NATO, and others, RIM has its own certification labs that speed up the approval process. RIM also developed a smart card reader so that when a user is away from his BlackBerry or PC, the Bluetooth reader blocks unauthorized use. The card is light enough to hang on a lanyard so users don't need to think about removing the access card every time they leave their equipment for a few minutes.

That security also includes a fail-safe provision against theft of information if a device disappears. When an employee reports a lost BlackBerry the company's IT department can change the password remotely, in case the user discovers the device wasn't really lost, it had just slipped between the cushions of the sofa at home. If after twenty-four hours the device has not turned up, IT can then send what's called a "kill command" that zaps all stored information so that even if an unauthorized person were able to gain access there would be nothing left to read.

In BlackBerry's first year, the relay centre acting as traffic cop could run on a single server. In 2009, RIM operates one of the largest private IP networks in the world. The BlackBerry infrastructure is now housed in large server rooms around the world and handles over 3 petabytes of data each month, which is 3,000,000,000,000,000 bytes of data, an amount roughly equal to the size of the digital library stored by Internet Archive, a non-profit organization based in San Francisco that stores periodic snapshots of the World Wide Web. In addition to security and performance for the subscriber, the carrier also benefits. The compression and efficiency of RIM's uniquely integrated solution, which provides the hardware, software, and services to deliver messages and other data, means reduced broadband use so the network can transmit more data on the same system, which has finite capacity. "The network is precarious, delicate, and expensive. Carriers aren't quite ready for everyone to be downloading hundreds of Web pages every second. It's wonderful for them. They know the traffic is clean and reformatted," said Barry Richards, of Paradigm Capital.

All along the way, the three eternal verities preached by Mike Lazaridis were maintained: concern for battery life, network conservation, and regular systemic updates. For example, it wasn't until February 2002 that the BlackBerry 5810 was unveiled at the COMDEX show held in Chicago. The 5810 looked like the 957 but was the first BlackBerry with both email and voice. Because the 5810 had dual bands, RIM was also able to use the device to expand sales outside North America.

In order to use GSM, the European standard established in 1987 by thirteen nations, RIM had to make significant investments to adapt its devices and systems. "Jim and Mike both had a vision. History has proven them to be dead-on," said Walt Purnell Jr., CEO of Motient. "A lot of folks thought it was a dumb idea, especially when you started combining voice with it. I mean, who needed another phone, just a clumsy phone? Motorola and Nokia make such sleek, sexy phones, who on earth would want a phone with a keyboard. Well, it turned out that a lot of people did." (GSM has become the world standard with 80 per cent of all users.)

It was also Lazaridis who decided to use Java software on

the BlackBerry 5800 series. At the time, there was no accepted standard among competing devices, but Lazaridis wanted something that was versatile, inexpensive, and could operate on any number of different networks. Switching to Java meant that all of RIM's software, written in a language called C++, had to be reworked. "Programmers love to rewrite their programs, so that wasn't so hard. But the hard part was slowing down the time frame in terms of investment, so if we were lucky, in two years we might be back to where we started," Lazaridis said in a reflective speech given at a conference in 2002. "We had to risk slowing down while we spent two years re-writing the first BlackBerry software. We had huge arguments over it."

The decision to use Java was important, however, because it made BlackBerry an open system that allowed thousands of independent developers to create new applications. Because RIM couldn't possibly figure out all the uses for BlackBerry on its own, it made sense for the company to give away developer kits so others could devise those uses. Adding Java also reduced production costs and weight because the software replaced one of the two processors. "It's like many things at RIM," said David Yach, CTO, software. "It requires a lot of conviction that you're right and the rest of the world is wrong. That's always a hard decision. There's a lot of smart people in the world. That's the culture. You have to back it up with facts and with data but the culture is, 'It's OK to be different from the rest of the world—but you've got to be right.'" RIM also sponsors gatherings for developers to hear their ideas and discuss the kind of applications that users needed. For example, a stockbroker might want a software application that allows investors to make wireless trades. Once such an application existed, he'd buy BlackBerry devices by the dozen and give them to his most active clients. In order to attract developers, as well as customers, to the first Wireless Enterprise Symposium hosted by RIM in Atlanta in 2002, RIM hired Jack Welch as a keynote speaker. His best-selling book, *Jack: Straight from the Gut*, had been published the previous fall. Welch commanded a six-figure fee, but his presence gave the inaugural gathering a cachet it wouldn't otherwise have enjoyed. Developers could return home and dine out for days on their "encounter" with Welch, who was widely regarded as the nation's best business strategist.

The first BlackBerry models with a colour screen, the 7200 series, were launched in 2003 and were followed by the 7100, the first BlackBerry that actually looked like a traditional cell phone with the "candy bar" shape. The 7100 also came with something new, a twenty-key keyboard that had two letters per key and used RIM's special software called SureType to guess what word the user wanted by referring to a 35,000-word database that grew in a user-customized fashion as new words were typed in. "Mike was challenging them to make the device skinnier. Somebody had the inspiration to say, 'Can we fit two letters on one key?'" RIM already had technology used for Asian-language keyboards where the situation was similar because a user was presented with a list of choices. "Then the creative juices started flowing. In this case, maybe we can create a better guess about what the user is trying to say. You can add a dictionary of words, go through the user's address book, and know the names," said David Yach.

New applications and technical innovations weren't the only avenues to increased sales. Price point mattered, too. In 2003, the new 6210 came with a redesigned circuit board and fewer sub-assemblies, thereby reducing RIM's production costs by as much as 40 per cent. As a result, carriers could use subsidies to cut retail prices, as long as customers signed up for a two- or three-year data plan.

The next big leap came in October 2004 with the 7290, the first BlackBerry to have quad bands so the same device worked in both North America and Europe. When Black-Berry was introduced in Spain in 2004, the country saw a faster rate of sales growth than any other European nation at the time. The November 11, 2004, issue of business magazine *Actualidad Economica* featured a cover story titled "*Locos por la BlackBerry*" and included photographs of senior managers using the handheld who, apparently, were suffering from the same CrackBerry disease as their New World counterparts, an "*adicción entre los ejecutivos.*"

The BlackBerry 8700, introduced in October 2005 after three years in development, came with a new Intel processor that sped up browsing, offered more memory, had a better phone, and offered a backlit screen and illuminated keys that dimmed in good light to extend battery life. "The 8700 was the riskiest, hardest project we had ever undertaken," said Lazaridis. "We wrote brand-new software, it was a brand-new chip—a Hermon processor from Intel, a brand-new RF [radio frequency] from RFMD, a brand-new power management chip that we designed, brand-new plastics, brand-new bright colour landscape display, brand-new radio stack from the ground up, brand-new EDGE RF base band and power amp, and it was the first time we'd put the antenna at the bottom. All to be delivered and certified by a certain date in the fall. We missed that original internal target date by only one month. That's pretty good in my book. The 8700 went on to be one of the most successful products we ever launched. That code, processor, and power chip live on today."

A review by Stephen H. Wildstrom in *Business Week* called the 8700 "a distinct improvement over previous models. The first thing you notice is that it's almost handsome compared with the utilitarian homeliness of the 'BlueBerry' 7290 it replaces," he wrote on November 10, 2005. "The silver-and-black case is a critical quarter-inch or so narrower, so you can operate it with one hand. Like the smaller 7100 series introduced last fall, the 8700 is far more phone-like than previous BlackBerrys, with proper red and green Send and End buttons and a phone-style 10-key dial pad in the keyboard."

When RIM celebrated its twentieth anniversary in April 2004, Lazaridis gave an interview in which he admitted that if he'd known all the ups and downs in the road ahead, he might not have set out on the journey. "But you are very young, very confident," he told Ron Deruyter, of the Kitchener-Waterloo *Record.* "Luckily, you are kind of blind to the enormity of what you are setting out to do."[3] The celebratory party for six thousand employees, investment bankers, community leaders, and students at the Kitchener Memorial Auditorium featured two groups— Barenaked Ladies and Aerosmith. "If we don't enjoy and celebrate our twentieth anniversary, what are we doing?" Lazaridis told the crowd before the concert began. "We should all enjoy this. We worked hard. This is our night."

Aerosmith lead singer Steve Tyler wore his BlackBerry on his belt throughout the show. "This is going to be the freakiest

---

[3] *Record,* March 6, 2004, p. F1.

crowd of all," he screamed at one point. "Let the freak out. Let it out." One of the songs Barenaked Ladies sang was "What a Good Boy." Everyone fell silent as the group launched into the sweet lyrics and soft melody. "*When I was born, they looked at me and said, what a good boy, what a smart boy, what a strong boy*," go the opening lines in the ballad that could have been written about Lazaridis himself as a child. Almost as one, the audience reached for their backlit BlackBerry devices and held them aloft. Mark Guibert described it as one of those surreal moments when the massive growth of the company became obvious—suddenly the company was big enough to fill a stadium with employees, spouses, and friends to watch two famous bands. "By 2004, the scale of everything we were doing was getting very big and so throwing a twentieth-anniversary celebration with Aerosmith and Bare Naked Ladies was actually right in line with the success and momentum and ambition of the company," said Guibert. "But it was still a bit of a shock and an eye-opener, in terms of understanding just how large we had become, when I looked up and around and saw this dark stadium filled with thousands of glowing BlackBerry screens, all swaying back and forth to the music."

CHAPTER FIFTEEN

CHAPTER FIFTEEN

A PEARL OF GREAT PRICE

IT IS JUNE 2006 AS MIKE LAZARIDIS takes the stage in the Enterprise Theatre in RIM 4, one of the two dozen buildings on the corporate campus in Waterloo. He greets the one hundred handpicked attendees at this weekly Vision Meeting, dims the lights, and rolls a four-minute video on the giant screen behind him. The first visual is a familiar face, the original BlackBerry with its rectangular green screen, followed by a swooshing array of successors, all accompanied by a background sound that's like an accelerating rocket heading for outer space. "The success of BlackBerry has been due to constant innovation in technology and leadership," intones the narrator while the newest model, not yet publicly announced, turns slowly through 360 degrees on the screen, like a runway model showing off a designer's latest look in Milan. "The innovative thinking behind the BlackBerry 8100 has continued this tradition and has resulted in the creation of the smallest and lightest smartphone in the market. To reflect this major step forward, we are evolving our approach to naming this product. Although this product has a model number, it has also been given a name that will live under the BlackBerry brand."

A few people move uneasily in their padded seats. A new name? "What's in a product name? A lot. Mark Twain once said, 'The difference between the right word and almost the right word is the difference between lightning and a lightning bug.'" To bolster the quote, Twain's words appear on the screen. There's even a pregnant pause between "lightning" and "a lightning bug," as if to underscore the difference or to imitate the time of ellipsis between a lightning strike and the roll of thunder that follows.

The soundtrack turns into an insistent drumbeat. "Naming a product is not a simple or easy task. Good names are distinctive, memorable, and flexible and a great name goes beyond describing features and benefits. Great names are like empty vessels that you can fill with meaning, personality, and powerful ideas. Great names can tell stories in less than a second."

Less than a second: the time it takes to send an email on its way. "BlackBerry is a perfect example of a great name. While at first encounter in 1999, it might have sounded odd in a market crowded with PageWriters, AccessLinks, and SkyWriters, BlackBerry was distinctive, memorable, and a perfect empty vessel for us to fill with meaning," says the narrator while newspaper articles about the launch appear, only to be swept away by unseen hands.

The words are now tumbling from the speakers, faster and faster, as the pace quickens. "The name for the 8100 had to help tell the story of a breakthrough product and convey the following personality and meaning: premium value, high-quality design, small, light, and sleek. The name also had to convey simplicity and be approachable without diminishing any of the status and professionalism already existing in the BlackBerry brand." Happy users are shown in various settings with keywords from the voice-over flashing onscreen to punctuate every major point.

"Our inspiration for the name came from the device itself. The 8100 will be the first BlackBerry to have an elegantly designed, backlit, white trackball placed in the centre of the device. This pearl-shaped trackball creates a new and innovative way to navigate on BlackBerry, and becomes the focal point for the device's premium industrial design," says the announcer while the handset fades into nothingness, leaving behind only the trackball like the Cheshire cat's smile in *Alice in Wonderland*.

There's a theatrical pause, then the announcement: "Introducing the BlackBerry Pearl." With that, the new name and the new handset appear together for the first time. "Why is BlackBerry Pearl a great name? Pearls evoke positive and appropriate images for the 8100. Pearls are valuable, stylish, and smooth." Not only is Pearl easy on the eyes, it trips off the tongue, too. "Linguistically, Pearl fits well with the name BlackBerry. It has five letters, like Black and Berry, so it creates a rhythm and is easy to say with BlackBerry. It sounds friendly, pleasing, and approachable. BlackBerry and Pearl are both natural and the words fit smoothly together. Like BlackBerry, Pearl is unique in the category and highly defendable, a name that competitors can't credibly copy or imitate. Pearls are small, smart, and stylish and so . . . is the BlackBerry Pearl." The final thirty seconds show variations of the handset and the name together, all leading to a concluding musical flourish while a female voice lovingly whispers, "BlackBerry Pearl," in everyone's ears.

When the screen goes blank, appreciative applause bursts from the audience. Although most attendees have worked on various aspects of the device during the last two years, this is the first time any of them have heard the name. They like it.

Equally important, they like being on the inside, knowing about "Pearl" before the general public, who are blissfully unaware of this latest iteration of the BlackBerry to be launched in three months' time.

Through the early days of RIM and well into the 1990s, Lazaridis often worked long into the night with engineers and developers. Today, his direct contact with the majority of employees is reduced, but Lazaridis tries to hold a vision meeting or other project meetings with different groups every week. This particular gathering began with the Pearl-naming video. Other sessions might kick off with current industry news or fun footage from a trade show such as the 2007 CTIA event when two former presidents, George H. W. Bush and Bill Clinton, showed up together at the Research In Motion booth and met the BlackBerry mascot.

Next, Lazaridis might demonstrate a prototype, pass along feedback from a major client, or reveal a recent idea, but his intention is always the same: inform managers and engineers about strategy, keep them jazzed up about what RIM is doing, and tell them how their individual contributions are helping the company. "The most important lesson in a vision meeting is that everyone is focused on the priorities. If you're not careful in an organization that grows, and you add layers of management, people can become lost because they aren't being exposed to other pieces of the organization and the overall business strategy," said Lazaridis.

In such circumstances, decisions can begin to look arbitrary. "It's very important to have enough of the company together to say, 'Look, you may think this is arbitrary, but let me show you the competitive and regulatory landscape, how we're valued as a company from a shareholder base, how reviewers, analysts, and competitors see us, what our strengths and weaknesses are, what the customers and carriers are thinking,'" he said. "If they don't see the point of all this, then they say, 'Well, this is fine, but we're just a for-hire shop because we're beholden to all these masters.' When you show them the complex integration of the landscape, the market, the regulators, it becomes, 'OK, I get it now.'"

Since the hour-long vision meetings began around 2001, it is usually standing room only. Given the size of the company today, the sessions are now by invitation only. No guests are allowed, no consultants or contract employees are admitted, not even a major supplier or carrier partner. "What's great about the vision meetings is I can simply be myself. I don't prepare in depth. I have a few slides that give me an idea, most of them written early in the morning when I come in before the meeting so I'm completely up to date," said Lazaridis. "The whole point is to fit through that funny-looking keyhole to the other side which is success. How do you get through that keyhole? You've got to contort a little bit to get through the keyhole and get on to success but you've got to show them how and why."

Both Lazaridis and Balsillie like to remain in touch with as many people as they possibly can in a firm that now has more than twelve thousand employees. "I used to walk around a lot, but with over twenty buildings here, and a bunch of other places around the world, I can't do it as much any more," said Balsillie. "It's amazing what you can do in a five-minute conversation rather than wait for people to come up to your office." Balsillie maintains that connectivity in part by chairing a Monday-morning meeting each week that begins at 8 a.m. sharp and usually ends at 9:30 a.m. The meeting includes a broad range of people from various sales and marketing groups. Local people join the meeting in person while others from around the world participate via conference call. There are individual reports from specific geographic areas and everyone is eligible to provide an update on what's been going on in their own spheres. "I write down what everybody says. It keeps me close to what's going on," said Balsillie.

Three years before Pearl had a name, the quest for RIM's first handset specifically aimed at consumers, not the business/enterprise market, began when Lazaridis told his engineers to build the smallest and lightest full-featured BlackBerry possible while maintaining the overall user experience that people had come to love about BlackBerry.

"What was really interesting was that every model they showed me was smaller than the previous one," said Lazaridis. "The production model was actually smaller, lighter, and better looking than the mock-ups. That doesn't happen very often. Usually when you go from concept car to production, they hardly resemble each other. They add another thousand pounds, they get bigger, have rubber bumpers on them, and it doesn't look anything like the designer car you saw at the trade show. This one actually looked better than the models."

With the lauch of the Pearl, BlackBerry's traditional trackwheel gave way to a centrally located trackball that allowed easy onscreen negotiation in all directions. Placed in the middle of the handset, the trackball also addressed complaints by left-handed subscribers about the awkward placement of the trackwheel on the right-hand side of all previous models. "I let decisions be made by others as much as I can, but there are certain decisions that I am very selfish about because they're 'bet the farm' decisions. The trackball was one of those decisions. As soon as I played with the trackball, I said, 'We're doing it.' Those are the kinds of decisions that I reserve the right to make. Some people loved it, some people thought it was the biggest mistake of our careers. Based on the results of our sales, it wasn't the majority who were against—but they were the most vocal."

For Lazaridis, there's no choice but change. "One of the best ways to stay relevant is to keep innovating. We've always had this saying that Intel inspired in us early on: 'Eat your own lunch at breakfast because you don't want someone else to eat it for you.' The idea is to improve all the things you hold sacred before someone else does. The laws of physics means there are certain things you can't improve and you use those as governors as to where not to waste time." Lazaridis also decided that he wanted the trackball to light up. The group argued with him, saying that the energy required would diminish battery life and the extra engineering involved would delay the certification process. "I just put my foot down and said, 'This is what we're going to do.' I rarely pull rank; that was one of the times I pulled rank. I wanted to get out first with that trademarked, centred, lit-up trackball. It connects the family of products so it's easily identified as a BlackBerry. It became iconic."

Lighting the trackball also led to the name. Lazaridis sat one evening in his darkened home theatre holding a prototype of the new handset while viewing a long, unfiltered list of potential names provided by RIM's marketing VPs. Suddenly, there was a moment reminiscent of 1984 when he saw the football player pirouetting on TV and came up with the company name. "I had just seen a commercial where a model was wearing pearl earrings. When I saw the handset light up in my hand for the first time, I said, 'Wow, that's a pearl.' So I just put Pearl on the list and forwarded it. The next day, we were all going 'Pearl, that's the name.' I'm not sure it was clear to everybody that I actually added the name the prior night."

First launched by T-Mobile in September 2006, Pearl not only offered email and a phone but also a digital camera, MP3 player, and memory slot. By Christmas, Pearl had become RIM's best-ever launch and was available through thirty-six carriers in twenty-two countries, including the United States, Canada, U.K., Austria, France, Spain, Italy, Germany, India, Hong Kong, Singapore, and Chile. At 4.2 by 2.0 by 0.6 inches and weighing only 3.2 ounces, "People were really shocked that we could make it this small," said Dennis Kavelman. "It's so small I forget which suit pocket it's in sometimes."

Praise was immediate. "There's a new sweet-spot champion, a do-everything phone that comes closer to the bull's-eye than anything before it: BlackBerry Pearl," wrote David Pogue in the *New York Times*.[1] "Truth be told, I wasn't expecting such a nice phone. It's nothing short of truly surprising. Black, thin, chromium-plated sides, very classy ... it's a BlackBerry in an evening gown," said Andre Boily in the *Ottawa Sun*. "It appears to have been designed not only for the professional woman or the businessman, but also for anyone who enjoys the finer things in life. It makes just about any other phone on the market appear old in comparison."[2] In the months that followed, other versions of Pearl were made available encased in red and

---

[1] *New York Times*, September 7, 2006.
[2] *Ottawa Sun*, November 10, 2006.

white. By June 2007, according to analysts' estimates, RIM had sold one million Pearls.

Marketing magazine named Research In Motion the 2006 Marketer of the Year and acknowledged the multi-million-dollar BlackBerry Pearl advertising campaign. The Pearl launch was supported by a range of activities, including point-of-sale items, electronic billboards in Times Square, co-op ads with the carriers, full-page newspaper ads, and London launch parties with starlets Tara Palmer, Sadie Frost, and Kelly Osborne. The ads and the blackberrypearl.com website featured five high-profile personalities demonstrating how the device helped them in their daily lives. They included *Generation X* author Douglas Coupland; Martin Eberhard, CEO of electric-car maker Tesla Motors; world champion snowboarder Gretchen Bleiler; actress Mariska Hargitay, who plays Detective Olivia Benson on *Law & Order: Special Victims Unit* and who founded the Joyful Heart Foundation for survivors of sexual assault, domestic violence, and child abuse; and Nina Garcia, fashion editor of *Elle* magazine.

In 2007, the campaign expanded to include the BlackBerry Mascot, a costumed character modeled after the smartphone, who had his own web page on MySpace, complete with videos, a naming contest, and comments from friends who've signed on to the social networking site. "We sent a crew out on the streets of New York with our BlackBerry Mascot and whenever they saw someone using their BlackBerry they'd ask them to tell us on camera why they love their BlackBerry," said Lazaridis. "It was pouring cats and dogs that day. It was unbelievable; it was flooding in the streets. Eighty people sat there under umbrellas telling why they loved their BlackBerrys. Some of them became YouTube ads, others went on our website. The whole production didn't cost very much and yet it had such an effect. Actually, everything we did that year seemed to have a big effect. In spring 2008, we were ranked with the highest-growing brand value. We grew nearly 400 per cent, three times faster than the second fastest-growing brand."

Pearl was soon followed by Curve, with its full QWERTY keyboard rather than Pearl's SureType, as well as a two-megapixel camera and a multimedia player. Next came the first dual-mode BlackBerry, the 8820, which provides both voice and data over either cellular or Wi-Fi networks in a handset with a world phone and built-in GPS. In 2008, three new BlackBerry models were released: Bold for high-speed 3G wireless networks; the Pearl Flip; and Storm, RIM's first touch-screen smartphone, one that mimics the feel of a QWERTY keyboard. In April 2009, the company launched BlackBerry App World, an online store with hundreds of free and for-purchase downloadable applications invented by developers who will receive 80 per cent of any revenue generated. In addition, a wide variety of new applications, such as Facebook, the video game Guitar Hero III, and music services such as Slacker, Pandora, Shazam, and XM Radio were made available on BlackBerry. "RIM's devices are very focused on what they do. They've been building from the ground up versus the other way around," said analyst Deepak Chopra. "They started from an environment where they didn't have much wireless speed or processing power, so they built what they needed very efficiently on platforms that didn't have a lot of power. As the power has increased, they've increased the amount of applications but they've been able to control the costs. The ability for someone who's not a techie to learn the device and to operate it is remarkably quick."

Since 2007, RIM has steadily increased its marketing efforts, both directly and in cooperation with its carrier and distribution partners. RIM's "Ask Someone Why They Love Their BlackBerry" campaign profiled many different types of interesting and successful BlackBerry customers who explained the reasons for their passion for BlackBerry. The subsequent "Life On BlackBerry" campaign included high-energy television commercials that showed fun scenes of people and activities all blending together and morphing into the shape of a Black-Berry smartphone. Another one of RIM's follow-on marketing campaigns was built around RIM's sponsorship of U2's global tour that opened in Barcelona in June 2009 and featured the band performing in a commercial that aired on the big screens in movie theatres, as well as on television and online. At the two-hour U2 concert in Toronto in September, where 25,000 of the 62,000 fans in attendance—the largest crowd ever at the Rogers Centre—were employees and guests of RIM, Bono made a point of thanking the company.

The two dozen songs performed by Bono and the group that's been popular for more than two decades ranged from "Sunday Bloody Sunday" to "Breathe," from U2's latest album, *No Line in the Horizon*. Above the stadium circled an airplane towing the slogan for RIM's current TV ad campaign, "Black-Berry loves U2." In conjunction with the concert, RIM released its new U2 Mobile Album. Developed in collaboration with the band, the app delivers music, visuals, and evolving interactive content.

RIM is expected to achieve approximately $15 billion in revenues in fiscal 2010, ending February 28, 2010. RIM's revenue of $3.9 billion for the three months ending November 28, 2009, comes 82 per cent from device sales, 14 per cent for service, and 4 per cent for software and other revenue. In RIM's first thirteen years as a public company, it grew its revenue by over 170,000 per cent and is the only company to have been included on the Deloitte Canada Fast 50 list every year since the award was created in 1998.

RIM keeps manufacturing costs down by leveraging device platforms across multiple models that are differentiated with various casings, features, and software, as well as support for different carriers.

RIM Manufacturing began production in early 1997 on just a single production line with fifty employees. Since that time, RIM has cost-effectively scaled its flexible manufacturing and distribution capacity globally with industry-leading contract electronic manufacturing partners while it continues to operate a manufacturing facility strategically co-located with Design and Corporate operations in Waterloo. The Waterloo plant was doubled in size in 2006 to 250,000 square feet, where employees work around the clock seven days a week on state of the art production lines. On a typical day, the production lines in Waterloo produce a variety of BlackBerry smartphone products. "Now we have quite a bit of flexibility in the event a line goes down, or part of a factory burns; you can pick up the slack in two other factories. The cost factor is not the key for us. Primarily we outsource for capacity reasons. Our factory, which we just finished expanding, is nearly all full," said Rick Landry, vice-president, manufacturing.

In addition to regular production runs, the Waterloo plant is used for prototype development and engineering work. "We debug the product, go through the early development and ramp phases of the product. We stabilize the product, get the yields up to the point where we are comfortable moving it to the outsourced partner so that they can be successful. If you have a problem in a plant in another country, it takes time. You have to put engineers on a plane or they ship product back to us to analyze. Here, it takes minutes or hours. Mike likes to call it the new product introduction centre, our lab," said Landry.

Every handheld contains hundreds of components from suppliers based all over the world. Manufacturing involves the use of scores of automated "pick-and-place" robotic machines each worth $750,000 to perform the initial assembly, but each and every device is completed by hand in a series of separate steps by individual employees who also calibrate and test the final product. Total time taken to create a BlackBerry smartphone from scratch and have it packed ready for shipping is two hours.

Debate about making Pearl, the first BlackBerry aimed at consumers, continued for months before launch. "These things evolve within a company. Not everyone gets it from day one," said Larry Conlee. "When Mike decided to build the 957 versus the 950, there was a whole bunch of RIM people who wondered, 'Why would we ever want to do that? Why would we want to put a big screen on it?' When we did the 7210, that was the first time we used colour screens. Again came the question: 'Why would we do that? People are reading email, it doesn't need to be in colour.' You always have these internal battles."

Pearl also required a different approach to sales. In the case of corporate buyers, the decision process is slow. Months of committee meetings and financial studies take place before a corporation commits to buying a new model for hundreds of employees. But Pearl was aimed at individuals and was to be sold at retail outlets, in addition to being sold through field staff, so

RIM had to estimate sales levels and be ready to supply devices in sufficient numbers to meet immediate demand—whatever that demand was. "We had to convince the carriers that this was a game-changer for us. This is not your old RIM, this is RIM bringing to the party a new product for a new market segment," said Conlee. "One of the things I did differently was to put together a production ramp plan that was steeper than anything we had ever tried to do. We said this is going to be different; this is going to be a big paradigm for us."

RIM also decided to rely on outsourcing more than in the past. The first phrase of production—where a few hundred units are produced, yield is poor, and problems are fixed—was begun simultaneously in early August 2006 in both Waterloo and at the Elcoteq facility in Monterrey, Mexico. By the time of the launch six weeks later, both plants were running well, so RIM felt comfortable halting production in Waterloo and relying totally on Mexican production. "Pearl by far exceeded any previous product in terms of how quickly we ramped the product, how much product we produced over a relatively short period of time, and also ramping it in more than one site," Landry said. "We ramped the Monterrey facility within two weeks of starting our ramp here, which posed a number of challenges for us. We basically had to allow our partner in to see all the warts in the early stages of the product ramp phase."

Outsourcing partners like Elcoteq can also have production contracts with other major manufacturers, such as Nokia, so walls are erected in the factory to prevent competitors from seeing each other's products in the final phases of development. "We've gotten better at products that are easy to build. We're using many of the same outsourcing partners that the large vendors are. All of that excess volume and capacity is not going to come from RIM's own facilities, it will come from our outsourcing partners," said Dennis Kavelman. "Our facility in Waterloo is going to become more and more a prototyping and developing facility. We're not bringing it down at all, it has a five million unit a year capacity. Those volumes are going to be very useful and critical in launching new products. As volumes increase, we're going to use our partners more."

Quality control keeps repair and return costs to a minimum. A subscriber usually receives a new handheld from the carrier in exchange for a broken device that is then sent to RIM for repair. Damage by dropping is the most common problem. Water issues are a close second. Matters are sometimes made worse when subscribers make the mistake of drying a soggy device in the microwave. Moving parts can also stop moving and dogs have been known to chew on devices. "Warranty returns are materially lower than other smartphone-type devices, so RIM has a satisfied customer base," said analyst Chopra. "How often is a BlackBerry touched during the day? If there was a way to plot usage time versus returns, I would think BlackBerry would be remarkably low considering how much people use it."

RIM's revenue does not just depend on adding new subscribers; current subscribers also upgrade to newer models. In fiscal 2009, for example, the number of net new subscribers grew by 11 million, but RIM shipped over 26 million devices. A majority of the additional 15 million units were sold to current subscribers upgrading to a new device, with much of the rest going into carrier inventory as RIM's distribution continues to expand. A portion of RIM's organizational growth has also come through acquisition. In March 2006, RIM acquired Ascendent Systems Inc., of San Jose, California. With Ascendent's software, when a BlackBerry subscriber's office phone rings, so does the

BlackBerry. Adding Ascendent meant BlackBerry users could have one phone number for both mobile and office calls.

Later that same year, RIM acquired two other companies: SlipStream Data Inc., of Waterloo, for its data compression technology, and Epoch Integration of Toronto, makers of software that helps corporate clients such as Time Warner, Interpol, and the U.S. Army monitor their networks. In a bid to expand usage among small- and medium-sized businesses, RIM also began giving away software to companies with fewer than fifteen employees in order to reach smaller firms that were likely to grow larger and buy more BlackBerry smartphones. In 2009, RIM paid C$130 million to acquire Certicom Corp., of Mississauga, Ontario, in order to perpetuate the alliance that RIM previously had with the data encryption specialist.

Since RIM opened BlackBerry to developers after moving to Java on the 5800, it has attracted over 175,000 developers to help enable the next wave of mobile applications. One of the more unusual software programs comes from the Diabetes Detection Institute and allows physicians to diagnose levels of diabetes by measuring the intensity of a vibrating BlackBerry placed on the arm or leg of a patient. Another application, called Naggie, reminds a BlackBerry owner to pick up milk on the way home. The settings can tap into the GPS locators and be so specific that a reminder goes off when you pass a neighbourhood convenience store. "Push email paved the way for the early success of this market, but a broad range of mobile applications will drive the next phase," said Lazaridis. RIM doesn't typically broadcast its future direction and strategies, so it's difficult for an outsider to know what else RIM has planned. "Even if you watch us closely," said Balsillie, "you'll only know 20 per cent of what we're doing."

CHAPTER SIXTEEN

THE FUTURE UNFOLDS

EVEN THOUGH MIKE LAZARIDIS GREW UP wanting to travel into space or make something that would go into space, in 1989 he turned down an opportunity to participate in Canadarm2, Canada's contribution to the International Space Station, because timelines were too long and working in the wireless world seemed more compelling. He was right to wait for his moment. In recent years, NASA ordered one thousand BlackBerry devices that the agency immediately put to use when a hurricane swept through Florida. "The BlackBerrys helped them manage everything, get through the hurricane, keep in touch with everybody," said Lazaridis, who later met with Sean O'Keefe, NASA administrator from 2001 to 2005.

O'Keefe told Lazaridis that he continued to rely on his BlackBerry. As he was driven home from work at the end of each day he was able to deal with emails and clear his evening for family time. "One day, there was a NASA astronaut asking all these questions. At first, Sean didn't quite grasp what was going on, but he kept answering the questions. The questions were: How is the shuttle investigation going, what have they found, when will it be put back into service? There was a sense of urgency," said Lazaridis.

O'Keefe became curious about the identity of his correspondent, looked him up on the internal system, and discovered that he was aboard the space station. Lazaridis added, "He's up there wondering when he's coming down. Here's this astronaut on the space station communicating to NASA and the conversation is being turned around to O'Keefe on a BlackBerry. So, I guess you could still say RIM contributed to the International Space Station in the end."

BlackBerry has become so integral to society that it has even been spoofed by Rick Mercer, the Canadian comedian who has his own CBC-TV show, *Rick Mercer Report*. Mercer has made a career out of teasing politicians, noting ironies in the news, and seeing humour in everyday events. In 2005, he created a short video skit about the addictive nature of Black-Berry that opens with Mercer entering a crowded office lobby while holding a BlackBerry in both hands. As he stares at the screen, thumbing a message, the voice-over says: "BlackBerry, from RIM Systems: text, web, email, power in the palm of your hand for the professional on the go." Because this professional is oblivious to his surroundings, he bumps into a painter's scaffold and falls to the floor as paint cans tumble on top of him.

In the next scene, Mercer has resumed his previous quick step, still working the handheld, but wears a helmet complete with chinstrap. As he strides along, his helmet strikes a succession of hanging flowerpots without causing him any harm. Next, Mercer emerges naked from the shower, eyes still glued to the screen, because the helmet has an antenna that boosts reception for those out-of-the-way locations. Clothed again and back in the lobby, he meets another BlackBerry user heading toward him.

The two execute a side-to-side dance, but pass safely and resume their forward progress because the email device has a camera that "broadcasts a picture of what's in front of you to your BlackBerry so you can always be looking at your BlackBerry."

In the final scene, Mercer is shown flying the optional red safety flag on his helmet that warns he's coming so he's able to successfully negotiate the crowded lobby while others veer wildly to avoid him. Posted on YouTube, the video has been viewed over 100,000 times.

Mercer's spoof is not the only video about BlackBerry to achieve popular fame. When BlackBerry Pearl was released, David Pogue, technology writer for the *New York Times*, created one of his weekly web videos that cast him as a chef concocting a BlackBerry from odds and ends in a juice blender. The stock-market blog Wallstrip offers an audition by a dead ringer for CNBC shoutmeister Jim Cramer nattering about RIM while using various props ranging from a Roman helmet to a ventriloquist's dummy.

There's even been a book in which BlackBerry plays a central role. *Financial Times* columnist Lucy Kellaway wrote *Who Moved My BlackBerry?*, a novel that was ostensibly by Martin Lukes, director of Special Projects at a-b glöbâl (UK), a character invented by Kellaway as a vehicle in her column for social satire on modern-day business. The book consists of a year-long series of email messages. The plot hinges on Lukes losing his BlackBerry, thereby revealing to his wife that he's having an affair with his personal assistant. *The BlackBerry Diaries* by Kathy Buckworth pokes fun at both the smartphone and modern motherhood.

BlackBerry has become so ubiquitous that it appears daily in newspaper stories, an accomplishment achieved by relatively few other consumer items. As with any success story, Black-Berry has attracted its share of detractors. "Without a doubt, the biggest thing to happen to the white-collar working world is the BlackBerry," said Marc Saltzman, author of *White Collar Slacker's Handbook*. "It's not easy being a white-collar worker today. Not only are you expected to work longer hours (nights, weekends, holidays, you name it), but thanks to mobile inventions such as cell phones, PDAs, BlackBerrys, and GPS devices, your boss can track you down wherever you may be. Isn't it ironic that 'wireless' devices are tethering us to the office even more so than before these inventions debuted?"

To fight back, Saltzman offers step-by-step instructions about removing the automatic signature at the bottom of all BlackBerry emails, the one that reads, "Sent from my Black-Berry Wireless Handheld," so the boss will think you're in the office when you're not. He also advises how to play background sound effects such as traffic noise while you're on the phone in order to disguise the fact that you're on a golf course filled with birdsong. There's even a program from ToySoft that provides a fake phone call at the discreet push of a button when you want to flee a meeting.

The device has become such an integral part of daily life that BlackBerry has been regularly seen over the years—without any payment for product placement—on such highly rated TV shows as *CSI: Miami, Law & Order, The West Wing, Sex and the City, Criminal Minds, Grey's Anatomy, 24,* and *Entourage.* Bloggers gleefully post paparazzi photos of celebrities using Black-Berry smartphones including Jessica Simpson, Sean "P. Diddy" Combs, Hugh Jackman, Sandra Bullock, Kate Hudson, Brad Pitt, David Beckham, Jennifer Aniston, Jay-Z, and Halle Berry, to name a few. There is even a dedicated celebrity-sighting website at www.celebrityblackberrysightings.com.

When Britney Spears told rapper Kevin Federline she wanted a divorce, her chosen instrument for delivering the blow was BlackBerry. A video crew that happened to be with K-Fed gathering material for Much Music's *Exposed* series captured an hour's worth of end-of-marriage messaging between a long-faced Federline and his wife of two years.

Praise for the BlackBerry has come from many quarters. "There is probably no more powerful a symbol of the change that wireless technology is bringing to daily life than the BlackBerry," said *Newsweek* in its April 4, 2008, issue. Ten years ago, "Only the obsessively connected wore pagers. To send the wearer a message, you called a living, breathing telephone operator who would type your words and send them along, making the device chirp like an agitated parakeet. The idea of a constant connection to the same email messages that resided on your office desktop PC was a foreign one. A decade later, living without that connection is almost unthinkable. For much of that, you can thank Mike Lazaridis, co-chief executive officer and founder of RIM."

Among the high-profile users is President Barack Obama who worked hard to keep his BlackBerry once he was elected to office. "One of the things that I'm going to have to work through is how to break through the isolation, the bubble that exists around the president," he said in an interview with ABC's Barbara Walters in November 2008. "I'm in the process of negotiating with the Secret Service, with lawyers, with White House staff ... to figure out how I can get information from outside the ten or twelve people who surround my office in the White House. Because, one of the worst things I think that could happen to a president is losing touch with what people are going through day to day." Said Lazaridis: "It shows you how important the BlackBerry is to people that use it!"[1]

In January 2009, Obama told CNBC, "I'm still clinging to my BlackBerry. They're going to pry it out of my hands." In the end, Obama was allowed to keep his BlackBerry.

Of all the erroneous allegations made about RIM over the years, the most persistent has been that some competitor is developing a killer device that will either end RIM's dominance or dispatch the company into oblivion. Analyst Mike Urlocker once drew up a list of all the killer products that had been billed by somebody as "BlackBerry killers." They included Palm 7, Qualcomm PDQ, Motorola PageWriter, Motorola T900, 3G, MSFT Exchange Server 2003, Compaq Ipaq, Ogo, Sidekick, Nokia E62, Sendo, Microsoft Stinger, and Pocket PC. To that list could be added other, more recent, mainstream candidates such as Palm Pre and Apple's iPhone. "I couldn't name another company that has been so consistently underestimated, even to this day," said Urlocker, a technology analyst with GMP Securities. "They don't follow a trend, they create trends. How could some company in Waterloo get that right? The reason is that Lazaridis stuck to fundamental principles of physics and engineering. He understood the limitations that a network, or a battery, or a colour screen imposed on devices."

According to Mark Guibert, there were many more products described as "BlackBerry killers" that didn't make Urlocker's list, but the constant barrage of hype over the years didn't distract the company. "When you're leading the market," said

---

[1] CBR Mobility, November 28, 2008.

Guibert, "other companies are going to compare themselves to you in an attempt to get a foothold and, particularly in the earlier years when RIM was smaller, lots of people assumed that the bigger, better-known companies would knock us out. But Mike and Jim did a brilliant job of instilling focus, diligence, and confidence in the culture of the organization. As a result, there has always been enough conviction in the company to inoculate it from the 'killer' hype."

Paradigm's Barry Richards experienced the same incredulity when he worked for CIBC Oppenheimer in San Francisco in 2003–04. "In California, it was heresy to think that RIM could compete with Palm. There was a lot of skepticism. We've had this wave every year or two about RIM's ability to compete despite having delivered all that they've delivered. I associate RIM with the New York Yankees. If you're from New York, you love them. If you're not, you hate them, even if you really don't know why, because they're so successful. Everyone seems to have an opinion, but not too many people are well informed. They might not know the history, they might never have looked at an income statement, but they have a thing about it."

Andy Seybold used to receive a call about RIM every month from someone on Wall Street who asked: "When are they going to fall? When is Microsoft going to finally catch up to them and be the killer?" According to Seybold, "The answer is: It's not going to happen. The wireless industry is not about a single operating system and a single device and a single set of applications, it's about people using cell phones that all have different requirements and needs and want different kinds of devices for different functionality. As long as we have that kind of market, RIM isn't going to go away."

Indeed, the smartphone market opportunity is still largely untapped. In 2009, RIM had 51 per cent of the North American smartphone market compared with 30 per cent for Apple and 4 percent for Nokia, according to Gartner Inc., a research firm based in Stamford, Connecticut.

RIM has succeeded not just because Mike Lazaridis and Jim Balsillie have technical and business skills and the capacity to innovate, but also because of the sheer force of their personalities. "Mike has an incredible ability to inspire and motivate. A lot of it comes from his clear focus and commitment to the future of the company. It also comes from the access that he has to the movers and shakers out there where he's meeting with prime ministers and heads of major corporations and thinking constantly about the next big opportunity in the marketplace," said Dale Brubacher-Cressman, who joined Research In Motion in 1988 as employee number five and retired in 2005, by which time the company had grown to five thousand employees.

RIM has grown so large that the annual Christmas party for Waterloo employees, formerly held at nearby hotels and the local Bingemans Conference Centre, had to be moved in 2006 to the RIM Park complex where the indoor facilities were big enough to hold the 3,500 employees, spouses, and partners who attended. In 2007 and beyond, the holiday celebrations had to be handled at departmental levels because the company had outgrown all the local banquet facilities with sufficient enclosed space.

The annual patent banquet has gone through similar growing pains. The event, held every fall in the ballroom of the Waterloo Inn, honours all RIM employees who were awarded patents that year. Individuals receive a plaque and have their photograph taken with Lazaridis. In the past, those employees who'd applied for patents but were still waiting approval (software applications can take up to six years) also attended. By 2006, the number of employees who had actually received patents had grown so large that applicants could not be included at the dinner.

Unlike many high-tech firms where senior managers come and go with unseemly haste, RIM's executive team has remained largely intact during the last ten years of fast-paced growth. Founder and co-CEO Mike Lazaridis, who launched the business in 1984, is still the visionary in charge, and Jim Balsillie, the co-CEO who arrived in 1992, continues to lead the business and strategy side. "If you were to liken it to military strategy, it's field level tactics that wins you a battle," said Dave Castell. "And it's picking the battles that you want to fight, and those you don't, that can win you the war in the end. That's what Jim is brilliant at. He knows what things are important and will fight for them. He'll be very focused on the practical elements of the deal."

That inner circle at RIM sets the tone for the organization, which remains relatively flat and flexible for a company of RIM's size. "I go back to my early days in cellular and the can-do attitude, the working hard, the passion to succeed, are all the same," said Larry Conlee, who came from Motorola in 2001 as the most recent senior recruit. "RIM has not developed the umbrella bureaucracy like Motorola. What we're trying to do from a management perspective is to try to keep that passion, that fire in the belly to win, to be successful, put your customer first, without letting the trappings of bureaucracy get in the way. That's the magic."

Vice-President of Organizational Development Elizabeth Roe Pfeifer has been involved in recruiting since she arrived in 1998. "When I was starting out we were all squeezed in one little building. Now I look out and see all the buildings and it's quite a feeling," she said. "RIM provided me an opportunity for my own personal development to grow to a point where not only do I have North American experience, I have global experience."

"Too many entrepreneurs focus on traditional sectors rather than knowledge-based ideas," said Lazaridis. "It's too easy to rely on your natural resources [in Canada] and not realize that people are natural resources, they're renewable and they are infinitely powerful. There are perfect examples where Canada has been a leader in a particular field and we're just going to have to learn what that recipe is and replicate it more. It's a mindset change, a cultural change. We've done it in the past," he said. "We can clearly do it again."

Even as they build RIM, Mike Lazaridis and Jim Balsillie continue to invest in the community, the country, and the global economy. In 2007, Balsillie donated C$33 million to create the Balsillie School of International Affairs on land beside the Centre for International Governance Innovation in Waterloo. The school will open in 2010. A second building, which will house other schools and programs, is planned for 2012. In addition to Balsillie's donation, Wilfrid Laurier University and the University of Waterloo contributed a combined C$50 million. Balsillie has also spearheaded the creation of the Canada-wide Canadian International Council (CIC). A partnership between CIGI and the Canadian Institute of International Affairs

(CIIA), the Canadian International Council will be housed at the University of Toronto. "The Americans have their powerful Council on Foreign Relations, which offers non-partisan analysis of international issues and integrates business leaders with the best researchers and public policy leaders. The British have long depended on the Royal Institute of International Affairs for the research that has assisted that nation to punch far above its weight. Similar institutions exist in Europe, Latin America, Asia, and in many developing countries. George Soros has been instrumental in the creation of the European Council on Foreign Relations. The CIC will be the Canadian player in this global network of foreign relations councils," Balsillie wrote in an op-ed article in the *National Post*.

The Mike and Ophelia Lazaridis Quantum-Nano Centre, built with C$50 million from the couple and C$50 million from the province of Ontario, will be home to the Institute of Quantum Computing and the Waterloo Institute for Technology. About two hundred researchers in both fields will work in the five-storey building scheduled to open in 2011 on the University of Waterloo campus. Neil Turok, formerly director of the Centre for Theoretical Cosmology at Cambridge and co-author of the popular science book *Endless Universe: Beyond the Big Bang*, joined Perimeter in 2008 after Howard Burton departed in 2007. Later in 2008, it was announced that Turok's former colleague Stephen Hawking had accepted a Distinguished Research Chair at PI, the first of many such postings. The total contribution to such institutions by Lazaridis, Balsillie, RIM colleagues, and governments at the local, provincial, and federal levels is C$700 million.

Beyond the money, the Waterloo region has become a cluster of excellence in institutions because of RIM's influence.

"We've been in the top ten in the Putnam—the annual MIT math exam—for ten years in a row and the computer science exam for the last five years," said Lazaridis. "Last year we were the only North American city to be in the top five. If you look at the other competitions we're involved in, the electric car, the solar car, we're getting higher and higher in all the ranks. The region has a great reputation for schools, including high schools. We've got a lot of advanced programs for advanced kids here. There is a real reputation for the advancement of mathematics, science, and engineering. If you look at the success of the universities and Conestoga College, there's a lot happening here. And it's not just RIM, but Open Text, Sybase, Google, and a lot of other companies here that are having a huge impact."

These institutions are only part of the legacy Lazaridis seeks to create. "If I can make engineering and science and research as important in every person's mind as I believe it really is, then I'll have achieved what I wanted to achieve. It's much harder than it looks because technology is moving so fast and because science becomes so advanced. We need to support these individual scientists and researchers who are doing this because they love what they do, because of the sheer joy of discovery. They aren't looking for big financial payoffs. To them the payoff is the intellectual excitement and reward of discovering something new in nature or solving a problem that will benefit mankind."

For Lazaridis, science and the support of scientific activity is an act of faith. "I don't fully understand what they're working on at Perimeter. I have a glimmer, I have an appreciation of the problem, or the complexity, or some of the work that's been done, but I don't fully understand what they're working on. I support them because I have faith in them, faith in what they stand for, faith in their education, their devotion. I have faith in them because I have seen the real results from the last one hundred years and what that's done to society. I know the benefits that will accrue to society should any of these individuals succeed in their quest."

Lazaridis goes on to say, "As a society the last thing we want to do is to play catch-up in that game because all the patents, all the discoveries, all the support industries, and the first movers happen around those discoveries and those universities and research centres. It's always been like that and that's what we're trying to create here. I have always believed that we are undervaluing the importance of science, scientists, researchers, and educators. If I can lift that so that it becomes one of the most important parts of the political debate, then mission accomplished."

According to Lazaridis, education for young people is the key. "I had the best education available to me in this country. I spent lots of quality personal time with some of the best educators that were available anywhere, I had access to the best tools and equipment from my high school through my university," said Lazaridis. "The big 'aha' moment occurred when I realized that I didn't need to work at Control Data to put all these skills to good use. I could work for others but I could still work on the projects I wanted to work on as opposed to the projects they wanted me to work on. The 'aha' moment for me was realizing those skills and all that investment in me had value and I could multiply that value."

By launching RIM, Lazaridis was able to turn his vision into reality. "It may seem naive now, but I had this real confidence in our abilities because we were solving very tough problems from an engineering point of view and we were armed with insight into the microprocessor world and how these circuits worked. There weren't a lot of people in this region, let alone Canada, that understood what we were working on, or what we had access to, or where we saw this technology going."

Despite his self-confidence and persistence, Lazaridis did not know where it was all going to end up. "In our wildest dreams did we know where BlackBerry was going to take us? No. But we did know that we had everything we needed and we had the best available in terms of experience, training, talent, and inspiration. We knew that, and that confidence never left us. It doesn't leave us today. We understand this stuff, we understand it deeply, it's part of our instinct. We're as good as anyone else, if not better. How can you ask for more?"

There will be bumps and unpredictable turns in the road ahead. RIM knows that its future cannot be predicted by looking at the past. While annual revenues have headed straight up, strategies for continued success require flexibility. "Competition is going to get more and more intense," said Larry Conlee. "It requires us to get better at what we do. The hard work is not over. The reward for hard work is more hard work, which is better than no work. I would like to see RIM continue to mature but not lose that entrepreneurial edge. If we can accomplish that as a management team we will be well served." At the same time, no newcomer is likely to catch up. "Because it's a regulated industry with standards you have to meet and pass before you're allowed to sell your products, there are concrete barriers to entry. You have to invest," said Lazaridis.

Another way RIM will remain in the lead is by continuing to believe that good ideas can combust anywhere, anytime, and that the company can act upon them quickly and effectively. David Yach recalls returning from a conference in late 2001 on a plane with Balsillie, who suddenly said, "I think we should host our own conference ... and I think we should have it in April." RIM was still a relatively small company and there was no venue, no agenda, no content, no sponsors, no vendors and less than five months to prepare for what became the inaugural Wireless Enterprise Symposium, now attended by over five thousand delegates annually. "We did it," said Yach. "The whole organization rallies and delivers." Even in its first year, the Wireless Enterprise Symposium was attended by one thousand people and lauded by exhibitors and attendees as one of the best conferences they'd ever attended.

For Balsillie, business is 5 per cent strategy, 95 per cent execution, so RIM focuses on execution in the full knowledge that most competitors cannot maintain a similar concentration. "You never modulate, you just don't stop, you never give advantages, and you count on the other person blinking. They'll have a reorg, or they'll quit, or they'll be overaggressive, or they'll do something erratic. Methodical predictability with a high function, high trust, high execution-centric organization is an unbelievably effective strategy," said Balsillie, who takes his work seriously but not himself. "Do your best, live for the day, go to bed, and do it again tomorrow. Don't live with regrets, don't over-scenarioize and don't worry about the future. That's all there is. The rest of it is just a grand illusion."

Research In Motion shipped its 75 millionth BlackBerry in 2009. In 1999, when BlackBerry was first launched, RIM sold a competitive advantage to companies, one that allowed employees to collaborate and make decisions at the speed of thought. BlackBerry took office email and turned it into wireless instant messaging without compromising security. Today, BlackBerry provides the ability to view, edit, and create documents, access the Internet and intranet, run multimedia applications and even replace the office desk phone.

The future looks equally exciting. RIM has over 500 carrier partners in 170 countries and more than 12,000 employees all focused on the future. "We do not rest on our laurels, we continue to hire the best and the brightest and we continue to invest in partnerships in every corner of the globe as well as in the fundamentals: innovation, operational excellence, and customer satisfaction," said Lazaridis. As a result, he believes BlackBerry will replace many of the functions now carried out by the laptop computer. "Just like the big computer mainframe gave way to the mini, and the mini gave way to the micro, and the micro fought it out with the laptop, there is a chance that BlackBerry may become sophisticated enough within the next few years that you'll never go back to your laptop. There is a chance that these handheld, wirelessly connected, highly efficient devices that are always on, always collecting data, always interacting with the entire information pool through the Internet, will replace your laptop. PCs will become media systems, which will be part of your big screen, but BlackBerry will be the core of everything, the central nervous system of what's going on. It will be managing everything from your handheld device, because that's where your customization is. The bulk of the media is either in a central store somewhere or at your cable or satellite provider."

As Lazaridis warms to his cause, he rises from his chair and roams around his office with its clear view of the University of Waterloo where many of the young minds study who will help

RIM. He long ago left the second-floor walk-up, yet here still hangs the print of the Porsche Turbo, albeit a bit faded but in a better frame, the talisman that his wife, Ophelia, gave him in 1984. "There has been a change over the last ten years in Canada in how we view education and how we view science and mathematics, engineering and entrepreneurship," said Lazaridis. "We have such an embarrassment of riches. We have so much good, fertile land and so many resources that the world's clamouring for. We have all the fresh water that we could ever want. We share a border with one of the world's largest trading partners. For most Canadians, the United States is just a few hours away by car. In some places you can walk across.

"Now, with all the trade agreements we have," Lazaridis goes on, "we've never been in a better position as a country. The only thing that I fear is that we become complacent in that success, in that comfort. When my family and I came here, we had nothing. My parents built it all up from nothing and we built RIM from nothing. There weren't a lot of roadblocks. There were trials and challenges, but government was supportive all along. The community was supportive. So, Canada has all this potential but we must continue to be a beacon of success and forward thinking."

The enthusiasm of Lazaridis is so infectious he could be a boy again, working in his basement, ideas a-bubble. "The world really understood the importance of communications when the 'red phone' between the Kremlin and the White House averted World War Three. Communications, and especially the Internet, are the most powerful weapons for worldwide stability and prosperity. The world has become flat because of communications. And we are fortunate to be in a position where we are influencing the evolution of communications around the world—our customers take BlackBerry everywhere and it has had an incredibly positive impact on the way people interact with information and each other. They can no longer imagine how they lived without it. And we just walked into it ... over twenty-five years." Twenty-five years to become an overnight success.

INDEX

Academy Awards, 55, 200
academic entrepreneurs, 229–30
AccessLink, 178–79, 276
Actualidad Economica, 271
Ada C. Richards Public School, 21
Adamou, Adam, 135–36
advertising, marketing, 192, 285
Aerosmith, 272–73
Agnew, Gordon, 230
Albright, John, 223
Alcatel, 228
Aldrin, Buzz, 98
All Points (Megahertz), 91
Allen, Sir Thomas, 210
Allen-Bradley, 56
Altamira Investments, 136, 137
"always on, always connected," 124, 179, 185, 264
Amazon, 11
Amdahl, Jim, 34
America Online (AOL), 188, 195, 264
American Express, 220–21
American Gas Association, 251
American Mobile Satellite Corp., 106, 161–62
Anderson, Pamela, 199
"angels," 51
Anglin, Greg, 34–35, 37, 41
Annan, Kofi, 220
Antonelli, Terry, Stout & Kraus, 239
App World, 284
Apple, 171, 173, 298, 296

Apple Newton, 76–77
application programming interface (API), 61–62
Apps, Eric, 138
ARDIS, 75, 125–26, 176 (*See also* DataTAC; Motient)
ARM Holdings, 110
Armstrong, Neil, 98
ARPANET, 32, 61
Arthur D. Miller, Inc., 73–74
Ascendent Systems, 289–90
AT&T, 75, 76, 103, 113, 123, 150, 151, 183, 239, 240
AT&T EasyLink, 64
AT&T Wireless, 260
ATMs, 105
ATS, 12
Automation Tooling System, 216
Avro Arrow, 16
Award for Canadian-American Business Achievement, 110
Ayre, Calvin, 230

"Baby Bells," 113
Balsillie, Carol (sister, Jim), 65
Balsillie, David (brother, Jim), 65
Balsillie, Heidi (wife, Jim), 67
Balsillie, James (Jim) Laurence
   art collection, 222
   background, 14–15, 65
   childhood, 65–66
   corporate persona, 10, 15, 17, 74, 81–82, 92, 122

credo, 305
education, 15, 65, 66–68
executive role-sharing, 81–82
family life, 15, 223, 227
health/fitness, 222–23
honours, awards, 67, 220
–Lazaridis, comparisons, 14–16
perception of by others, 16, 70, 82, 125
philanthropy, 13–14, 214–17, 300–1
physical appearance, 15
presentation skills, 136, 142
role, 15, 70–71, 81
stock options, 14, 132, 196
visionary, 215, 268
work ethic, 66, 67, 222, 227
writings, 69, 83, 249–50
Balsillie, Laurel (mother, Jim), 65
Balsillie, Ray (father, Jim), 65
Balsillie Centre of Excellence, 13
Balsillie School of International Affairs, 13, 216,
    219, 300
Banc of America Securities, 186
Bank of Montreal, 133, 134, 137, 138–39
Barclays Global Investors, 14
bar-code scanning, 53, 54, 84
Barenaked Ladies, 16, 187, 272, 273
Barnstijn, Michael, 47–48, 50, 51, 53–54, 62, 64,
    70, 71, 82, 86, 99, 100, 113, 142, 167, 217–18
Barse, Jack, 74, 164, 169–70, 208–9
Basir, Otman, 230
Battelle, John, 228
batteries, 20, 53, 91, 97, 98, 99, 103, 105, 108,
    109, 120, 124, 155, 164, 268
Bell, Alexander Graham, 9, 79, 240–41
Bell Canada, 95, 150
Bell Mobility, 104, 176, 260
Bell Northern Research, 228
BellSouth, 64, 74, 93, 100, 102, 106, 113–23,
    125, 126, 140, 156, 157–60, 161,167, 168,
    169–70, 174, 176, 177, 194–95, 240
BellSouth Enterprises, 114, 119, 123, 159
BellSouth Mobile Data, 114, 119, 160, 194
BellSouth Wireless, 123
Belzberg, Brent, 129
Ben & Jerry's, 192
Benioff, Marc, 190
B.F. Goodrich Canada, 30
Bennett Jones (firm), 225
Bernard, Bob, 191–92
BlackBerry
    accolades, 188–89, 282, 295–96

addiction metaphor, 189–90
and business etiquette, 193
business team, 170
category, 168–69
celebrity endorsements, 202, 294–96
competition, 178–79
design, 175–76, 177, 267
detractors, 294
and downtime, 168, 181
early adopters, 188, 199, 265
ease of use claim, 169
brand value, 11
desktop, 177–78, 184–85
global reach, 202, 249, 260–73, 282
impact, 18, 128, 245–46, 257–59, 263, 291–96
injunction threat, 246, 248–50, 251
launch, 174, 179
market share, 10, 264–65
media reaction, 178, 188–89, 190, 192
naming process, 170–73, 276–77
precursor business model, 158–59
pricing, 175, 176–76, 191, 270–71
sales approach, 176, 179–85, 194–95, 287–88
samples, 181–82, 183, 185, 294–95, 200–1, 235
security architecture,183–84, 191, 267, 269, 290
status symbol, 185
steering committee, 167–69
subscribers, 11–12, 189, 192, 197, 199–200, 238,
    245–46, 249, 251, 262–65, 283, 289, 290
BlackBerry, 957, 184, 191–92,195
BlackBerry 5800, 110, 269
BlackBerry 5810, 268
BlackBerry 6201, 270–71
BlackBerry 7100, 202, 272, 287
BlackBerry 7200, 270
BlackBerry 7290, 271
BlackBerry 8100, 275–77 (See also Pearl)
BlackBerry 8700, 271–72
BlackBerry 8820, 284
BlackBerry Diaries, The (Buckworth), 293
BlackBerry Enterprise Server (BES), 184–85,
    258, 263–64
BlackBerry Internet Service (BIS), 264
BlackBerry killers, 296–97
BlackBerry Mascot, 283
"BlackBerry Prayer," 193
Blanchard, James, 251
Blavatnik, Len, 68
Bleiler, Gretchen, 283
BMO Nesbitt Burns, 141, 194–96
Board of Patent Appeals and Interferences, 252

Bodog.com, 230
Bohm, David, 36
Boily, Andre, 282
Bold (smartphone), 11, 284
Bombardier, 12
Bono, 285
Brazile, Donna, 199
British Telecom, 228
Brock, Rick, 68–69, 70, 129
Bronfman, Edgar, Jr., 13
Bronfman, Sam, 13
Bronfman, Yefim, 210
Brown, Dan, 220
Brubacher-Cressman, Dale, 54, 55, 71, 100, 104, 113, 180, 298
Brzustowski, Tom, 214
BT Cellnet, 195, 261
Buckworth, Kathy, 293
Budgie, 41, 42, 43, 44–45, 86, 173
Bullfrog, 99–106, 111–12, 114–15, 140, 142, 155–56, 161
Burton, Howard, 205–8, 214, 301
Bush, Barbara, 199
Bush, George H.W., 278
Bush, George W., 199, 220
Bush, Jeb, 259
Bunsow, Henry, 250–51
Business Week, 178, 272

C.A. Delaney Capital Management, 136, 137
CAD (computer-aided design), 34, 231
Campana, Thomas, Jr., 239, 242
Campbell, Don, 210, 225
Campbell, Kim, 83
Canadarms, 57–58, 291
Canadian Business Hall of Fame, 220
Canadian Business magazine, 10–11
Canadian Chamber of Commerce, 238
Canadian Clay & Glass Gallery, 218
Canadian Imperial Bank of Commerce, 85
Canadian Institute of Chartered Accountants, 134
Canadian Institute of International Affairs, 300–1
Canadian International Council, 300, 301
Canadian Pacific Railway, 190
Canadian War Museum, 218
car phones, 80
Carkner, Steve, 83–84, 85, 92, 100, 134
Carleton University, 228
Carragher, Mark, 150
Case, Steve, 188

Casio, 103
Cassiopeia Elo (PC), 90
Castell, Dave, 167–69, 172–73, 176, 177, 184, 191, 227, 299
Casteneda, Carlos, 35
CDS–100 sign system, 47, 49, 50–51
Cellular Telecom & Internet Association, 245
central processing unit (CPU), 40
Centre for International Governance Innovation (CIGI), 13, 215–16, 218, 223, 300
Centre for Theoretical Cosmology, 301
Certicom, 230, 290
Chamberlain, Russ, 108
Chamberlain, Savvas, 236
Chaudhuri, Sujeet, 212–13
Cheriton, David, 230
China Mobile, 263
Chopra, Deepak, 17, 284, 289
Chrétien, Raymond, 110
Church, Mark, 100
CI Mutual Funds, 183
CIBC Oppenheimer, 186, 297
CIBC Wood Gundy Securities, 144
Cingular, 123, 245, 257–58
Cisco Systems, 245
Citibank, 81
Citicorp, 265
Citigroup, 268
Clark, Marion, 107
Clarkson, Gordon (firm), 67, 151
Clinton, Bill, 76, 199
CNET Editor's Choice, 163
Cochrane, Tom, 148, 187
Cognos Inc., 54
Colvin, Geoff, 190
COM DEV, 12, 129–30, 142, 150, 160–61
COMDEX (trade show), 90–96, 268
Compaq Computer, 150, 195
Compuserve, 64
Computer Advertising Signs, 45, 46
Conestoga College, 302
Conlee, Larry, 151–53, 262, 287, 288, 299, 304
Control Data Corp., 32–34
Cooley, C.E., 107
co-op students, 14, 29, 30, 31, 32–34, 36, 37, 149, 175
Cooper, Andrew, 216
Cork, Ken, 215, 225, 226
Corman, John, 46, 52
Corman Custom Electronics, 44
Corman Manufacturing, 46, 56, 63

Council on Foreign Relations, 254, 301
Cowpland, Michael, 228
CrackBerry, 18, 189–90, 271
Credit Suisse First Boston, 162–63, 188
Creo Inc., 228
Crossing the Chasm (Moore), 264
Curtis, John, 216
Curve (smartphone), 11, 284
Cyber 205 (computer), 33

Da Vinci Code, The (Brown), 220
Daley, Cathy, 222
Dalhousie University, 220
Dalsa Inc., 12, 230
Damon, Matt, 199
Dantec Systems, 30
Dasani, 173
DataTac, 106, 161
David Suzuki Foundation, 219
Davidson, Ernie, 55–56
Davis LLP, 210
de la Renta, Oscar, 200
De Niro, Robert, 220–21
de Saint-Exupéry, Antoine, 18
DeGeneres, Ellen, 220, 221
Delaney, Ian, 135
Delgado, Carlos, 200
Dell Computer, 162, 188, 200
Dell, Michael, 200
Deloitte Canada, 286
Dept. of Communications (Canada), 80
Dept. of Industry (Canada), 198
Deruyter, Ron, 272
Diabetes Detection Institute, 20
DigiSync Film KeyKode, 54–55
Dittberner Associates, 73–74
Doc Martens, 192
DoCoMo, 59, 263
Doll, John, 249
donut rule, 148, 153–54
Dow Jones World Technology Index, 196
Dowd, Maureen, 199
Doyle, Denzil, 228
Dubinsky, Donna, 91–92
Duell, Charles H., 248
Dykes, Ron, 119

Eagan, James, 245
Easson, John, 141–42, 143, 195–96, 197
Eastman Kodak, 228, 239
eBay, 132, 133, 192, 255

Eberhard, Martin, 283
Ebert, Roger, 90
Edmonson, Peter, 87, 89
Edper Financial Group, 133
Einstein, Albert, 77, 210, 226
Elcoteq, 288
electronic film counter, 52–55 (*See also* Digi-
Sync)
electronically programmable logic device
(EPLD), 48
Elmasry, Mohamed, 32–33
email
addresses, 156–57, 160, 163–65, 169–70
development, 59–77
early adopters, 90
impact on corporate culture, 234
popularity, 89–90, 158, 163, 179
(*See also* push email)
E-Mail Addresses of the Rich and Famous (Godin),
89–90
Emmy Awards, 55
Empire Club of Canada, 236
employees—RIM
donations, 218–19, 230
donut rule, 153–54
expertise, 87–89
interviews, 87–88
loyalty/commitment, 8, 9–10, 47, 63, 139, 229
motivation, 55, 149, 160
number, 88, 105, 134, 154, 180, 201, 233, 279,
298
patents, 298–99
stock options, 48, 131–32, 139, 142, 147
student hires, 148–49, 235–36 (*See also* co-op
students)
"Enchanted Garden" event, 62
end-to-end solution, 175, 177
English, John, 215, 216
Envoy, 75
EO Personal Communicator, 76
Epoch Integration, 290
Ericsson, 59, 60, 61, 62, 72–74, 83–84, 85, 86, 87,
102, 103, 124, 127–28, 208, 240, 245
Ericsson Mobidem, 72
Eritel, 60
Ernest Manning Award, 219
Ernst & Young, 67
Estill, Jim, 82, 181, 223
Etheridge, Melissa, 220
"evangelists," 176, 180–82
Evertz Microsystems, 54

Excite, 228

Fabian, Justin, 170, 172–73, 180, 181
Facebook, 284
Fargo, John, 251
Fasken Martineau (firm), 238
Fast 50 list, 286
fax machines, 75, 160
Federal Business Development Bank, 134
Federal Communications Commission (FCC), 80
Federman, Lynne, 257
"few chip package" concept, 98
Fidelity (mutual fund), 14, 202–3
Fiedler, Mark, 119
Financial Post, 162
Financial Times, 293
Finnegan (IP law firm), 241
Fiorenza, Cosimo, 225
FIRE (microprocessor dev tool), 51
Fonn, Karen, 219
Foote, Cone & Belding, 171
Forbes, 102, 192, 255
Fortune magazine, 10, 190
Fortune 500, 158
Franz, Dennis, 55
Franz, Tom, 97, 107, 110, 123
Fraser, Rob, 135–36
Fréchette, Louise, 216
free trade, 69, 307
Freedom (PCMCIA card), 90
Fregin, Doug, 21–22, 23, 26, 27, 37, 39, 40, 41, 43, 46, 47, 48, 50, 51, 53, 54, 57, 70, 71, 142, 149, 209, 221
Frezza, Bill, 72–73, 74, 124
Frost, Sadie, 283

Gabarro, Jack, 68
Gasoi, Frederick, 52–53
Garcia, Nina, 283
Gardner, J.D., 119
Gartner Inc., 194, 298, 298
Gates, Bill, 90–91, 227
Geddes, Keith, 230
General Magic, 75
General Motors, 45, 49, 54, 86
Generation X (Coupland), 283
Genuity Capital Markets, 17
George, Alan, 213
Gibson, Dunn & Crutcher, 188
Giffin, Gordon, 251

Gilhuly, Barry, 167
Gillett, Terry, 96, 97, 98, 102, 103, 106–7, 109–10
Glenayre Technologies, 178–79
Glick, Marty, 251
Globe and Mail, 211, 215
Gluskin Sheff + Associates, 136, 137
GMP Securities, 296
GoAmerica, 162
Godin, Seth, 89–90
Golden Thread Charitable Foundation, 218–19
Goldman Sachs, 81
Gonnet, Gaston, 230
Google, 228, 230, 264, 302
Gordon Capital, 162
Gore, Al, 76, 199
Gore, Kristin, 199
Governor General's Award, 134
Graffiti (software), 75, 189
Grand River Regional Cancer Centre, 217
Gray, Linda, 50
Griffin, Jason, 111–12, 155
Griffiths, Brad, 136–37, 138
Griffiths McBurney Partners (GMP), 135–37, 138, 143–44, 183
Group of Seven, 222
Grove, Andy, 190
GSM/GPRS (General Packet Radio System), 266, 268
Guibert, Mark, 101, 114, 148, 154, 155, 160, 170, 172, 173–74, 178, 192, 200, 201, 258, 273, 296–97
Guild, Paul, 212
Guitar Hero III, 284

Hagey, Gerry, 30
Hales, Ernie, 26, 30
Handspring Visor, 189
handwriting recognition technology, 75, 77, 93, 189
Handi-Talkie, 80
Hargitay, Mariska, 283
Harrell, Mike, 114, 119
Harrowston Inc., 129
Harvard Business School, 67–68
Hawking, Stephen, 214, 301
Hawkins, Jeff, 91
"heartbeat," 124
Heche, Anne, 55
Heidrick & Struggles, 151
Heinbecker, Paul, 215, 216, 263
Helms-Burton Act, 135

Hertz, Heinrich, 79
Hewlett, Bill, 229
Hewlett-Packard (HP), 72, 101, 109, 150, 168, 170, 229, 264
Hightower, Neale, 121, 169–70
Hind, Hugh, 150
Hobbs, Bill, 74
Hobbs, Jim, 114–15, 119, 1210–21, 124, 160, 169–70, 194–95
Holland & Knight, 188
Hollywood, 55, 199, 200
Holzer, Jessica, 255
Home Hardware, 44
Honeywell, 63
household appliances, 98
Howrey LLP, 243, 245, 251
Hu Jintao, 220
Hutchison Telecom, 261

IBM, 48, 67, 106, 133, 161, 188, 264
Idol, Billy, 90
Imperial Oil, 30
Industrial Research Assistance Program, 55
InfoWorld magazine, 178
Inside the Tornado (Moore), 168
Institute for Advanced Study (Princeton), 207, 209
Institute for Quantum Computing (IQC), 13, 213–14, 301
Institute for Theoretical Physics, 207
Institute of Chartered Accountants of Ontario, 220
Integrated Centre for Optimal Learning, 219
Intel, 11, 5, 81, 93, 95–102, 106–11, 123–24, 125, 140, 171, 174, 188, 190, 245, 271
Intel Achievement Award, 110
Intel Capital, 101–2
Inter@ctive Pager 800, 106, 161
Inter@ctive Pager 900. See Bullfrog
Inter@ctive Pager 950. See Leapfrog
Interconnection Services, 119
Intermetrics, 51
International Data Corp, 179
International Property Owners Association, 249
International Space Station, 57–58, 291, 292
Internet Archive, 267
Internet Message Access Protocol (IMAP4), 125
Internet White Pages, The, 89
iPhone, 296
Iridium, 240
Ironclads (video game), 35

IT managers, 183–85, 191
Itronix Corp., 105–16

J. Zechner Associates, 136, 137
Jack: Straight from the Gut (Welch), 270
Janus, 14
Jarmuszewski, Perry, 87
Java software, 268–69, 290
Jiddu Krishnamurti, 36
Jobs, Steve, 125
Johnston, David, 13–14, 214, 215, 223
Jones Day (firm), 241, 242, 245
Jordan, Royce, 157
Joseph E. Seagram and Sons, 13
Joyful Heart Foundation, 283
JRC Canada, 104, 150

Kavelman, Dennis, 133–39, 140, 143–44, 147, 148, 153, 182, 183, 190, 196, 219, 282, 289
Kavelman-Fonn Foundation, 219
Kaiser Resources, 63
Kawasaki, Guy, 168–69
Kennedy, Ted, 90
Kenney, David, 242
Kerr, David, 133
keyboards, 93, 99, 101, 116–17, 154–55, 175, 178, 179, 189, 194, 268, 270, 272
Kidman, Nicole, 220
kill command, 267
Kitchener Industrial Coalition, 69
Kitchener-Waterloo, 12, 105, 227
Kitchener-Waterloo Art Gallery, 218
Korb, Joseph, 257
Korthals, Robin, 211, 223–24, 225
KPMG Canadian Region, 225
KPMG Peat Marwick Thorne, 134
Kraft, 81
K–W Community Foundation, 219
K–W Hospital Foundation, 219

Laflamme, Raymond, 214
Landry, Rick, 104–5, 150, 156, 286, 287
laptops, 74, 106, 178, 242, 306
Latham, John, 100–1, 104, 106, 130–31, 266
Lawrence, Sharon, 55
Lazaridis, Cleopatra (sister, Mike), 21
Lazaridis, Dorothy (mother, Mike), 19–20, 21, 27, 29, 43, 49, 307
Lazaridis, Mike
    background, 14, 15, 19–21
    –Balsillie, comparisons, 14–17

celebrity status, 220–21
childhood, 20–28
corporate persona, 9–10, 15–17, 58, 50, 81–82, 84, 88–89, 107, 112–13, 121, 149
credo, 24, 27, 34, 35–36, 169, 211, 268, 302–3
early inventions, 22, 23, 25–26
education, 15, 21, 23–25, 27–41, 49
entrepreneurship, 34, 35, 36–37, 41, 127–28
executive role-sharing, 81–82
family life, 15, 44, 115–16, 223, 224, 225–26, 227, 232
honours, awards, 219, 220
on innovation/entrepreneurship, 232–33
interviewing technique, 87–88, 206
perception of by others, 16–17, 36–37, 41, 55, 63, 65, 120–21, 125, 206, 221, 223–24
philanthropy, 13–14, 47, 207–12, 213, 216, 301–2
physical appearance, 15, 206
presentation skills, 53–54, 120–21
residences, 21, 34–35, 37, 42, 46
role, 15–16, 81
spirituality, 36, 226
on students, 231–32, 236
stock options, 14, 132, 196
virtuous cycle idea, 236
visionary, 164, 209, 210–11, 213, 268, 299, 303–4
work ethic, 22–23, 24, 100, 132, 227, 278
Lazaridis, Nick (father, Mike), 19–20, 21, 22–23, 43, 49, 307
Lazaridis, Ophelia (wife, Mike), 115, 221, 223, 225, 232
Lazaridis, Paul (uncle, Mike), 19, 21
Leapfrog, 101, 102–3, 106–7, 111–12, 114, 116, 126, 161, 162–63, 167, 194
accolades, 163, 164
advantages over Bullfrog, 155–56
appearance, 154–55
launch, 154
BellSouth purchase order, 122
manufacturing, 155–56
presentation to BellSouth, 119–21
white paper, 116–19
wooden models, 120–21, 140, 142
Leben, Will, 171–72
LED (light-emitting diode), 45, 49, 119
Leggett, Sir Anthony, 213
Lehman, Bruce, 248
Leibovitz, Annie, 220
Lenahan, Bill, 113, 123

Levin, Gerald, 188
LeVine, Ken, 265
Levy, Steven, 252
Lewis, Allan, 167
Lexicon Branding Inc., 170–73
Lexington Financial Group, 67
LG Medical Tech, 150
Linkert, Barry, 100, 167
Lipman USA Inc., 105–6
Little, Herb, 64
Little Prince, The (Saint- Exupéry), 18
L.L. Bean, 192
local area networks (LANs), 31–32, 48
Long, David, 243
Los Alamos National Laboratory, 214
Lotus 1-2-3, 67
Lucent Technologies, 245

MacCallum, Louise, 113, 217–18
Macintosh, 168
Magna, 12
Maplesoft, 230
Marco, 75
Marconi, Guglielmo, 79
Marketing magazine, 283
Marleau Lemire, 138
Martin, Paul, 213
Martin, Roger, 133
Maskus, Keith, 254–55
Massey-Ferguson, 12
Matthews, Terry (Sir Terence), 228
Mauldin, Earle, 102, 114, 119, 123, 159–60
McGuinty, Dalton, 213
MCI Mail, 164
McMaster University, 87, 220
McMurtry, Don, 89, 100, 114, 147, 153, 180, 172–73, 194, 219
Megahertz Corp., 91
Mennonites, 226–27
MENS Club, 84
Mercer, Rick, 292–93
Merrill Lynch, 183, 186, 188, 194, 195
Mersch, Frank, 136
Meucci, Antonio, 240–41
Meyer, Charles, 150, 237–38, 239, 241
Michel, Paul, 246–47
Microsoft, 90–91, 102, 117, 125, 174, 179, 180, 227–28, 240, 264, 297
Microsoft Exchange, 179
Microsoft Exchange/Outlook, 175
Micsinszki, John, 23–24, 28–29, 39, 287

Midland Walwyn, 138
Mike Lazaridis Theatre of Ideas, 210
Mike and Ophelia Lazaridis Quantum–Nano
    Centre, 301
Mikula, Ben, 144
Milunovich, Steven, 183
miniaturization, 96, 97, 98, 105
Mitel, 228
Mobile Computing and Communications magazine,
    163
Mobile Data Report, 18
Mobile Data World Conference, 62
mobile point-of-sale terminal (MPT), 85–86, 91,
    104
mobile virtual network operators (MVNOs),
    158–59, 259–60
MobiLib, 62, 63
MobiLib-Plus, 64
MobiTalk, 62, 64
Mobitex Operators Association, 62, 208
Mobitex Protocol Converters (MPCs), 83–84
Mobitex technology, 59–64, 73, 74, 75, 80, 83,
    96, 100, 103, 105, 106, 112, 113, 114, 116,
    120, 122, 124, 125, 128, 155, 164
MobiView, 64
Moore, Geoffrey, A., 168, 264
Moore, Gordon, 97
Moore, Mike, 138–39
Moore's Law, 97, 98, 108
Morrison, Debbie, 218
Morrison, Don, 150–51, 152–54, 218, 234, 260,
    262
Morrison, Scott, 183
Morgan Stanley, 194
Morse code, 79
Mossberg, Walter S., 189, 193
Motient, 106, 162, 268 (*See also* American
    Mobile Satellite Corp.; ARDIS)
Motorola, 9, 61, 75, 80, 84, 87, 88, 91, 99, 101,
    102, 141, 151, 152, 154, 155, 178, 240, 264,
    268, 299
Mousseau, Gary, 63–64, 164–65, 167, 184, 219,
    234
MSN, 264
Mulroney, Brian, 83
Murray, James B., Jr., 80
muscle memory, 93, 99
MySpace, 283

9/11, 246, 257–59, 263
Naggie (, 290

naming process, 171–74, 275–77, 281–82
NASA, 47, 291–92
NASDAQ, 182-183, 185–86, 188, 190, 195,196
National Basketball Association, 200
National Film Board, 52–55
National Gold Medal, 134
National Research Council (NRC), 51, 55, 228
National Sciences and Engineering Research
    Council of Canada, 214
Nationsbanc Montgomery Securities, 144, 182
NATO, 267
Nature Conservancy, 219
Neale, David, 16, 60, 64–65, 103, 104, 159, 191–
    92, 194, 201, 208, 254
NEC Computers, 103
Netscape, 182
network operating system (NOS), 33
network operations centre (NOC), 176, 177,
    266
New Technologies Products (NTP), 239
New York Times, 199, 282, 293
Newsweek, 192, 252, 295, 295
Nextel, 260
Nike, 192
Nikom, 104
Nobel Prize, 213
Nokia, 84, 229, 264, 268, 288, 298
Noranda, 225
Nortel Networks, 12, 206
Novatel, 103
NTP Inc. v. Research In Motion Limited, 237–53
NTP v. Palm, 255

100 Fastest Growing Companies List, 10
O'Brien, Conan, 202
O'Donovan, Val, 129, 130, 142, 161
O'Hara, Robert, 125, 175
O'Keefe, Sean, 291–92
O_2 (mobile telecom operator), 261
Obama, Barack, 295
OEM radio, 87, 88–89, 90, 105–6, 140, 162, 266
Ogilvy & Mather, 220
Ohm's Law, 21
Ontario Development Corporation, 127–29
Ontario Ministry of Industry, Trade and Tech, 130
Ontario Securities Commission (OSC), 132
Ontario Teachers' Pension Plan, 225
Ontario Technology Fund, 130
Open Text, 12, 150, 230, 302
Oracle, 188, 264
Order of Canada, 220

Order of Ontario, 220
Osborne, Kelly, 283
Osmond, Donny, 202
Ottawa Sun, 282
Outlook Express, 125, 170
outsourcing, 288–89
over-the-counter trading, 138, 139
Oxford English Dictionary, 230

Packard, Dave, 229
packet data, 124
packet switching, 60–61, 136
pACT (personal air communications), 103–4
PageMart, 240
PageNet, 162
PageWriter, 178, 276, 296
Palm, 75, 91–92, 102, 189, 193–94,255, 262, 264, 297
Palm Pilot, 91, 93, 167, 181, 189
Palm VII, 179, 191, 296
Palmer, Tara, 283
Panasonic, 105–6, 111–12, 155
Paradigm Capital, 142, 185, 261, 268
Paradigm Research, 42, 297
Parsons, Graham, 139
"Patent Abuse" (Balsillie), 249
Patent Office. *See* U.S. Patent and Trademark Office
patent reform, 249, 253–55
patent trolls, 238, 240
patents, 30, 220, 237–55, 298–99
Pathiyal, Krishna, 237
Pavilion (PC), 170
PC World, 192
PCMCIA cards, 90–91, 92, 133, 140
PDAs, 75–77, 96, 106
Pearl , 11, 277–78, 280–90, 287–88, 293
Pearl Flip, 284
peer-to-peer messaging, 103, 164
Peet's coffee, 192
Pentium, 96, 110, 171, 173
peripheral vision, 99
Perimeter Institute, 13, 207–13, 214, 220, 221, 225, 231, 301–3
Perot, Ross, 74
Personal Communications Showcase, 154
Persson, Ake, 127–28
Peterborough Collegiate and Vocational School, 66
PIN numbers, 156–57
Piper Jaffray (co), 186

Pirner, Tom, 60–61, 62
Pirsig, Robert, 35
Placek, David, 170–73
Pocket PC (Microsoft), 117
Pogue, David, 293
Polaroid, 239
Porter, Michael, 68
PowerBook, 171
Profit magazine, 163
Purnell, Walt, Jr., 125–26, 161–62, 268
push email, 11, 125, 175, 178, 179, 184, 264, 290

quality control, 104, 289
quantum mechanics, 213–14
quantum theory, 35
Qualcomm, 240
QuickBooks, 134
QWERTY, 99–100, 101, 116–17, 154–55, 284

radio frequency (RF), 86, 87, 89, 90, 271
Radio Shack, 40
radio waves, 79–80
RadioMail, 73, 74, 75, 164
Raiffe, Howard, 68
RAM Mobile Data, 73–74, 75, 93, 99–100, 106, 112–14, 123, 124, 127, 156, 157, 158–59, 164
Ramparts (gateway), 164
Ramsay, Anne, 55
random access memory (RAM), 39–40
Rare (eco reserve), 218
RBC Dominion Securities, 143–44
Reach for the Top, 25, 29
Reagan, Ronald, 242
Record (K-W), 69, 272
Roy Studio Collection, 217
read-only memory (ROM), 39–40
ReFlex technology, 155
Regional Bell Operating Companies (RBOCs), 127
Reid, John, 225
Reiter, Alan, 17–18, 188
Re$earch Money Conference, 231
Research and Tech Park (UW), 229, 230–31
return on life (ROL), 181
Rich List (Sunday Times), 68
Richards, Barry, 142, 185, 202–3, 261, 268, 297
Rick Mercer Report, 292–93
RIM
    accounting system, 134
    acquisitions/construction, 197–98, 289–90
    awards, 110, 283

bank loans, 133–35, 137
billing system, 176–77
competition, 123, 126, 154, 159, 178–79, 191, 193–94, 233–34, 296–97, 304
corporate costs, 201–2, 218, 226, 233, 269
corporate culture, 87–89, 114, 130, 147–48, 152–53, 233–35, 297, 299
donations, 205–19, 230, 301
early years, 41–58
future, 304–5, 306–8
global reach, 8, 10, 11, 12, 14, 17, 202, 220, 233, 282, 286, 300–1
goes public, 140–45, 182–83
governance processes, 132–33
government assistance, 198
headquarters, 12
incorporation, 43
investment in, 14, 51–52, 71, 123, 127–45, 182–83, 188
logo, 50
management team, 149–53
manufacturing, 104–5, 140, 155–56, 221, 286–89
market capitalization, 9, 10, 11, 136, 144,183, 190, 196, 253, 298
naming, 41–52
new carrier strategy, 259–63
offices, 49–50, 82, 95, 104–5, 134, 154, 197–98
patent lawsuit, 237–53
possible acquisitors, 101–2, 133–34, 137
prospectus, 140–41
revenue, 10, 54, 57, 69, 84, 91, 106, 130, 133, 178, 190, 202, 265–66, 285–86
share prices, 190–91, 195–96, 197, 202, 203, 211, 212, 253
stock options investigation, 132
stock symbol, 183
US markets, 185–203
vision meetings, 275, 278–80
(See also employees—RIM)
RIM Box, 64
RIMGate, 64, 164
RIM Park, 218
Roe Pfeifer, Elizabeth, 150, 233–34, 235, 300
Rogan, James, 248
Rogers Cantel, 158–59, 174
Rogers Centre, 285
Rogers Communications, 16, 59–60, 93, 183, 260
Rogers Wireless, 60–64, 103, 162, 208

Rogers, Ted, 59–60
Rosehart, Robert, 215
Rotman School of Management, 133
Royal Bank of Canada, 133
Rules for Revolutionaries (Kawasaki), 168–69

Saltzman, Marc, 294
"seeding," 183, 184–85
salesforce.com, 190
Salmon, Walter, 68
Salomon Smith Barney, 188, 265
Sammy's Hill (K. Gore), 189
Samsung, 84
San Francisco Chronicle, 253
Sandvine Corp., 12, 228
Saucier + Perrotte, 209
SBC Communications, 123
Scientific Research and Development, 198
screens, 93, 99, 105, 117, 120, 189, 191, 270, 287
Search, The (Battelle), 228
Sema Group UK, 103
Seybold, Andy, 16–17, 102, 105, 160, 174, 177–78, 185, 221, 297
SG Cowen, 186
Shah, Sandeep, 108
Shanghai University, 235–36
Shaw, Chris, 35, 40–41, 43, 44
Sheritt International Corp., 135
Show Low project, 107–10
Siemens, 84
signs system, 41, 42, 43, 44–45, 47, 49, 50–51, 86
Silicon Valley, 34, 74, 179, 228, 229, 237
single-mailbox integration, 165, 219
Skytel, 156, 162, 177, 240
SkyWriter, 276
SlipStream Data, 290
Small Business Development Corp., 52
Smith, Larry, 36–37, 41, 50, 210–11
Smits, Jimmy, 55
Smithsonian Institution, 163
Snyder, Peter Etril, 43
Sobieraj, Sandra, 199
sound symbolism, 172
SoundView, 186
Spar Aerospace, 57
Spence, Patrick, 183
Spencer, James R., 241–44, 247, 248, 250, 251–52, 253, 255
spirituality, and science, 35–36
Sprint, 164, 240
SS Tech, 128–29

Stanford University, 171, 228–29, 230
start-ups, 229–31
Stork NV, 70, 128
Storm (smartphone), 284
Stout, Donald, 239, 240
Student Venture Loans, 43
Stymiest, Barbara, 133
"Success Lies in Paradox!", 116–19, 155
Sullivan, Gerry, 30, 230–31
SuperComm conference, 163
SureType, 270, 284
surface mount technology (SMT), 55–56
Sutherland-Schultz Ltd., 56–57, 68, 69, 70, 81,
    128, 129
Swain, Harry, 215
Swain, Philip, 238
Swedish Telecom, 60
Sybase, 150, 302
Symbol Technologies, 105–6
Symons, Mary, 66
Symons, Tom, 66
SYNNEX Canada, 82

386 technology, 106–7, 164
3Com, 240
Tasker Electronics, 56
TD Asset Management, 14
TD Bank, 225
TD Lancaster, 138
TD Securities, 138
"Tech 100" list, 10–11
Technology Horizons Ltd., 142, 161
Technology Partnerships Canada, 198
Technology Triangle, 12
TekNow, 239, 242–45
Telecommunications Hall of Fame, 220
Telefund Canada, 239
telegraph, 77
telephone, 79, 240–41
Televerket, 60
telex, 74
Telsa Motors, 283
Telus, 16
Tendler, Benson, 150
Terman, Fred, 229
TerreStar Corporation, 162 (See also Motient)
theoretical physics, 207–12
Thompson, John
Time magazine, 220
Time Warner, 188, 290
T-Mobile, 202, 260, 282

tombstone (notice), 143–44
Tong, Ophelia, 43–44 (*See also* Lasaridis, Ophelia)
toothbrush, 48–49
Toronto Blue Jays, 200
Toronto Stock Exchange, 144, 183, 190
touch typing, 93, 99, 116–17
Tour (smartphone), 11
trackball, 277, 280–81
trackwheel, 111–12, 120, 155, 280
trademarks, 171, 173
Trent University, 66, 220
Trieu, Congquay, 108
Trilogy Systems, 34
Trinity College (U of T), 66, 217
trucks, 60, 105, 120, 158
Trudeau, Garry, 77
Tubbs, Graham, 95–96, 97, 106, 107, 110
Tucson project, 97, 100, 107, 110
Turok, Neil, 301
Twain, Mark, 247, 276
two-in-a-box matrix, 81
two-way paging networks, 8, 118, 120, 136, 141,
    155
Tyler, Steve, 272–73

U2, 285
UNICEF, 179–80
Uniform Evaluation (UFE), 134
United Nations, 215, 216, 263
Université Laval, 220
University of Ottawa, 228
University of Toronto, 66, 133, 167, 217, 301
University of Waterloo, 13–42, 47, 49, 61, 82, 87,
    148–49, 150, 167, 197, 205, 207, 210, 212–20,
    225, 229–30, 300
University of Windsor, 37, 41
UNIX, 32, 33
Urlocker, Michael, 162–63, 200, 296
U.S. Court of Appeals for the Federal Circuit,
    244, 246
U.S. Dept. of Defense, 32
U.S. Dept. of Justice, 113, 248–49, 251
U.S. District Court for Eastern Division of
    Virginia, 240–43
U.S. military, 188, 290
U.S. Patent and Trademark Office, 239, 245, 248,
    252, 253, 255
U.S. Robotics, 91, 92, 102, 133
U.S. Securities Exchange Commission, 132
USA Today, 190, 192
Usenet, 47, 87

value-added resellers (VARs), 179
Vanstone, Scott, 230
Vasilliou, Mike, 71–72
Verizon, 245, 260
Viking Express, 72, 74
VISA, 85
VisiCalc, 67
Vodafone, 202, 261
VoiceStream, 260
Volker, Michael, 51–52, 54, 65, 144–45

Wall Street Journal, 178, 189, 192, 193, 239, 253
Wallace, Jim, 240
Wallstrip (blog), 293
Walters, Barbara, 295
Wandell, Matt, 87–88
Washington Post, 192, 253
Waterloo (ON), 12, 228, 229, 301–2 (*See also* Kitchener-Waterloo)
Waterloo Community Foundation, 217–18
Waterloo Institute for Technology, 301
Waterloo Maple, 214, 266
Waterloo Pump, 30–31
Waterloo Regional Children's Museum, 218
Watt, Lynn, 225
Welch, Jack, 199, 200, 270
Wente, Margaret, 215
Werezak, David, 150, 167, 170, 172, 173–74
West, Terry, 50, 57, 95–96, 109, 110
Westinghouse, 70, 128
Wetmore, John, 133
W.F. Herman Secondary School, 23–25, 27–28
White Castle, 192
White Collar Slacker's Handbook (Saltzman), 294
Wildeboer, Dellelce, 138
Wildeboer, Rob, 138
Wildstrom, Stephen H., 178, 273
Wiley, Rein & Fielding, 240
Wilfrid Laurier University, 134, 149, 214, 215, 216, 217, 220, 300
Windows CE, 90–91
Winfrey, Oprah, 22
Winland, Thomas, 241
Winston, Harry, 200
Wireless Enterprise Symposium, 270, 305
Wireless Intelligence Group, 17
Wireless Internet and Mobile Computing Newsletter, 105
Wireless Internet & Mobile Computing (co), 188
Wireless Nation (Murray), 80

Woerner, Klaus, 216
Wood, Ken, 22, 26–27
Woods, Tiger, 220
Working Ventures, 135–36, 137
World Wildlife Federation, 219
Wright, Doug, 42, 215, 225

X.25 network, 63–64, 164
XM Satellite Radio, 162
XScale technology, 110

Yach, David, 150, 219, 234, 269, 270, 305
Yahoo!, 228, 264
Yankee Group, 141
Yorkton Securities, 138
Young Presidents' Organization, 68
YouTube, 283, 293

Zen and the Art of Motorcycle Maintenance (Pirsig), 35